MY LIFE, MY STAGE

MY LIFE, MY STAGE

by

ERNEST STERN

LONDON
VICTOR GOLLANCZ LTD
1951

Translated from the German manuscript
by Edward Fitzgerald

Printed in Great Britain by
The Camelot Press Ltd., London and Southampton

CONTENTS

My first costumes

CHAPTER I

VIENNA

"From head to foot in egg yolk—that's me."

"He seems to prefer spinach for me."

It was behind the scenes of the full-dress rehearsal of "*Die Krone*", a piece by the German playwright Emanuel von Bodmann, and apparently two of the actors didn't altogether approve of my colour scheme. And they talked so loud that it was impossible for me not to hear what they said. I had started off on my career as a stage designer with a daring experiment, and their witticisms were not exactly encouraging.

I can hardly claim that I was a conscious pioneer in the movement for the visual reform of the stage. In fact, I was a complete tiro; I didn't even know that such a movement existed. But at least I had instinctively avoided the usual thoughtless jumble of colours which was so popular in stage costumes in the 'nineties and which had so often spoiled my own enjoyment of otherwise good performances. "Motley is the enemy of colour" is a sound artistic maxim.

As an artist and a painter, I was offended by the senseless confusion of colours, and I wanted to avoid it in my own first attempt, so I had coloured my characters according to their roles. The princes were in black; the princesses in white; the duenna in violet; and the other roles in green, yellow, grey, etc. As it turned out, my efforts were noted and approved by the critics proper—to the astonishment of the facetious actors.

The scene of this, my first attempt to conquer the stage, was Munich, which at that time was a centre for the performance of

Vienna

Wagner's operas. Musically speaking, the standards were very high, but unfortunately the performances were hampered by a traditionalism which was so deeply rooted that even the slightest change was denounced as a sacrilege. Siegfried, Lohengrin, Elsa, Brunhild and all the rest were almost comic figures and all the illusion was destroyed—so much so that even naïve members of the audience could appreciate the justice of the caricatures which appeared in the comic papers. Even the repeated protests of the many groups of artists which played an important role in Munich life made no difference— at least, not where Wagner was concerned. The tradition was sacrosanct. Occasionally an artist would be called in to assist in some new staging, but that didn't happen often, and even when it did his work was invariably hamstringed by the interference of "influential persons".

Many years later, in 1910, at a time when scenic reform had long won the day elsewhere, I was offered an appointment as Chief Costume Designer for the Munich State Theatres—by that time I was already with Reinhardt. The job carried with it a very good salary, a flattering title and the prospect of highly interesting work, but when I came to examine the proposed contract I found one clause—just a few words—which, properly interpreted, meant that the Chief Costume Designer would have to reckon with the interference and criticism of a highly-placed personage. It probably meant that one of the princesses would decide whether the costume designs met with her approval and, above all, whether they were in accordance with her ideas of decency and propriety.

I turned down the tempting offer. A colleague of mine who occupied a similar position at the Berlin State Opera House had, for instance, to ensure that all the actresses and singers wore corsets. Her Majesty the Kaiserin Augusta Viktoria insisted on it.

But perhaps I ought to say something about how I came to be an artist in the first place. Before I went to Munich and devoted myself to art, I was in Vienna, which, in the nineties was the centre of art and culture for south-east Europe. I was a Roumanian, and for us Roumanians Europe began in Vienna. I was sent there in the first place not to study art, but accountancy, bookkeeping, the credit system—in fact, in everything likely to be of use to me in my future business career. But the imperial capital on the Blue Danube had so much to offer in the way of distractions that learning to be a business man seemed very dull.

At home my only acquaintance with the wonders of the outside world had been through the pages of the illustrated papers, but now those wonders were all around me: splendid architecture from many periods, picture galleries chock full of masterpieces, fascinating coloured posters on the streets inviting me to visit the theatres. The first that aroused my interest I remember was one outside the famous Burg Theater. It was for "Julius Cæsar". I already knew that the author was a playwright named Shakespeare. We had his collected works—in a German translation, of course—in our bookcase at home. I had never read the play, but I knew that there were battle scenes in it with prancing horses—ours was an illustrated edition—and that greatly interested me, so I bought a ticket. In some excitement and great expectation, I sat on a bench in the gallery and awaited the appearance of the Romans on horseback. But the people on the stage just talked and talked, and there wasn't a sign of a horse from beginning to end. That was a disappointment, and yet my first experience of the theatre made a deep impression! Romans in togas, golden helmets, shining breast-plates and shields. And the Forum with its majestic columns!

No, on the whole I was quite satisfied with my first performance, though I did subsequently complain to my uncle about the missing horses. He told me solemnly that I should have to go to London to see it staged that way: the horse-loving English insisted on it, he said. Very well, I decided, I would— some day.

Goethe, Schiller, Calderon, Shakespeare, Molière, all the great classics were in the repertoire of the Burg Theater, and thanks to a company of really first-class actors and actresses the performances were of the highest quality.

The relatives with whom I was staying encouraged my search for culture, and they contributed a small weekly sum to pay for further visits to the theatre. In this way I saw "Faust", "Hamlet", "A Midsummer-Night's Dream", "Maria Stuart" and a great many other classics. I became a standing-room regular in what was called the Fourth Gallery, which was the cheapest part of the house. After rushing through my school work, I would join the queue at the box-office. Most of the people in the queue were enthusiastic youngsters like myself—some of them would-be actors and actresses. Of course, we had our star cult in those days too, and after the performances we would dash round to the stage-door to cheer Faust, Mephisto, Lady Macbeth or Juliet once again.

Unlike most of my new friends I never felt any desire to be an actor. Unconsciously my main interest turned to the purely visual aspect of the stage, and gradually my taste began to develop. In particular, I grew interested in the origin of the scenes I witnessed, and I would search through the picture galleries of Vienna, studying the works of Veronese, Dürer, Cranach, Longhi and others purely for the costume interest, and in this way I began to learn the forms and peculiarities of the various styles and epochs, whilst the Viennese scene itself, with its Gothic, Renaissance and Baroque churches and its Rococo and Empire palaces, taught me to distinguish the characteristic styles of building.

My critical faculty was awakening. Although for those days the standard of the Burg Theater productions was on an astonishingly high artistic level, I often boldly decided that this or that visual effect could have been better achieved in a different fashion.

From childhood I had painted, drawn, cut out and pasted together, and made things with coloured paper, cardboard, gold and silver paper and so on. Inspired by an illustrated travel book called "The Far East", I built Chinese and Japanese towns with bridges, pagodas and walls. And when at last they were completed and painted I would set light to them and enjoy the conflagration. And when one town was destroyed in this way I would start building another.

No one ever specifically drew my attention as a youngster to the colourful, half-Oriental street life of my own town. My interest in the gay dresses of the peasants and in particular in the colourful rags of the gipsies, arose naturally and without prompting. I had a marvellously illustrated book of "Greek and Roman Sagas" and, using it as a model, I made myself helmets, breast-plates and shields, and with a wooden sword I would wreak great execution amongst my enemies—tall thistles which grew luxuriantly in our courtyard.

Apart from the theatre and the art galleries, there was very much else in imperial Vienna to distract me from the dull monotony of my enforced studies—for instance, the splendid military parades and the magnificent religious processions through the streets. On my way to school I would choose detours which led through the older quarters of the town—very often quite out of my way. Little red lamps glowed in the mysterious gloom of archways before pictures or statues of saints and martyrs. Under great balconies supported by impressive caryatids, gates would swing open to allow grand carriages drawn by proud and splendid horses to roll out into the streets. On the box sat impressive coachmen with three-cornered hats, powdered wigs and fine liveries. The flames of innumerable candles glowed softly in splendid churches and to the swelling peal of the organ processions of monks and nuns in the garb of their orders trod the aisles. And on ancient façades, over enormous windows, were sculptured coats of armorial emblems, or the heads of helmeted and bearded warriors, the grinning faces of satyrs or chubby-cheeked cupids with garlands in their hands.

On the Feast of Corpus Christi the traditional procession wound through the streets from the Hofburg to St. Stephen's Cathedral, and then the route was covered with strips of red carpet whilst rows of soldiers knelt on either side. Behind the baldachin above the Host carried in a monstrance walked the white-uniformed old Kaiser Franz Joseph carrying a feathered hat in his hand, and followed by a brilliant cortège of ecclesiastical dignitaries and high-ranking officers resplendent in their gala uniforms.

There was always "music in the air" in the town of Mozart,

Vienna

Beethoven, Schubert and Johann Strauss, though it was chiefly of the gayer, lighter sort, and Franz von Suppé, Millöcker, Lehar and others conquered the world with their operettas. The people of Vienna sang and danced their way through life despite all the trials and troubles of political life in imperial Austria, and when we regulars of the Burg Theater felt a desire for something a little lighter after the classics there were many other theatres to provide it. I did not often go to the opera in those days—not so much because I cared less for the operatic art as the fact that I didn't know the people in the queue so well.

There was a very popular song at the time which declared that there was only one imperial capital and that was Vienna, and only one princess and that was Pauline Metternich. It was a tribute to the general popularity of the wife of the second son of the famous Metternich, the Austrian Ambassador to the Court of Napoleon III, where she played a great role as arbiter of social life. Richard Wagner, for instance, owed his introduction to Paris to Pauline Metternich, whose ingenious ideas for balls, masquerades and performances of all kinds endeared her to the gaiety-loving Parisians. Now she was back in Vienna, an old lady, but she still played the same role.

It was thanks to her encouragement and support that the famous "Music and Theatre Exhibition" took place in Vienna. The official placard for the exhibition showed the figures of Thalia, Euterpe and Melpomene, the muses of drama, music and the dance. A specially constructed theatre, equipped with what were then the very latest technical devices, produced plays and performances of all kinds in all styles and in many different languages. In a specially constructed mediæval market-place set up in the exhibition grounds mystery and morality plays were performed daily as well as the delightful Merry-Andrew comedies of Hans Sachs. The leading European theatres had set out their treasures, and, in particular, there were marvellous rarities from India, Japan and China.

I spent all my free time—and a good deal of it that wasn't free—in eagerly studying the wonders of the exhibition, which strongly reinforced my growing conviction that my place in life was not at a desk in an office. But even when I was safely in my classroom I had only to look out of the window and there were three fine buildings to attract the eye. In the distance surrounded by green was the columned rococo building of the Polytechnic, and then, rather nearer, there was the Concert Hall, whose façade was decorated by representations of musical geniuses done in gold, and, nearest of all, the Künstlerhaus. And in a row on its roof looking down at me reproachfully as I sat at my desk were the busts of Raphael, Rubens, Michelangelo and Rembrandt. Architecture, music and painting: all three seemed to conspire to warn me that my place in the world was elsewhere.

My fate was soon decided. The drama "Hero and Leander" of the Austrian poet Grillparzer was being performed again at the Burg Theater after a long absence from the programme. The gallery queue was particularly long, and if you wanted a good place you had to rush breathlessly up a series of long flights of steps which seemed almost endless. On the way I overtook a girl who had apparently abandoned the struggle. She took my fancy and I promised to save her a place if I could. I managed to do so and she thanked me warmly.

She was fair-haired, with blue eyes and an engaging smile, and I was more than ever taken with her.

"I suppose you're going to be an actor like everyone else up here?" she said in the pause.

My vanity made me unwilling to confess that I was at the Commercial Academy, so I lied and said that I was studying art; it sounded so much finer and more romantic. She was an artist too, it appeared, and she invited me to visit her studio and bring along some of my sketches.

Susanne, my new acquaintance, had a studio—it was really only an attic room—under the roof of the house next to the theatre. The cracked and shabby walls were covered with her sketches and paintings, and it was all very romantic to me. Despite my commercial studies, I was also doing a certain amount of sketching and designing so, in fact, I had something to show her. Her verdict on my work was so encouraging that in my enthusiasm I embraced and kissed her there and then, and at the same time I plucked up courage enough to confess my deception. She introduced me to a private school where I was able to draw from the nude in the evenings when my relatives supposed that I was at the theatre. And in my teacher I found a good friend who offered to let me work there during the day as well without extra payment. This I did and after that the Commercial Academy saw me no more.

Sooner or later, of course, the whole thing had to come out, and it did. Let me pass over the embarrassing scenes when my relatives discovered that I hadn't been near the Academy for weeks. Nothing mattered now; the die was cast. I had decided that in the autumn I would go to Munich, and in the meantime I studied as hard as I could for the entrance examination to the Academy of Art there.

In the meantime, Susanne and I became close friends and I was in her studio almost every day. It was not long before I began to notice how hard up she was. One day I went to her attic studio at an unusual hour and found her in a rather primitive but highly effective and fantastic costume consisting of strips of coloured materials, glass beads, feathers and one or two other odds and ends, and she confessed that it was one of the home-made costumes she used as a dancer with travelling troupes to supplement her income.

As my school of drawing was closed in the summer months and I urgently needed further practise before I went to Munich in the autumn, I hired models and drew from them in Susanne's studio under her direction. She possessed all the qualities of a good teacher, unerringly drew my attention to the essential characteristics of my models and prevented my wasting my time in unnecessary details.

For some time I had been wondering how I could help her out a little without actually offering her money, and then an idea occurred to me. I complained about the waste of time caused by my having to go out to eat in a restaurant, and suggested that I should eat with her in the studio. She agreed to this, and from that time on I bought the food for both of us. Susanne in her turn suggested that I could save the money for a model and she offered to be not only teacher but model as well. She had a large mirror in the studio which she so arranged that whilst she was standing model for me she could also see and control my work. When the time came to cook she would throw on something or the other to cover her nakedness and then prepare the meal for us both.

In the two months which we spent together in this way before I left for Munich I learnt a very great deal, and when I finally left Vienna I carried away the memory of a generous personality and a charming woman.

Susanne poses in between the cooking

CHAPTER II

MUNICH

THE WINDOW OF MY hotel overlooked a square. A broad
street with gabled houses on either side led into the square
through a wide archway. The houses and the arch itself were
decorated with long blue-and-white striped Bavarian flags.
Crowds were gathered in the street and the square. A band
could be heard in the distance coming nearer. After them came
a standard company and drummers followed by a long procession of men in mediæval costume shouldering crossbows.
The crowd cheered and yodled and the crossbowmen answered,
swinging their feather-decorated hats gaily. It was my reception
within an hour of my arrival in Munich, and I took it as a
good omen.

It was a glowing September day in 1896, the beginning of
the famous October Celebrations, which are held in the
meadow at the foot of the giant statue of "Bavaria" and last
for two weeks. The streets were full of peasants and peasant
women in their colourful local costumes out to enjoy themselves, and the townsfolk were just as gay. The fine old houses
were decorated with garlands. All the public-houses were busy
taking in supplies, and great drays each drawn by four magnificent horses and loaded with huge barrels of beer were a
prominent feature of the streets. With smoked meats, *Sauerkohl*,
Salzbretzeln and beer, the Bavarian heaven was about to open
its gates.

The next day I found myself a room at 11 marks a month,
including breakfast.

There was a whole week before I sat for the entrance examination of the Academy and I used it to get acquainted with
the town. Although I was fairly well supplied with money, I
went carefully, but I did buy myself a copy of Murger's "La
Vie de Bohème" as a sort of programme and guide to the life
which I felt was now awaiting me.

Theatre tickets were cheap in Munich too, but the two State
Theatres, the one in authentic rococo and the other in equally
authentic Empire style, could not compete with Vienna,
though Munich's fame as a centre of the arts was well founded.

Although the House of Wittelsbach had not the resources of the Habsburgs, the various Wittelsbach kings, and in particular Ludwig I, had encouraged the arts in every possible way. The Pinakothek with its collection of Old Masters is world-famous, and the Glyptothek with its sculptures, including the complete pediment groups from the Temple of Ægina, is not far behind. New streets and squares of classic buildings with their colonnades and their neo-Greek propylaeum styles had been built around the old quarters. Berlin critics, jealous of Munich's fame as an art centre, have sought to belittle the town and its new architecture as pompous and theatrical, and although perhaps there is something in their criticisms, I found it all very exciting and, as it turned out, it was a splendid preparation for my future work as a scenic artist.

The old part of the town with its Gothic churches and its mediæval gabled houses and gateways is romantically situated on the Isar, a green and frothing river which rolls swiftly down from the mountains. All these old buildings were carefully preserved with German thoroughness and piety, and everywhere there was an impression of comfort and well-being. Unlike Vienna, the Gothic here was not oppressive, the Renaissance was lighter, and the barock and rococo more playful and charming. Even the saints seemed less austere in Munich, and the bronze statue of the crowned virgin on the square in front of the Town Hall, the "Patrona Bavariae", was always decorated with flowers. And the form was matched with gay colour. Munich was not an industrial town and it did not suffer from the typical smoky sooty-grey drabness industry brings with it.

The mountain sky over the town was clear and blue, usually with a few white clouds for contrast. Not far to the south the chain of the Alps was visible, and the town was cooled and enlivened by the mountain breezes.

Such were my first impressions when I arrived in the September of 1896, and first impressions go deep. "Live and let live" was the general rule of life in Munich. Its comfortable citizens were never in a hurry and there was no heavy traffic on their streets. They had time to stand and stare and enjoy the pleasant things around them, and amongst those pleasant things were the attractive dark-eyed girls of the town.

For me in particular one of the most charming sights of the Munich streets was the peasants and the peasant women and girls who came into the town from the surrounding country, dressed up in their delightful local costumes, filling the squares, markets and churches with gay colour. Before long I never went out without taking a sketch-book, and when, many, many years later, I began to design the costumes for "White Horse

Munich

Inn" I found that I had done the greater part of the preparatory work already.

I was to spend the next twelve years of my life in this environment, and it was invaluable to my training as an artist. Munich was Catholic and Conservative, even reactionary, and the Catholic Church had an important word to say in everything. And yet the general atmosphere was astonishingly democratic. Cleverer heads than mine have noticed that, and many have put it down, rightly I think, to the democratic influence of the wine of the country, the good rich Bavarian beer, and, in particular, to the manner of its drinking.

If you want it at its best it must be drunk fresh from the barrel, and to take it that way you must go yourself to the place where it is sold and drink it on the spot. And thus it comes about that in Munich you will find a socially very mixed crowd around the beer pumps. The high officer, the member of the Town Council and the artist rub shoulders with the porter, the carter, the worker and the clerk; each contentedly drinking his "*Mass*". I have seen princes of the blood royal enjoying their mug of beer at the "Brauhaus" standing in the crowd with Tom, Dick and Harry, chatting about the events of the day, offering their humbler fellow citizens a cigarette or a light. And the priests of the church in their black cassocks are there too, enjoying the rich dark beer every bit as much as the leather-shorted peasants around them. That sort of thing makes for democracy and a certain social understanding.

The intimate association of all classes of society in the *Frühschoppen*, or morning beer, is an important social character-istic of Munich and the same phenomenon is repeated in the winter carnival, which introduces an astonishing period of masked liberty. Tolerated, even encouraged by the Catholic Church, which realizes in its wisdom that the revels are followed by the Ash Wednesday of inevitable remorse, the town gives itself up for two whole months to enjoyment and revelry. The numerous artistic communities, to one or the other of which we art students all belonged, took a leading part. For months we would work hard preparing the most fantastic designs and working out new and original ideas for the scenery and costumes. We did everything ourselves, carpentered, hammered, plas-tered, erected, cut and shaped materials, sewed and painted. The practical experience I acquired in the building up of such unreal worlds was subsequently to stand me in very good stead.

"We're fellow countrymen, aren't we?" a good-looking young fellow asked me one day, and then began to talk Rou-manian. His name was Max Klang, and he was already a painter whilst I was still only in the drawing class. We students certainly learnt as much, if not more, from each other as we did from our teachers, so that when Max suggested that we should share a studio I readily agreed.

A few days later we had taken a studio with one room attached, and, as far as I was concerned, the *Scènes de la Vie de Bohème* could begin. Of course, we had to have a house-warming.

"Lazare will have to come with his guitar," said Max. "I'll make Turkish coffee and we'll dance."

I already knew Lazare, a Russian, who was in my class, a cheerful fellow and a good companion. Max also mentioned the names of several others he intended to invite. That was all very well, but, with my mind prepared by Murger, the idea of drinking coffee and dancing with my fellow students seemed a little tame and I said so.

"What do you mean, without women?" Max asked in astonishment. "Aren't there several families in this house with grown-up daughters?"

"Yes, but we don't know any of them," I objected.

"What does that matter?" he replied. "We soon shall."

And we did. He went to all the doors, introduced himself and invited the girls, and four of them came to our house-warming.

"Why aren't you dancing?" he asked me, and I had to confess that I couldn't dance.

"What!" he exclaimed. "You can't dance, and carnival time's just round the corner. That won't do. Dancing's more important than drawing and painting during the carnival."

And so I had to take dancing lessons. There were a dozen or so helpless, clumsy youngsters like myself, all rather nervous and shy, lined up for lessons, and the old dancing teacher or his bony partner would seize us and drag us round and round the floor. An elderly female played a jangling piano in one corner of the room, and we waltzed around counting the steps out loud, or stood against the wall and watched the other learners. I never did learn to dance properly. Somehow or the other it never went into my bones. I danced so badly that I rarely had courage enough to ask a girl to dance with me, and before long I had forgotten the first thing about it.

"The underworld" was the theme of my first great carnival. It embraced the kingdom of Satan as well as that of Pluto— that is to say, both the mediæval and classical. Each class at the Academy chose its own idea and was entirely responsible for the decoration, the design and the costumes. Our class chose "The Kitchen of Old Nick's Grandmother." It was a fearsome hole with bats hanging from the ceiling. From cracks in the stone walls leafless branches stretched out fantastically like bony arms over a great hearth on which a tremendous cauldron bubbled. Old Nick's grandmother, a frightful old witch, stirred around the devil's broth in the cauldron. On the branches above her other witches perched like evil birds. The hearth also served as a platform for the singers.

At the entrance Greeks, Romans, fallen angels, skeletons, courtesans, ghosts, demi-virgins, and gods piled into Charon's bark and were ferried across the Styx, splashed on the way by water nymphs. On the other side they entered through the open mouth of an enormous Medusan head into the presence of

The Nether World. Carnival Munich

Pluto, who then condemned each dead soul to kiss his wife, Persephone. After that the visitors wandered over fields of asphodels in which maidens danced to the flutes of fauns and satyrs. Venus could be observed at her toilet; the great founders of world history, Nero, Robespierre, Napoleon, Torquemada and others were there, and there was also a Pythia who oracled in between selling hot sausages. In the menagerie of the singer Orpheus, who, of course, tamed wild beasts with his melodies, were gorillas and highly coloured apes in cages, clinging to the bars, drinking beer and joining lustily in the singing. And after many other such amusements there was a gigantic three-headed Cerberus painted yellow with red splotches. Visitors went through the wide open mouth of the middle head and came out at the tail end into a vast hall full of drinking, dancing, singing, shouting people. Three orchestras, whose members were fantastically costumed, played, often simultaneously, and the noise and merriment were enormous.

Mexican Montezumas and Indian Grand Moguls, figures from the Arabian Nights and the Roman Bacchanals, characters from Memphis and the mysterious jungle—they all gave each other a rendezvous at Munich's carnival. It was not only young people who enjoyed themselves. All classes, all ages (almost) and both sexes gave themselves up to the spirit of carnival. And then there were very many visitors from all parts of Germany and even from other countries to see, and join in, the fun.

With the great demand for costumes of all sorts, there were a large number of firms in Munich which hired them out. On one occasion I came into rather closer contact with one such firm when I needed costumes for satyrs and fauns for a Bacchic procession. I suppose I must have shown some practical and original ideas, because the proprietor of the concern asked me if I would like to work for him. The fact that he proposed to pay me—if modestly—for my services was agreeable and at the same time it flattered my vanity. It represented the first money I had ever earned by my own unaided efforts. At the same time the experience was very valuable: I learnt the peculiarities of various kinds of materials, silks, satins, and so on; how to decorate materials; how to find effective substitutes for costly materials of all sorts, and so on.

With Ash Wednesday it was all over again for another year. "Enjoy yourselves harmlessly here and return to your duties refreshed and strengthened" was the inscription on the gate of one of the Munich parks. I took this friendly exhortation very much to heart, and when the Carnival was over I returned to my work with renewed vigour and determination. I already knew my place in life: it was at the easel. And my task was to draw and paint my fellow men—and women. All else was subordinate to that, a mere background. I sketched and I painted ceaselessly: old and young, pretty and ugly, and above all I drew and painted from the nude. The male body is logic; the female is harmony. There is movement even in a resting body. The creative artist, painter and sculptor, sees beauty where the inartistic can see nothing.

"Realism" was the great slogan in those days, and it was much misunderstood by the layman, who thought it meant the deliberate avoidance of the beautiful.

My new teacher, Professor Franz von Stuck (I was now in my second year as a student of painting), was not fond of the slogan.

He was interested in form and colour, in simplicity, in the avoidance of the accidental and non-essential. He never failed to realize when we had "painted ourselves silly", and as he was young then and no pedant he would tell us to give it up for a few days and try something else. And when that happened the enthusiasts of "Realism" would exclaim triumphantly: "See! Even your own teacher realizes that academic painting isn't everything. Paint your charwoman. Paint a broken flower pot. Paint an old boot. . . ."

I now lived in a small studio of my own in the north of the town. Opposite me on the same floor was an old lady who

My second studio in Munich, 1887

painted. The door of her studio was almost always open on a scene of great disorder. And in the middle of it there she sat in a torn overall and painted flowers. One day when I had been sent home from the Academy for a rest because I was thoroughly off form I decided to try my hand at "Realism". The studio of my neighbour with its unmade bed, the intimate items of female clothing hanging over the stove to dry and all the rest of the chaos struck me as a suitable subject.

She had always been very kind, almost motherly to me, and I asked her if she would allow me to take her studio as a model. She readily agreed, but suggested that I should do better to paint the special bouquet of flowers she had ordered for the next day.

"Flowers!" I exclaimed. "No, I want a realistic subject," and I burst forth in a torrent of ill-digested phrases about "Realism".

"But flowers are real enough," she objected.

"Maybe," I replied, "but they're pretty-pretty, and Realism spews out the chocolate-box type of thing."

"Just as you like," she replied tolerantly. "Come along tomorrow and you can paint realism to your heart's content."

The next morning I presented myself with my materials and to my surprise I found the door of her studio closed. "Just a moment", she called out when I knocked, and then after a moment or two: "Come in."

I went in and on a table stood a great sheaf of lovely orange lilies in a blue vase and posed next to them was the old lady in the altogether. Astonished and embarrassed, I stood there gaping.

"Don't stand there," she said, and she quoted at me: "a broken flower pot, an old boot, your charwoman. . . . Well, imagine I'm your charwoman and by chance I'm next to these flowers, which I hope won't prevent your painting a thoroughly realistic study."

I recall this incident as typical of the freedom of outlook which existed amongst us, and the ease which with we ignored the usual conventions. The old lady—Fräulein Clothilde was her name—belonged to a category much despised by us: the so-called paint-wives, on the analogy of fishwives, and sometimes the names they were called were even more insulting. In our view they had no right to exist at all. At first I was a little impressed and put to shame by the helpfulness and interest of the old lady, and by the way in which she was prepared to put herself out, but before long I had come to the facile conclusion that really she was only doing her plain duty. Because we were art students we were inclined to think the world belonged to us, and to take it as a matter of course that everyone should share our views of our great importance. We were outwardly recognizable by our soft hats and our velvet jackets, and we were much spoiled by the citizens of Munich. We were granted credit by long-suffering tradesmen in the locality, and in the cafés and places we frequented our animal spirits were not resented. The regular "Local" of my particular crowd was the Café Elite, and later on this brought us in the honoured title of "The Elite Group." We drank coffee in the afternoons and beer in the evenings—if we could afford it, but the waitresses had instructions from the proprietor never to worry us by asking what we wanted to eat and drink. And when our disputes on art grew wild and noisy neither the proprietor nor the other guests took any notice.

It was round about this time that two illustrated weeklies were founded in Munich, one of them to become world-famous: "Die Jugend," which was more literary, and "Simplizissimus," which was more political and satirical. "Simplizissimus" in particular gathered a remarkable band of illustrators and artists around it. Its political, military and social caricatures were not only witty and original, but artistically absolutely first-class.

Inspired by "Simplizissimus," our group began to draw in a similar style and we bought ourselves a large sketch-book which remained in the Café Elite and was at the disposal of anyone who wished to sketch in it. Thanks to these coloured caricatures and cartoons, my friend Alexander Salzmann and I sometimes obtained commissions from both "Simplizissimus" and "Die Jugend." In fact, before long I earned more money by my illustrations and my caricatures than by my painting, although my first exhibition brought me in not only very favourable notice from the critics, but also membership of the most modern group of artists of the day, the Munich Sezession.

The most important thing for me was, of course, my gradual drift—if that is the word for something on the whole rather deliberate—towards my ultimate profession of scenic artist and designer. The unconscious beginnings had been made in Vienna, thanks to my theatre enthusiasms, which opened up a new world to me. But even before I had ever been inside a theatre, as a schoolboy at home in Bucharest, it had given me great pleasure to decorate and embellish all too-dull looking objects. In our dining-room at home there was an enormous cupboard with glass windows through which one could see a higgledy-piggledy mass of things which always offended what was no doubt the beginnings of my æsthetic sense. I drew and painted three large and decorative Chinese on paper and pasted the result inside the glass to cut off the objectionable view. I also took a large piece of cardboard, bent it into the shape of a screen and painted it with cranes and lotus flowers to cover an old iron stove whose ugliness also offended me. And for all these undertakings I had a constant admirer, friend of the family, Dr. Servatius, an imposing figure with a big dark brown beard.

"Marvellous!" he would exclaim, examining the latest piece of my handiwork. "The boy's a born decorator."

I didn't know what a decorator was then, but it was clear that it was a term of praise, so after that if anyone asked me what I wanted to be when I grew up I always answered: "A decorator."

CHAPTER III

I TREAD THE BOARDS

ON ONE OCCASION a cabaret was organized in Munich in connection with an artists' celebration and I appeared on the stage in a one-man "musical sketch." What the audience got was hardly what it expected, but it proved highly successful. I was provided with charcoal and a huge sheet of paper six foot by four, and as the music played so I sketched whatever the music suggested to me. Not only that, but my lines moved in time with the music: to a waltz they moved gracefully; to a polka they moved jerkily; to a march they went smartly, and

My rhythmical drawing (Cabaret)

so on. As soon as one sketch was completed the sheet was torn away and another one was ready beneath it for the next attempt.

Some sort of "talent scout" must have observed my efforts because shortly afterwards I received an offer to appear in the famous Munich cabaret, "The Eleven Executioners," and I accepted it. The Paris-style cabaret was introduced into Germany around the turn of the century. In Munich it owed its introduction to the Frenchman, Marc Henry, who made a

witty and amusing compère. His mental agility and presence
of mind were extraordinary and he was never at a loss for a
sparkling riposte. His Franco-German in itself was very funny
and Munich audiences took him to their hearts rapturously.
He also sang French songs and amusing little ditties, whilst his
German colleagues sang or recited daring and satirical verses,
and belaboured stick-in-the-mud and reactionary tendencies,
mocking at the Philistines and cocking a snook at the authorities.
And as they were all young, and poets and artists, they praised
love to the skies, particularly the "free" variety. Sketches with
pungency and point were played and a number of women also
took part. Amongst "The Eleven" there were several first-class
musicians and composers. The lute and the guitar were used
together with the piano, and there was even a small orchestra.
It was something quite new for Germany. The title of the
cabaret, "The Eleven Executioners," was intended to suggest
that judgement was sharp and execution summary in the battle
against reaction and obscurantism. At the beginning of each
performance the whole eleven appeared in red cassocks and
sang the "Executioners' March."

Whilst I was on the stage doing my turn I wore such a red
cassock with a hood and a black mask, and I was billed as
"Tobias Loch," so that my real identity—not that it mattered
much in those days—was a secret. My turn was also successful
before wider audiences; so much so that Marc Henry asked me
if I would go on tour with him. Apart from the fact that the
pay was good, the tour included Austria and many German
towns, and this would give me an opportunity of seeing many
things I wanted to see and studying many different kinds of
architecture, because during the day I should be free, as
my turn required no rehearsal.

Eight of us went on tour, including one woman, Maria D.,
who appeared always in a very elegant and sophisticated black
dress with a train. It fitted her like a second skin, but apart from
that it was decently closed right up to the chin. In this attractive costume she sang highly modern chansons, with great
effect. The first stop was Nuremberg, with which I was already
well acquainted, so I knew just where to go to do my sketching.
The famous cobbler and poet Hans Sachs was a real person to
me and Wagner's "Mastersingers" music was in the air. I
hummed it enthusiastically as I sketched the wonderfully
preserved old buildings, the churches, the gabled houses and

the town walls. Faust and Mephistopheles emerged from Dürer's doorway, and Goetz von Berlichingen rode in the Burghof on his great war-horse. With all its past glories, Nuremberg was not content to rest on its laurels as a centre of South-German culture. It was a modern, go-ahead town and it manufactured many things, from delightful toys to railway locomotives. In addition, it had a very fine line in roast sausages and strong dark beer. I have always felt it a particular tragedy that the Nazis had to choose Nuremberg for their headquarters and thus bring about its destruction.

In Wuerzburg there were the Tiepolo frescoes in the baroque episcopal palace. Bamberg and Regensburg came next, followed by Coburg with the massive statue of Adam and Eve, our first parents, both covering what it is usually thought ought to be covered with huge fig-leaves held in still huger fists.

In Graz, our first stop in Austria, we had a smart audience which consisted chiefly of officers of the local garrison. They didn't take us very seriously, but they were hospitable with the usual polished aplomb of the aristocratic Austrian, and they gave us a wonderful banquet in celebration of our visit.

In Pilsen we drank the famous light beer of the town and ate ham dumplings, a local speciality. In my spare time I busily sketched the town walls as though I had foreseen that quite a number of years later, in 1914, I should design the stage setting for a Reinhardt production of "Wallenstein's Camp," which is laid before the walls of Pilsen. In Prague we were lucky in having a French compère and it won us the sympathies of the anti-German Czechs. The spring mists gave the gothic and baroque buildings of the town an unreal and fantastic appearance, and the Hradschin Castle on its heights was reminiscent of a Doré engraving. The historical buildings looked forbidding and gloomy, and their windows, surrounded by stonework flourishes, looked more suitable for defenestrations than letting in the sun. On the tower of the famous Alt-Neuschule in the Jewish quarter was a Jewish emblem, and set in it was a clock with Hebrew characters. In the gloomy interior bearded old Jews sat and patiently copied the Rolls of the Thora. The Jewish cemetery made a tragic impression; it was so overcrowded that the tombstones leaned against each other like heavy volumes in some well-stocked library. Even at that time I found the atmosphere in the Jewish quarter tragic and oppressive, and it was as nothing to what was to come. The famous Habima Theatre has translated this atmosphere to the stage in its repertory piece, "Dybuk".

From Prague we travelled to Dresden. By that time it was spring. The trees were coming into leaf and many bushes were flowering. The splendid baroque buildings looked airy and graceful in the sunlight. I am afraid we didn't go down particularly well with the Saxons nor they with us, but at least for me personally the visit was not wasted.

Breslau was our next stop. Like all Prussian towns in those days, Breslau maintained the old obligation for acrobats, tight-rope walkers, actors and other wandering vagabonds to report their presence to the police within twenty-four hours. That applied to us, so we went to the police station in a body, where each of us was subjected to a close and conscientious examination by zealous police officials. When we told them our professions: singer, reciter, musician, etc., all went well—they were accustomed to such things—until it came to my turn. "Musical-Sketcher" was what I was called. That floored them; they had never heard of such a thing, and I was subjected to a long and searching examination, and a debate began in which one official after another joined until everyone available was assembled to solve the difficult problem. In the end they insisted that the description was an error; it must mean music-copyist, and as music-copyists were not subject to the obligation to register themselves for a short stay they washed their hands of me.

Apart from this preliminary, our stay in Breslau was particularly pleasant. Enlightened audiences flocked to our performances and at the hotel of the Rügmer brothers, where we put up, they told us they were delighted to have artists as guests instead of the usual commercial travellers, and we were waited on hand and foot and thoroughly spoiled. And every evening our theatrical colleagues of Breslau would foregather to dine with us at the excellent table the Rügmers kept. I noted in my diary at the time:

"To-day we left Breslau for Stettin with bunches of violets which had been given us as a parting gift. Even under close police supervision life can be pleasant."

The continuation of our tour in Pomerania, Mecklenburg and Schwerin was neither very successful nor very pleasant. We found the inhabitants of the northern plain as cold as their climate and they regarded us as vagabonds and paupers from backward Catholic Bavaria, though in reality Catholic Bavaria was almost a centre of light compared with this part of the world, where reaction and obscurantism was much more narrow and deep-rooted.

Our tour was in the hands of the usual theatrical agents, and they had shown not the slightest understanding for the particular nature of our performance, which was of a more intimate and sophisticated character, and could not be expected to appeal to audiences in many of the places they sent us to, with the result that we often performed to half-empty houses and the takings were small, often not enough to meet expenses. As for me, once again the thing was not a dead loss, and I discovered that for an artist Stettin, Rostock, Stralsund and the other ports had their own attractions: a fishing boat full of wriggling silvery fish coming in to land its catch, a lovely old-fashioned sailing boat, even a steamer putting in to set down passengers; and then amongst numerous modern buildings without character, there were still worthy representatives of the old nordic brick gothic to be recorded in my sketch-book.

When we arrived in the old and well-preserved Hansa town of Luebeck we were able to forget the cold, narrow Prussianism of the northern plain. Here the people were of the sea rather than the interior, and their nature was totally different. They looked outwards towards the sea and not behind them towards Berlin. They were Germans, yes, but they had retained their own maritime character untouched—or at least they had at that time. I filled a whole sketch-book with the typical pointed gable houses of the lovely little town with its atmosphere of prosperity and confidence. Luebeck is the scene of Thomas Mann's "Buddenbrooks", which is the story of a Luebeck family, a sort of tarter, more astringent, "Forsyte Saga", which had already attracted a great deal of attention in Germany at that time.

In Flensburg I made my first sailing trip and enjoyed it tremendously. My diary notes: "We (that is, Henry and I) cut through the waves with a strong wind behind us and the spray flying in our faces, tasting salt on our lips and running down our cheeks. . . . We tried to think of the best comparison to convey the sensation as the boat swayed. Henry, the Frenchman, found that it reminded him most of lying in the tender arms of a woman. I found the experience too cold to remind me of anything of that sort. Fortunately, we put in from time to time at places where the typical hot grog of the northern water front was readily available."

We played for a few nights in Kiel, Wilhelm's naval base. And as we were, so to speak, in the lion's den, we considered it our duty to stress the satirical character of our performance. It was the time of the Boxer troubles in China and an international expedition was there under the command of the German Field-Marshal Waldersee. We let ourselves go at his expense even at the risk of coming into conflict with the censorship, but, in fact, we found the naval officers, who made up the greater part of our audiences, particularly receptive for our type of wit and humour, and our stay there was both pleasant and profitable.

Much encouraged, we set off for Hamburg, where we were quite confident of success. Our performances there were given in a modern art gallery, served, so to speak, to the Hamburgers as a special artistic titbit, but unfortunately we found that the local inhabitants had no interest in modern cabaret art and often we seemed to outnumber our audiences. As Tobias Loch, the "Musical-Sketcher", I found our stay in Hamburg depressing, but as Ernest Stern, the artist, it was highly valuable and enjoyable. Not only was there plenty of grist to my artistic mill, but whilst we were there I received news from Munich that three of my pictures, which I had put into an exhibition, had been sold. And to add a touch of interest and consolation to the event, they had been purchased by a Hamburger, a Herr von E., a descendant of Heinrich Heine, a native of that city, though you wouldn't think so if you looked for any memorial to him in the town on the Alster.

Our tour was not doing so well and we were even considering breaking it off altogether when we were approached by an educated and enthusiastic young man who told us he owned an art gallery in Bremen and was anxious that we should appear there. So off we went to Bremen, exchanging one Hanssatic town for another. We liked it in Bremen and fortunately Breman liked us, and the takings once again began to look more satisfactory. In addition, we got to know a literary group which called itself "The Golden Cloud" and did a great deal for us. And then there were the *Worpsweder*, a group of artists who lived in and around the village of Worspwede and painted life-size oxen and cows, and also took a collegial interest in us.

I found good booty for my sketch-books, particularly the wonderful old Rathaus, which, fortunately, survived the bombings during the Second World War, and the stone figure of Roland before it. On the upper floor is still the old council chamber from which the town was ruled. The great beams are carved with fish-tailed mermen—for a change—and on the walls are paintings of frigates and whales. Down below in the cellar stand "The Twelve Apostles", as twelve great wine-barrels are called.

Bremen was the last town in the tour for me. The others went on to Osnabrück, but I preferred to call it a day and I returned to Munich. On two subsequent occasions I went on short visits to Berlin and Vienna at Henry's invitation, but after that my short-lived career as a "Musical-Sketcher" came to an end.

CHAPTER IV

PODOLIA

THANKS TO MY professor in Munich, Franz von Stuck, I
became the art teacher of a Russian Count of Franco-Polish
extraction named Orlovsky, who was an attaché at the Russian
Embassy in Munich. His position was a sinecure, because
although the Bavarian Government had to have a diplomatic
corps to minister to its vanity, all the real relations between
Russia and Germany went through the Russian Embassy in
Berlin. The Count had a luxurious studio in which he did a
certain amount of painting and sketching from the living model.
He was not without talent, but he was a dilletante. After he had
worked for perhaps an hour or so, friends would begin to look
in and then his Italian manservant would serve cakes and
liqueurs and the work of the day was over.

Orlovsky was a practising Catholic, which should have
prevented his duelling, but didn't. He was also a member of
a Bavarian knightly order whose chief object was to pay special
honour to the "Immaculate Conception of the Blessed Virgin".
On a number of occasions I found him in his studio posing
before the mirror in the full dress blue-and-white uniform of
the order. When summer came and the Munich Russian
Embassy began its extended summer holidays, he invited me
to come with him to his Podolian estate in order that he could
continue his artistic studies there under my supervision. As an
added inducement, he pointed out that I should find plenty
of things worth painting there. It sounded very attractive and
my Russian friend Alexander S., who had told me a good deal
about the beauties of his homeland, urged me to accept, and
as the Count proved willing to invite Alexander as well as
myself, I accepted. It was a marvellous opportunity to see
something of the mysterious land of golden cupolas and wild
Cossacks and at the same time be diplomatically protected
from the attentions of the Russian police and the Ochrana.

Count Orlovsky and I met in Vienna—Alexander was to
follow later—and together we went to his Podolian estate.
There was a third member of our party, a Frenchman, M.
Metais, introduced by Count Orlovsky as a leading fencing

master. Apparently Count Orlovsky intended to keep his hand
in at other things besides painting.

Podolia was, of course, not Russia proper, but there were
plenty of strange and interesting things to be seen there.
Orlovsky owned a large estate which embraced the town of
Proskurov, though "town" is a rather ambitious word to apply
to a higgledy-piggledy collection of buildings and huts of all
sorts, most of them dilapidated. There were peasants in typical
Russian peasant garb, Jews in long caftans, Tsarist police and
soldiers, many horses and tremendous flocks of geese, and the
neighbourhood consisted of lakes and birch woods.

Orlovsky's house lay in its own grounds in the middle of this
conglomeration. The annual fair was about to take place at
Proskurov when we arrived, and the Count considered it his
duty personally to invite all the Polish aristocracy within a
day's journey to be his guests during the fair, and he took me
with him. Driving from estate to estate over roads full of ruts
between endless stretches of agricultural and grazing land, we
would pull up at the front door of a white- or yellow-painted
house and be assisted to alight by servants in Old-Polish
liveries. It was like entering another world, one which lay at
least a century back in history. In style the interiors of these
country gentlemen's houses were usually either involved
rococo or formal empire. On the walls hung the portraits of
ancestors, some in powdered wigs, others, with bristling
moustachios, wore the famous *Konfederatka*, the typical square
topped Polish cap. The local landed gentry were all rather
stiff and conventional in a bygone fashion and they all spoke
Polish with a large admixture of French. Russia itself lay far
away and it seemed not to exist at all for these Polish aristo-
crats. They all accepted Count Orlovsky's invitation, but, as it
seemed to me, with some reserve, and when I mentioned my
impression he confirmed it, saying that all these people dis-
approved of his activity (if such it could be called) in the
Russian diplomatic corps as something bordering on treachery
to the cause of Polish independence.

When we had finished inviting the Polish noblemen, Orlovsky
informed me that we must now journey to Kamenets-Podolsk
to invite the Russian Governor. The town lay in the extreme
south-west corner of the Tsarist Empire, almost on the Austro-
Hungarian frontier. It sprawled up a hill around which flowed
the Dnieper, almost turning the town into an island. The

houses stretched up the hill in disorderly terraces, and on the brow of the hill was a large church. Its slim-columned tower was topped with a crescent on which stood a statue of the Blessed Virgin. This unusual style of church architecture betrayed the history of Kamenets-Podolsk. Originally the town had been in the hands of the Turks and the Tartars, and the tower with its crescent had been the minaret of the mosque. The conquering Poles had turned the mosque into a Catholic church and planted the Blessed Virgin on top of the Mohamedan crescent.

We stayed two days in the town, during which the Count, in full diplomatic uniform, paid his respects to the Governor, whilst I spent my time sketching. On our way back we used

Russian "rest house"

the broad military highway, which, in the absence of a railway up to the frontier, was kept in very good order. Now and again on our journey we passed forbidding-looking buildings surrounded by high walls. Their small barred windows indicated that they were some sort of prison. The count stopped in front of one of them.

"Sketch that," he said. "It's a Russian rest house. Gangs of convicts deported to Siberia spend the night here on their long journey. These places mark the end of one stage and the beginning of the next."

It appeared that such buildings were situated at definite intervals throughout the country to Siberia, each marking a day's march for the prison columns. Mother Russia protected her children from the wind and the weather at nights.

When we got back to Proskurov we found that preparations for the annual fair were far advanced. Flagpoles and bunting had appeared in the muddy streets and a small town of wooden huts had sprung up on the fair ground. The streets were already full of horse- and ox-drawn carts. Tremendous herds of cattle had been brought together for the annual market, to which, of course, the fair was merely an appendage. A lively trade was already proceeding in various agricultural products, whilst crowds of peasant women and girls clustered round booths selling various knick-knacks. They were all in their festive clothing and made a colourful picture. Their traditional high boots of multicoloured leather were slung over their shoulders —it was easier to walk in the mud with bare feet. Large numbers of police had been brought in for the great occasion and each of the grim-looking guardians of the law wore an equally grim-looking revolver in a large holster prominently displayed at his waist. Cossack squadrons were there too and occasionally they trotted through the streets on their wiry little ponies. Whatever else happened, the authorities seemed determined that order should rule, for this was more or less a frontier area and its Polish-Ruthenian-Jewish population was not remarkable either for its love of or loyalty to the Romanovs.

The local beer and schnaps houses were not sufficient to meet the enormously increased demand of fair time, and so temporary ones had been erected, and there were even bars on wheels which went around to see that everyone got enough to drink. There was music too, and many of the drinking houses had engaged bands. Vodka was cheap and at fair time it flowed ceaselessly. In some respects too, the Tsarist bureaucracy was of a liberal mind, and other physical enjoyments were also catered for. Political freedom was not allowed, but circuses were encouraged; they helped to distract men's minds from other and more dangerous things.

One of Count Orlovsky's servants had been given to us— that is, M. Metais and myself—to show us around because he spoke broken French. Whilst he was guiding us around the fair ground he suddenly shouted excitedly:

"*Très jolies mademoiselles! Très bien, beaucoup jolies*", and he pointed to two carts surrounded by cheering men waving their caps. The carts were loaded with furniture, which seemed to consist mainly of beds, and throned on top of it were a dozen or so women who were singing and waving back at their admirers.

It was difficult to agree with our mentor when he insisted that they were very pretty, but at least they were all in great good humour—or appeared to be—and they sang and shouted and blew kisses to the men. We followed the procession and saw it stop in front of a dilapidated house, whereupon scores of willing hands helped to unload the furniture and carry it into the house under the watchful eye of a couple of grinning police-men. And so one of the most important fair-ground amusements

Jewish houses, Ukrainia

of the annual Proskurov market was established: the temporary brothel.

Gradually Count Orlovsky's house filled up with his guests, and one four-in-hand after the other rolled up to the house and disgorged its occupants. Finally the Governor himself arrived, complete with a retinue of Russian officers. The whole house was in festive mood and every evening a string band played in the large dance hall. But it was very interesting to note that even though they were all guests of the count, they tended to fall fairly obviously into two groups, the Poles and the Russians, and the two groups maintained only polite and formal contact with each other. The musicians, all bearded Jews, represented a third independent racial group—they refused to drink even a glass of water in this Christian house. By this time Alexander had arrived, and he and M. Metais and I formed a sort of neutral group maintaining amicable relations with all the others.

There was to be racing in connection with the fair. A proper course had been marked out, and a number of the count's guests had brought their horses to take part. One of them, a certain Count G. had brought three. He was a tall slim man, with the typical sinewy strength of the sportsman. He spoke perfect German and he often talked to Alexander and me about art in general and the painting of horses in particular. It appeared that he was the owner of a stud farm in Volhynia, about three hours ride away over the borders of Podolia. We discovered that he was not a "Russian" Pole, but an "Austrian" Pole and actually a serving officer in one of the Austro-Hungarian cavalry regiments. At the same time he was a landowner in Russia. There were often odd situations in the frontier districts.

"Oh, so our worthy host wants to study art, does he!" he exclaimed when we explained to him how it was we came to be in Proskurov at all. "Another of his whims. Well, if you get tired of Xaverius (Count Orlovsky's Christian name) you can always come over to my place."

The fair was over and all Count Orlovsky's guests except us and M. Metais had gone. Now, we thought, he'll have time for his art. But pistol shooting came first, and the count practised steadily in the garden for some days, and after that he practised fencing with M. Metais, and insisted that Alexander and I should take advantage of the opportunity to learn. We did, until our arms ached, and then the count went back to his pistol practice. After this had gone on for a number of days he went off on a visit to a fellow nobleman and left us to do what we liked with our time, so we sketched and painted. He returned one night, but he was gone again before we were up the next morning.

In this situation we received a letter from Count G. reminding us that his invitation was still open, and so we decided to accept it. We hired a carriage and set off to Volhynia, leaving a disconsolate M. Metais kicking his heels—at least we could paint on our own, but it wasn't much fun for him to practise fencing on his own. We arrived at Count G.'s estate and found that he lived in a *Schloss* on a hill, built in the playful style of 1820. Above the entrance arch was a coat of arms with lilies, and servants in blue liveries wearing belts whose buckles bore the same device, assisted us to alight and escorted us into the *Schloss*, where we were welcomed in the entrance hall by

Count G. himself in riding dress with brown top boots. A pack of hounds and a few Russian Borzois were collected at the door waiting for him. The countryside around was flat with many birch trees and a chain of lakes, but the park in which the house was situated was hilly and wooded. Not far away were the paddocks and stables.

The house itself was charmingly in style. The high pointed windows of the various salons, done out in red, green or yellow tapestry, looked out on to well-kept grounds with ornamental shrubbery and flower beds. On the walls was a fine collection of English sporting pictures. The furniture was all in Empire style.

At that time Count G. was a bachelor, though later he married an American heiress. Somewhere out of sight was a housekeeper who saw to it that everything went smoothly in *Schloss Novosielica*, and go smoothly it did, though we never once set eyes on her in all the six weeks we were there.

Count G. wanted us to paint his horses, and in that respect his wishes were precise. He was not interested in the artistic portrayal of his horses, and when we painted our first *plein-air* pictures and were very satisfied with the result our host looked at them critically and then observed politely:

"I beg your pardon, gentlemen, but my mares are brown and I see you've given them light-blue backs. How do you account for that?"

We explained to him that the glossy sheen of his horses' coats reflected the blue sky on their backs like a mirror, and that was how an artist saw them therefore. He listened with attention as we propounded our theories and assured us that he found it all very interesting. He was even prepared to admit that there was something in it. . . . But . . . would we kindly paint such pictures for our own amusement and for him would we paint in the usual style of English horse portraiture which was, as a sportsman, what he wanted? He urged us to study his English sporting prints and pictures, none of which, of course, strived at the slightest artistic effect, but set out to be a faithful portrait of whatever equine model was represented.

We did most of our work on the horses in the early morning before the flies began to bother them and make them restive, and we did our level best to translate their lovely lines: nostrils, head and ears, neck, withers, back and tail, with accuracy, and to reproduce their colours just exactly as they were, irrespective of the lighting. A stable boy was always with us armed with a fly swatter to drive away any interfering insects.

For our private studies, our "coloured fireworks" as he called them, he kindly placed the whole of his "hippological material", as he termed it, at our disposal—with the one exception of his magnificent and highly valuable stallion "Er", which we were allowed to paint only his way—I think he felt that in the case of this marvellous beast anything else would have been a sacrilege.

Count G's Castle, "Novosielica"

In addition to his horses, Count G. had a kennel full of dogs of all sorts, hounds, Russian Borzois, bull terriers, wire-haired and shaggy terriers, most of them whelped at Novosielica. Only one dog, and she was a bitch, Miss Pickles, was ever allowed into the house. In the mornings the whole lot would wait in silent expectation for him to appear, and when he finally did scores of ears would be cocked awaiting the longed-for word. If it were spoken they would spring to their feet barking joyfully and follow at his heels. If nothing was said, they would mournfully watch him as he disappeared.

Otherwise the pack was in charge of a low-browed, pock-marked "boy" named Zdenko, and once a week a peasant pony was slaughtered for their food. Count G. was not a hunting man, but he had no objection to his dogs enjoying themselves, and they raced around in the neighbourhood hunting rabbits, hares and rats, and occasionally capturing a wild duck or two. I watched them at work and I was astonished at their skill and how they co-operated with each other instead of each playing for his own hand.

Count Orlovsky had his fencing master from Paris; Count G. had his tennis trainer from Vienna, and we played tennis, a game which was by no means so popular or so well known then as it is now.

Schloss Novosielica had only candle lighting and no bells. If we wanted anything we just clapped our hands and this was heard in the servants' hall, where there were always up to a dozen liveried lackeys waiting to answer any such summons. When they had nothing else to do they sat on a long bench in the servants' hall and in front of them was a large cage containing a live owl.

Count G. was, of course, an impassioned horseman, and he often took us with him on horseback. I had never been on a horse in my life before, but thanks to the count's tuition and the fact that every consideration was shown to me I didn't do so badly.

He also took us with him on many of his social calls. As neighbours invariably lived at some distance from each other, the carriage would be made ready on such occasions and Count G. would drive. I remember two of these visits in particular because in each case they were to real eccentrics. Unfortunately, I have forgotten their names, but the visits I remember very well.

"I owe old X a visit," the Count said one day. "He hates my visits, but there's nothing he can do about it, and it amuses me. First of all he doesn't like my ways and secondly he's such a stinking miser that he counts every lump of sugar you put in your tea at his place. And yet he's a millionaire and possesses what I believe is a remarkable collection of porcelain. I don't know much about such things, but you gentlemen, being artists, will probably get a great deal of pleasure out of it".

We drove off to visit X, and his porcelain, G. on the high box and Alexander and I inside. When we came to the gates of X's house we found them closed. G. cracked his whip and whistled once or twice, but there was no sign of life and no one made any attempt to open the gates.

"The old fox probably saw us coming and had the gates closed," said G. "I'll show him," and he laughed.

The carriage pole between the two powerful horses was iron-shod and extended well beyond their heads. G. backed the carriage and then, with a crack of his whip and shouts of encouragement, he urged the horses forward against the closed doors. The powerful shaft crashed against the gates, which groaned but did not give way, so G. backed again and tried a second time. This time the gates burst open and we rolled through in great style, the two horses galloping grandly up to the entrance of the long low-lying house.

I did not understand the Polish greeting of the baldheaded man who came running down the steps to greet us, but when he then welcomed his guests in French it was apparent that he was making the best of a bad job. He also immediately apologized for not being able to entertain us with anything to eat or drink, as his kitchen staff was away. G. gave a hearty laugh at this.

"It's just what we expected," he observed, "but these two gentlemen are artists; they haven't come for anything to eat, but to have a look at your collection of porcelain."

"What a great pity!" said X at once. "But the window shutters of the salon are fastened down and there's no light."

By this time we were in the hall of the house.

"*Ach!*" exclaimed G., "that's all right; I'll soon see to that," and without waiting for an invitation he pushed open a pair of double doors on one side of the hall and strode into a dark room.

"Stop! Stop! my good friend," cried X. "There will be an accident in the dark. Let me," and he hurried after G., but, too late—from the room came a sudden sound of smashing china.

When we followed our bald-headed host, G. had pulled open the shutters and the light which streamed in showed fragments of broken china on the floor. The collection was so large that there was no room for it to be displayed properly; all the glass cases and tables were full and there were many pieces of beautiful china on the floor. There was only a small path free from one room to the next, and G. strode on. Again there was the sound of breaking china and then the crash of shutters.

"Herr Count!" shrieked our host in the last accents of despair. "Monsieur le comte. Please don't take the trouble to open the shutters yourself. Ivan! Sashka! Come quickly. Open the shutters."

Two manservants appeared as though from nowhere and he urged them on to haste in a mixture of Polish and French.

"Ah! Ivan and Sashka, so you're back again already. Splendid," we heard G. call from the third room. When we went in to him he was holding a beautiful tureen up for our admiration.

"Look at that!" he exclaimed admiringly. "Alt-Meissner, I believe. A masterpiece."

Our host hurried up to relieve him of the work of art and he did succeed in saving the tureen itself, but G. still held the cover, which was decorated with fruit in relief and most delicately coloured.

"*C'est tres fragile, cher comte,*" stammered our host in a fright "*Soyez prudent, je vous prie*. It's one of my rarest pieces."

But G. gaily held the lid up to the light to show us its delicacy. The lid slipped through G.'s hand and fell to the floor, where it broke.

"That's what comes of being hungry," he said with a malicious grin. "We've driven for several hours to see you, my friend, and the fresh air gives one an appetite. But it's all right now, isn't it? There's Ivan and Sashka to attend to us."

"Yes, yes," murmured the unfortunate man, collecting the pieces of his valuable tureen lid from the floor. "Of course. I beg of you, please go into the dining-room."

In the dining-room the table was already being laid, and the snack we started off with developed into a banquet, because every time G. proposed that our host should show us some more of his collection he had new delicacies brought in and new bottles uncorked. And when G. mentioned the Meissner, Sèvres and Nymphenburg figurines a battery of champagne arrived.

We finally drove off in a state of great physical contentment, G. waving his whip in the friendliest possible fashion to our host, who stood forlornly on his front steps and watched us go.

"That's the way to punish an old miser," said G. with deep satisfaction. "He wouldn't have given us so much as a cup of tea."

The other strange neighbour G. took us to visit was a very different type. He was an old bachelor. His father had been Polish and his mother Russian, and his French was liberally interlarded with Polish and Russian. He was wearing a Turkish dressing gown and on his fat fingers were many fine rings. His house was full of costly but tasteless furniture, and the walls were covered with aggressively flowered tapestry. All around hung oil paintings in pompous, much-ornamented gold frames, and their subjects were all the same: naked women.

On our arrival tea was served by a middle-aged woman dressed discreetly in black. So far so good, but the very excellent and dainty sandwiches which followed immediately were served by a slim and pretty young woman somewhat heavily made up, who smiled rather more invitingly than the occasion seemed to call for. A wonderful dish of cream was then brought in by a voluptuous and deeply *décolleté* blonde in a pink dress. And finally preserved fruits were served on a silver tablet by a young woman in an Oriental fantasy costume. A gold-embroidered Zouave jacket left her neck and arms bare. Wide transparent harem trousers were fastened at the ankle with heavy silver buckles. From the small turban she was wearing a thin veil hung down over the top half of her face. Her arms and hands, and particularly her bare feet were loaded with jewellery. G. looked at the girl appraisingly.

"Your latest, *cher ami?*" he inquired. "I can't remember having seen her before."

Our host stroked his jet-black and obviously dyed moustache proudly and nodded.

"She's pretty, don't you think? She can also play the piano, and she reads excellently aloud."

When we had finished tea, our host offered us cigarettes and led us into another room, in which three other young women, lightly clothed and revealing a good deal of their charms, were sitting on a red sofa. He also introduced us to a raven-haired Jewess named Maniushka, his favourite. According to him, Jewesses knew the art of love-making better than any other women.

"That's the way he likes it," said G. as we drove off. "Maybe he's a wise man to live the way he wants. Who knows? He doesn't harm anybody."

In between such visits we continued our painting, and when we had had enough of painting horses and dogs we were provided with peasants and their ox carts and peasant girls in their national costumes. We also went around finding our own motifs, and there was no shortage. We had plenty of time to ourselves, because G. was just as restless as O. He would go off for days at a time, and once or twice he even went to Kiev and Warsaw. By this time I had done about a dozen portraits of G.'s horses in the style he liked and I felt that I had made a generous return for his hospitality, so when I suddenly experienced a violent desire to re-visit my Roumanian homeland I packed up my own pictures and off I went

Bucharest

CHAPTER V

CHILDHOOD AND FAMILY

WHEN I ARRIVED HOME I found everything very satisfactorily the same as usual. My grandparents—who were
more parents than grandparents because I had been left an
orphan when I was hardly three years old—still had their meals
at the same old round table under the same old lamp. For
hors d'œuvres there was still cold chicken and the cold fish known
as "Lakerda", and, to follow, my grandfather still invariably
sliced up a ripe melon. When he had eaten he still wandered
round the room pushing a picture straight here and there, sat
down at the piano and played a few accords, and then went off
to have his siesta. On the night-table beside his bed was still
the same old copy of Schiller's "Don Carlos", and the book-
mark was still in the page on which the Marquis Posa begged
King Philip: "Sire, give us freedom of thought!"—a demand
which was to send German audiences into ecstasies of applause

many years later. After his nap my grandfather still went to his favourite café to play chess whilst my grandmother sat on the balcony and took the air.

The older we get the more clearly we can remember many of the things of our youth. We can recall whole scenes in all their details so that—at least the artists amongst us—could set it all down just as it once happened, particularly as in childhood, as we all know, the sun is always shining and the days are always bright. For example, I can see myself very plainly

Grandma and cook discussing the menu

indeed in a sort of Little Lord Fauntleroy costume, a velvet dress with a large lace collar and red stockings. My French governess, who taught me to read out of a leather-bound book, had colourless hair and bony fingers and wasn't in the least what the words "French governess" conjure up. In the hall sat my grandmother near the geraniums rocking gently in her chair and the light streamed in on the scene through wide windows and broad glass doors with coloured panes of glass through which the sun threw yellow, green and red blobs on the carpet. And there was my small table on which I drew, painted, pasted and cut out. On the broad steps which led to the next floor the cook Julie would squat and discuss the day's menu with my grandmother.

Opposite, visible through the windows and doors, was my grandfather's business premises, a one-storied house. He had only to cross the courtyard to go from his business to his home and vice versa. Leon Lempart was a big, broad-shouldered and very upright man with a moustache of which he was very proud. By that time it was already going grey and he brushed it carefully with some stuff out of a tin to keep its colour. He had light grey eyes, a kind face and a friendly smile, and I loved him very much. Not only that, but I greatly admired his imposing figure and the great dexterity with which he seemed to manage everything which came his way.

In his long low warehouse opposite there were piles of military shakos, helmets and caps of all kinds, because he was a purveyor by royal appointment to the Roumanian Army. He made any required kind of military headgear. Such machinery as was necessary was housed in an annexe, and it had been manufactured according to his own designs. Although he had many men working for him he still liked to do the cutting out himself, and for this purpose he used a magnificent pair of cloth shears on an enormous and highly-polished cutting-out table. In addition to military headgear, he was also famous for his gentlemen's hats: top-hats, opera-hats, bowlers and so on.

My grandfather had come to Roumania from Russia as a young married man with two growing daughters, assisted by his older brother who was already well established and prosperous as a dentist. He had decided that hat-making was a good line, so he went to London and Paris to study the trade. By 1873 he was already in a position to exhibit his own models at the Vienna Exhibition, and he won a gold medal. In 1877, at the time of the Russo-Turkish War, Roumania was the ally of Tsarist Russia and Bucharest became the headquarters of the Russians. The numerous Russian officers temporarily stationed there ordered their white summer peaked caps from their fellow countryman. Money was no object whatever to them, and Leon Lempart did very well. It was in this period that he bought the Boyar house and site on the main street of the town, in which I spent my childhood and adolescence.

His elder daughter, Bella, married Leopold Stern, a Roumanian, who had studied at Leipzig University and received the degree of Doctor of Philosophy. I was their son, but owing to their untimely death I hardly knew them.

His younger daughter, Annette, was a very pretty, dark-haired girl. I used to listen fascinated when she played the piano and sang. I can see her now, a delightful picture in a close-fitting light-coloured dress with a bustle, sitting at her piano against a background of red wallpaper in her boudoir. Not only did I listen to her with fascination—I can still recall her beautiful rendering of Schubert's "Trout"—but I gazed at

In my bedroom as a small boy

her with fascination too. She was the dream of all young aunts, I think. Her room gave on to the salon, and on the other side was my grandmother's room with its white wallpaper and great moss roses.

The room in which I slept had four windows and a white-tiled oven. Above my bed a carpet with a life-size lion realistically woven into its pattern hung against a wallpaper of light blue with sprays of golden flowers. I remember all the wall-papers very clearly and when I visited the Musée des Arts

Décoratives in Paris in 1900 I met them all again as examples of French wallpapers of the Second Empire.

"Below stairs", behind the dining-room, was the cook's domain. There were always several servant girls in the house and they were all dressed in Roumanian national costume. That was in the days before Roumania introduced the conventional black-and-white dress for domestic servants. I liked the coloured embroideries on the blouses and aprons and the coloured beads and gay kerchiefs of Annica, Ileana, Leanca and whatever their names were, just as I loved all the old costumes of my semi-Oriental country. The fruit and vegetable seller who came into our courtyard selling his wares in two loaded baskets carried over his shoulder on a pole was dressed all in white with black embroidery, and he wore a pointed hat of astrakhan fur. There he would stand, for present-day eyes a totally improbable figure, calling out his wares in a sing-song voice. In my youth he, and many like him, were everyday figures. Another one would come in a somewhat similar get-up crying, "Mielu! Mielu!" He had skinned lambs for sale which he carried slung along a pole. The milk-woman, dressed in a green and yellow leather jacket lined with fur, would drive into the courtyard with a small highly-decorative two-wheeled trap drawn by a pony. The peasant who carried in our firewood from his wagon wore a decorated smock made of sheep's wool, round his middle was a black, brass-buckled belt and on his feet were *opanken* of pigskin in which he moved noiselessly. And as for the gipsies who came around with their wares in baskets on their arms, their sharp features were framed in the most fantastically coloured scarves, and as they offered their goods for sale—perhaps already cooked and still steaming corn on the cob carefully wrapped up in a white napkin in their baskets—they might have been pirates from any romantic production. Then there was the tinker who would repair anything on the spot. If the cook had something to mend out would come his workshop and be set up at once. He would dig a small hole, make himself a charcoal fire, get his bellows going and before long the job was done.

All day long there was a never-ending procession of such highly-coloured and fantastic types through our courtyard. From my table I could see them through the window, and when anyone of particular interest arrived I would run out into the yard to get a closer look. And if I liked to go to the other end of the thistle-grown yard I could look over the wall into the barracks square of the town gendarmerie. I regarded this troop of men, uniformed in the French style, with a somewhat proprietary air, because my grandfather supplied their shakos, which were splendid affairs with horse-hair plumes. From long watching, I knew every word of command and every bugle call. When the cook-house call sounded off I went to eat, and when the retreat was blown at night I returned unwillingly indoors.

There was also a small door in our courtyard which led into the courtyard of the house in which the other Lemparts lived. This was the family of my grandfather's elder brother, the dentist. There was a great deal more liveliness in their house than in ours, because there were not only sons and daughters living there, but also sons-in-law and daughters-in-law. And there was always a well-filled dish of sweets in the drawing-room. . . .

The family of my father, the Sterns, lived in another part of the town, and once a week I would visit them accompanied by Janos, my grandfather's porter. Janos, as his name indicated, was a Hungarian. He came from "over there", which was the Roumanian way of referring to those who came from the other side of the Carpathians. At the time I just accepted the fact that the Sterns and the Lemparts had nothing to do with each other, and even later when I began to wonder I never asked any questions. When members of the two families met at the syngaogue, perhaps on one or the other of the great Jewish holy days, they would recognize each other with a nod, but no more. Gradually I realized that the Sterns, most of whom had been to a university and followed one or the other of the professions, felt that the Lemparts, who were "in trade", weren't good enough for them. This was true in particular of the eldest brother Stern, my uncle Adolph, who was a lawyer and extremely conscious of his social superiority to "the hat-maker", as he always called my grandfather. He was strongly supported in this attitude by his eldest sister Clara, my aunt, a fine-looking woman with a sharp tongue, who was unwilling to forgive my grandfather his trade or overlook the, to her, unfortunate fact that her deceased brother, my father, had married old man Lempart's daughter, whereas, as a doctor of philosophy of Leipzig University, he ought to have done much better for himself. As she grew older she even got it firmly fixed into her mind that in some strange way my grandfather was responsible for my father's early death.

This Aunt Clara had married very well, i.e. she had married into a lot of money, and she kept my grandparents on the paternal side. I remember my other grandfather, Gedalia Stern, a silent, white-bearded old man who had been a jeweller. When I knew him he spent all his time doing fretwork, making large and complicated contraptions such as bird-cages in the shape of gothic cathedrals, highly decorated cupboards, filigree waste-paper baskets and so no. One day he went out like a light.

Grandma Stern

I don't think he ever paid the slightest attention to me at any time.

His wife, my grandmother, a sprightly little person, was quite different, and she made a great fuss of me. She was of an independent character, and right up to the last she insisted on having her own home, and I visited her up to my twelfth year, when she died. She had been born in Roumania at a time when the country was a Turkish province and her way of life was still Oriental. For instance, her favourite way of sitting was cross-legged on a low divan. With her hair carefully enclosed in a fine white shawl, and wearing a wide, reddish-brown scurtica trimmed with fur, she would sit there and drink cup after cup of Turkish Mocca, and—a point which interested me in particular—there was always a silver dish full of the most wonderful Turkish confections to hand.

Both sides of my family attached great value to the pleasures of the table, and their menus were not only varied, but prepared with love and care. Thanks to our varied origins and antecedents, Roumanian, Hungarian, Russian and Turkish specialities came to the table, and, in addition, the tasty dishes of the Jewish cuisine. All sorts of vegetables, fruits and poultry were readily available and also the delicacies of the Danube and the Black Sea. And never in my life have I tasted such exquisite sweetmeats, confectionery and pastries as were obtainable in those days from the Polish, Greek and French pastrycooks of Bucharest.

At last the time came for me to go seriously to school, and I started in the *Institut François* where the teaching languages were both Roumanian and French. Grandfather Lempart intended to make a businessman of me, but although as my guardian he was entitled to do what he liked, he preferred to consult the Sterns, who, although they contributed nothing to my upbringing, nevertheless thought themselves entitled to protest vigorously—and my Uncle Adolph did—at the idea of making the son of the doctor of philosophy a businessman, i.e. another "hat-maker". However, Grandfather Lempart thought that a business career was the right thing for me and so from the *Institut François* I went to the *Evangelische Schulanstalt*, where the main teaching language was German. Then I was sent, as the reader already knows, to the Commercial Academy in Vienna, where I greatly pleased the Sterns by upsetting my grandfather's plans for me and deciding to become an artist. I was sorry about that, but there can be little doubt that my decision was the right one. It certainly did not break my grandfather's heart and for years he supported me liberally whilst I was still a student. I think he hoped that one day I should come to recognize that trade had a golden background, whilst painting only had golden picture frames. But in the end he, too, realized that I was right, and one day he said to me generously:

"My boy, I can see that you have chosen the right thing for yourself and the one best in accordance with your capacities. Go ahead and God bless you."

When I returned to Roumania for the last time in 1913, the

last year in which the world was ever again to know anything like normality, the last year in which it still seemed reasonably solid and secure, the old man was dead, and when I visited his grave there was a fresh wreath of violets, placed there by his former workmen.

But that was much later, and on my first visit he was still alive and active and things were much the same as when I had left. True, the little girl, my cousin, who had been eight years old, was now a young woman. The cabs no longer made such a racket as they rolled over the stony streets, because they now all had rubber tyres, and there was a good deal more electric lighting. What a gentle hand progress had so far laid on the place! All the picturesque old types were still there in their traditional costumes, still thronging the market place, which still had all the old familiar smells. The sides of the bridge across the muddy river were still hung with gaily-coloured carpets and embroidered peasant shirts for sale, and as I stood looking at them a voice greeted me:

"Welcome home. The young gentleman has not altered very much."

It was Leanca, the daughter of Paraschiva, now become a robust, blooming peasant woman. Leanca, who had been one of our servants, was selling her wares on the market, and from the white shawl wound in a special fashion around her head and shoulders I saw that she was married. The eyes that looked up at me were still those of the Byzantine mosaics at Ravenna—except for their merriment.

"Leanca!" I exclaimed with pleasure. "How are you? And how is your mother? Is she still hale and hearty? And does she still weave carpets and do such marvellous embroidery?"

"Thanks be to the Blessed Virgin," she replied, "at fifty she looks like my elder sister instead of my mother. She still lives in the same old house in the maize-fields near the dykes and carries her goods into town on her back. I send my two children out to her sometimes."

Tzatza (or "aunt") Paraschiva was one of my most delightful childhood memories. One day when I came home from school—I was about nine years old at the time—Leanca met me excitedly.

"Mother's upstairs," she whispered. "In the drawing-room with the ladies."

For me anyone who could weave such wonderful carpets and

embroideries as Tzatza Paraschiva could was something of a fairy and I rushed up to the drawing-room. There she sat on the sofa. Her hair was enclosed in the stiff white *broboada*, which was the head-covering of married women, and her dark eyes looked at me in a friendly, motherly fashion. Her *camascha*, or peasant blouse, was gold-embroidered, and the long wide sleeves came down over the backs of her hands as she sat there. Her voluminous skirt was black, embroidered with silver. Round her waist was a belt of red leather ornamented with beads. She reminded me, sitting there in her Sunday best, of a richly decorated ikon.

"Tzatza Paraschiva has agreed to take you and your friend Toma to her house for the summer holidays," my grandmother announced, and Tzatza Paraschiva smiled and nodded, and her voice when she spoke was like music.

I had heard a lot about Paraschiva's house from her daughter Leanca, about the endless maize-fields, the lines of willows, the geese, the ducks, the turkeys and the wolfhound Puiu. Up to then I had always spent my summer holidays with one or the other of my relations, but now the idea of spending them at Paraschiva's house with my friend Toma, who was the son of an official, was wonderful. Like all Roumanian children in those days, both Toma and I had full Roumanian national dress: a short white jacket embroidered in black, a wide-armed blouse drawn in at the waist by a broad leather belt, felt breeches and a sort of sandals of pigskin, *opanken*, the whole crowned by a hat of sheepskin.

Dressed in this picturesque costume, which is ideally suited to Roumanian climatic conditions, we were escorted by Leanca, who was very young then, to the market-place, where "Uncle Stan's" cart was waiting for us. We climbed into it and the cheerful old greybeard whipped up his three horses harnessed *troika* fashion and off we went, first over the uneven streets of the suburbs and then on to the dusty country roads. This in itself was a marvellous start to our holidays, and on our way we saw the whole countryside spread out before us in all its summer glory. There were shepherds on mules taking their flocks into Bucharest, peasant carts drawn by great bison, bands of wild-looking gipsies with their caravans and their animals, and then —like the icing on the cake—a whole squadron of gaily uniformed cavalrymen jingling back into Bucharest from country manoeuvres, their trumpeters occasionally sounding a lively tucket. In the afternoon we came into a neighbourhood of maize-fields and lakes shining in the sun between wooded hills, and then, just as we had passed a little church painted all white, our cart stopped before a wattle hedge in front of a farmhouse. The door was wide open and as we pulled up with a great shouting and trampling of hooves and rattling of harness a slim and pretty girl with blonde pigtails came, or rather was dragged out, holding on to a great wolfhound. That was obviously Leanca's younger sister, Florica, and the dog Puiu.

"They're there!" she cried. "They're there!"

And almost immediately Tzatza Paraschiva appeared behind her in her handsome peasant dress, carrying in her left hand the inevitable spinning staff resting against her hip. It is hardly ever out of the hands of Roumanian peasant women, who still go on spinning even when they are walking around. Tall, upright and well-made, she stood there in an ungirdled *camascha* which reached almost down to her bare, well-shaped feet.

"Welcome, boys," she cried. "We're happy to have you."

The house was low and long and whitewashed. The high maize-thatched roof, which formed deep eaves right along the front of the house, was supported by columns of wood painted blue and making a sort of veranda over a long low stoop. In front a fire was burning in a shallow hole in the ground. A pot was simmering over it and other cooking utensils stood around. Between the blue wooden columns there were lines from which hung the various half-finished garments on which Paraschiva was working: embroidered *camaschas*, aprons, cloths and so on, a colourful sight.

All of us, "Uncle Stan" as well, then sat round the primitive cooking hearth and had our meal—*ciorboa*, thick soup; *mamaliga* with sheep-milk cheese (the Roumanian national dish)—and I don't think I ever ate a meal that went down better. To the left of the house was an orchard which stretched down almost to the lake. Over the lake the white houses of a small village glimmered in the sunlight between the green of the trees. Great flocks of ducks were swimming on the lake, occasionally rising into the air, wheeling round and settling down again. And all around stretched great fields of maize, with stalks already as high as a man. What a place it was for two youngsters to spend a holiday! There were small islands in the lake surrounded by sedge and rushes; perfect settings for playing Robinson Crusoe.

And there was a boat to get to them. And if it was Red Indians we wanted to play, there were plenty of feathers of all kinds for our headdresses and various ways of colouring them.

From my ninth year onward I spent several holidays with Tzatza Paraschiva, and although it was a clear case of calf love, when I went to see her again as a young man of twenty-four, I was still quite excited at the idea, although she was now a woman of fifty. And when I saw her again I was not disappointed. My judgement as a youngster had been right; she was a beautiful woman and the years had dealt very lightly with her. She recognized me at once and her face lit up with friendly welcome.

"There you are again, my son."

And there was a motherly and tender quality in her voice and her beautiful eyes shone. Everything was the same as usual, except that there was now a charm and feminine attraction in her which I could see and appreciate as a man, but which I had felt only vaguely as a child. Her manner was as natural as ever, and she made no attempt to apologize for her primitive peasant household to me, the young man from the big towns, used to higher, or let us rather say, more sophisticated standards of comfort. There was the fire still in the same hole in the ground, and the simple meals of *ciorba* and *mamaliga*, which tasted as good as ever. Florica was no longer there; she was out somewhere in service. And the old wolfhound was dead.

Tzatza Paraschiva knew that I had become an artist, a painter of pictures. For her that was something like the old monks who painted ikons, and she was very interested. As I talked to her she went on with her own work, holding the *camascha* material taut between her toes and her left hand whilst she did the coloured embroidery with her right.

I had brought her various presents: coffee, confectionery, a collection of coloured silk threads for her embroidery, a leather case with various sized needles, and, as the *pièce de résistance*, a large album with coloured illustrations of Roumanian decorative motifs, *Motifs Anciens de Decoration Roumaine*, assembled by Marguerite Miller-Vershy. I translated the title for her, and, beaming with pleasure, she turned over the pages with great care, making little exclamations of admiration at the illustrations. But the text caused her to shake her head sadly.

"Even if it were printed in Roumanian and not in a foreign tongue, I couldn't read it," she said despondently. "When I was a young girl they didn't teach us to read."

That was rather a surprise to me. I had never thought about it. As a youngster I had been firmly convinced that she could do everything, but, of course, it was the usual thing amongst the older peasants: none of them could read. They "had no book", as the saying went.

"Never mind, Tzatza," I said consolingly. "You are an artist in your own line. No one can weave and embroider like you can. Your work might well be exposed in a museum of beautiful handicraft work; it's so good."

At that her face lighted up.

"Three of my *camaschas* are already there," she exclaimed exultantly, and she ran into the house and came out with a large faded envelope on which was printed: "Ministry of Education". It was addressed to: "The Widow Mircea Paraschiva, near the Village of Balta, Ilfov District".

The letter inside was from the Curator of the then newly founded Museum for Folk Handicraft and it thanked Paraschiva for the exhibits and invited her to attend the formal opening of the museum by Her Majesty Queen Elizabeth. The Queen had always supported Roumanian peasant handicraft, and by her example she had encouraged upper-class Roumanian women to wear the old national costumes. On special occasions she herself appeared so dressed.

"And did you go, Tzatza?" I asked.

"Indeed I did," she replied, "and all the fine ladies there were dressed in our peasant costumes with wonderful necklaces and ear-rings. And they chose me to give a bunch of roses to the Queen."

"That was because you were the most beautiful, Tzatza," I exclaimed.

"It was twenty years ago and more," she replied, "and I was younger then."

"Those twenty years have gone by and left hardly a trace," I declared.

She looked at me for a moment, said nothing, but shrugged her shoulders and changed the subject.

Of course, I sketched and painted her dozens of times, whilst she span and embroidered and whilst she did her cooking at the fire. On one occasion I even persuaded her to let me paint her with her hair uncovered. This, she thought, was not quite proper for an older woman, but in the end she agreed, and for the first time I had an opportunity of seeing just how rich and beautiful her hair was. It was usually covered up either with the *broboada* on formal occasions or a *tulpan* around the house. She put flowers in her hair for me and let it flow as though she

Roumanian Church

were still a young girl, and really, the years seemed to fall away from her. She looked at the portrait with naïve enthusiasm, but I was not altogether satisfied and I explained that I was more a painter of figures than faces. I feared that I had not done justice to the original.

Thirty years later I was to recall Paraschiva again and in particular the way in which she cut her *camaschas* and joined the long edges together with coloured wool. It was when I was designing the costumes for Sir James Barrie's "The Boy David". I wanted a simple but effective style of tunic for Saul, Samuel, David and the Philistines and Hebrews. Paraschiva's designs had just that touch of the primitive antique which I required.

Berlin

CHAPTER VI

BERLIN

In Munich I was always poking around in second-hand bookshops, and once, amongst heaps of books piled up on the floor, I came across an unbound copy of a volume of Shakespeare illustrated by an unknown artist whose work impressed me tremendously. The bookseller was unable to tell me who the artist was. I found one or two other volumes, but still there was no clue to the identity of the artist. And then one day I was hardly in the door when the bookseller came hurrying forward waving a book and crying, "John Gilbert." He had found the first volume, on which it said: "Illustrated by John Gilbert." I bought the four volumes for a small sum and carried them home in triumph to study at my leisure.

On the way, what should I see but a poster of the Royal Hoftheater advertising a performance of "A Midsummer-Night's Dream". I was so struck by the coincidence that I determined to go and see it. At home I carefully read the piece and studied John Gilbert's illustrations, and I decided that the way he had chosen was the only fitting way to illustrate Shakespeare. Although I had been rather disappointed with the Munich theatre after Vienna, I bought a ticket and went to see "A Midsummer-Night's Dream", in the hope that the people at the Hoftheater had been inspired by my new hero, but again I was disappointed.

Theseus and the lovers were the usual theatre Greeks posturing before the usual banal and orthodox scenery. Bottom and his fellow tradesmen were quite funny, but nothing like John Gilbert's conception. I hoped for better from the woodland scenes, but no, there they were, just the same as usual, with Titania in a long skirt with a train, fairies out of an old-fashioned ballet, and Puck in rose tights and a light blue frock. And what made it worse was that the part was taken by a woman—Gilbert had made Puck a proper boyish imp. Depressed at the experience I went home and studied Gilbert's illustrations again and determined to go round to the theatre the next morning and open their eyes to the way things should be done. When I woke up I did no such thing, but the reputation of the Royal Hoftheater was mud in my eyes.

In January 1905 I saw photos in some of the illustrated papers and read enthusiastic criticisms of a performance of "A Midsummer-Night's Dream" in Berlin, staged by a new name, a pioneer named Max Reinhardt. I had just been offered a job as artist on a Berlin weekly, the "Lustige Blätter", and so the prospect of seeing Shakespeare as John Gilbert had imagined him became real again.

After a most unpleasant crossing from Harwich we landed in Hamburg. That may seem a strange way for a man to get to Berlin from Munich, but there was a good reason for it. I wanted to get married. The lady was German whilst I was Roumanian. That would have meant endless difficulties in Germany, so on our way to Berlin we went to London and got married there. In Munich an artist was a somebody; in Berlin —apart from certain circles—he was a nobody, and we felt ourselves something like the advance guard, and forlorn hope, of an army left far behind. However, once we had got into touch with various painters and illustrators we gradually began to feel more at our ease. I had a regular income from the "Lustige Blätter" and at the same time I had ample opportunity of doing other work that pleased me. But although we lived in Berlin from 1905 to 1933—fatal date in German history—we never really felt ourselves at home.

When we arrived Reinhardt's "A Midsummer-Night's

Dream" was still running, and, of course, we went to see it. This time even my high expectations were not disappointed, although, to tell the truth, there was very little of my beloved John Gilbert in Reinhardt's staging. Reinhardt's main efforts had been devoted to the woodland scenes. Heavy plastic trunks of trees jutted here and there out of a rolling grass-covered glade. It was a northern wood and not the usual tropical or Mediterranean affair. From time to time during the performance—for instance, when the lovers chased each other— the wood revolved. That was all splendid, but unfortunately Theseus, Hippolyta and the lovers were still the stereotyped stage Greeks. However, the tradesmen were much better, proper roystering English bumpkins; and the lion in Pyramus and Thisbe was yellow with a splendid mane of golden shavings. The fairies were no longer the depressing ballerinas of old-fashioned performances, but slim and elegant girls in close-fitting green tights and green wigs.

On the whole the performance and the presentation were a delight. There was only one fly in the ointment for me—Puck again. The role was played by a slight female creature in a shaggy wig, a piece of leopard skin round her bosom and horrible yellow-brown tights. Puck—a wraith of a girl instead of a broth of a boy—spoiled my first experience of Reinhardt's "Midsummer-Night's Dream". It annoyed me; first of all because the role called out for a boy, and secondly because I hated his tights and his womanish legs, strutting and straddling in a vain attempt to make believe they were masculine. I think it was from that moment that it was war to the death between me and all tights—and let me say at once that Reinhardt was subsequently one of my strongest allies in the struggle, and so was Gertrud Eysold, that very Puck whose otherwise lovely legs had annoyed me so much.

A few months after that performance of Reinhardt's "Midsummer-Night's Dream" I unexpectedly received a letter inviting me to come to the Deutsches Theater—Reinhardt's theatre —for an interview. I went, of course, most curious to discover what it was all about. They came to the point straight away:

"Have you got time and inclination to design the scenery and costumes for Offenbach's 'Orpheus in the Underworld' quickly?"

I was beside myself with enthusiasm. What an opportunity! The house of Orpheus in a landscape. Olympus with the gods.

Eurydice's boudoir in the underworld, complete with Bacchanalia. The prospect bubbled in my mind like champagne. I could have sat down and started there and then, but first of all I had to see Reinhardt himself. We were introduced and we sat down opposite each other whilst I waited in vain to hear his ideas on the subject. He looked at me in a friendly fashion with his rather prominent light-coloured eyes and let me do the talking.

"Orphée aux Enfers." Operetta for Reinhardt, 1906

"Should I use the revolving stage?" He left it to me. Did he want Jupiter, Juno, Orpheus and all the rest in the usual classic costumes? He left it to me. Did he want the scenery realistic or stylistic? "It's an operetta, remember," was all he would say. It was only when I was leaving and had promised him that I would let him see my first sketches in a day or so that he suggested that the landscape in which the house of Orpheus was situated might look good with fruit trees in blossom. I didn't care for the idea at all; it was too pretty-pretty, *Kitsch*, to use our favourite expression, but still, Reinhardt was Reinhardt even then, and so Orpheus had his blossoming orchard. All the other scenes I designed completely according to my own ideas.

When I came to design the costumes I made the usual beginner's error of forgetting that men and women had to wear them and that they must therefore, from that point of view at least, be strictly practical. My designs were too much influenced by my experience as a cartoonist and illustrator. In addition, I didn't know that the designs were then handed over to a theatrical costume firm for execution and that every detail had to be explained to them. However, on the whole the production of "Orpheus in the Underworld" went well, although quite a number of things were different from what I had planned. The fault lay largely with Reinhardt's own people, who, when they failed to understand my designs, didn't bother to come to me for explanations.

After the first performance the "Arena", a Berlin magazine invited me to write an article on the production, and this I did, at the same time criticizing various errors, insufficiencies, omissions and so on in a would-be humorous vein, and describing how Reinhardt had occasionally torn his hair out in comic despair.

After the article appeared I was again invited to come to the Deutsches Theater for a discussion. This time Reinhardt received me at once.

"I've read your article," he said. "You've got a lot to criticize, Herr Stern. If you think you can do it any better, what about it?"

I left that interview as Costume and Scenery Director of the Reinhardt Theatres.

It was all very heartening, but at the same time there were difficulties. In Munich I had been primarily a painter. When I had moved to Berlin I had become primarily a caricaturist. Now I was suddenly a designer and the collaborator of Germany's leading theatre reformer. Three different tasks. At a pinch one could perhaps, after all, serve two masters—but three?

However, the first effect of my new job was a very considerable increase in my income, which sprang from 300 to 750 a month—not too bad an income in those days.

I had signed up with Reinhardt without first informing the publisher and owner of the "Lustige Blätter", who now had misgivings in case my new work should have an unfavourable effect on my work for him, but who at the same time adopted the role of my "discoverer" and appealed to me to admit that the engagement on his paper had opened up the world for me. There was a lot of talk about opening up the world in those days,

C

particularly in Berlin, which was invariably referred to as a "world town", a world centre of the arts, a town of unlimited possibilities, and so on. A zealous and ambitious propaganda by interested parties pushed the idea manfully. Numerous exhibitions showed the latest French developments in painting; Impressionism became all the mode, and there were plenty of "art patrons" eager to buy the works of Seurat, Gaugin, van Gogh and so on at high prices. The Press did its share to stoke up the publicity and there were constant articles on "the development of artistic life in the Reich's capital", and so on. Artists who showed ultra-modern tendencies in their work were encouraged to come to Berlin from the provinces and often assisted to do so.

There was nothing official about all this. Prussian Berlin, the upper circles of the administration, remained indifferent; they were not interested in painting and sculpture, unless the paintings happened to be of patriotic subjects—Frederick the Great, for example—or the busts those of Hohenzollern princes and grandees, and they regarded the whole affair as a racket organized by self-seeking art dealers—Jews, of course—and boosted by their kept Press. But we artists profited by the situation. As a member of the Munich Sezession, I was now elected a member of the Berlin Sezession. There was nothing to stop my continuing my painting and my exhibiting, particularly as I now had a private studio in the Deutches Theater, and that still seemed my chief work to me.

An iron door leading to the attic floor of the theatre opened on a room distempered in cobalt blue. It was ornamented by a number of real suits of Japanese armour and it served me as a sort of reception-room. Behind it was a roomy studio with my pictures, my easel and materials and a big designing table. On that table was my bible: my Shakespeare illustrated by John Gilbert. In addition there was a five-volume edition of Racinet's "L'histoire du Costume" and a series of costume lithographs by Jacquemin.

Despite my great interest in the theatre, I did not know much about the various tendencies already vigorously at work in many countries to reform and revive the theatre. I had seen one or two of Gordon Craig's designs in "The Studio" and read one or two Press notices, but apart from that my equipment in experience and knowledge was very small, and now here I was, an active and inadequately prepared warrior at the heart and centre of the battle, because it certainly revolved in particular around Reinhardt.

"Orpheus in the Underworld", my first real venture into the theatre, was produced in the Neues Theater, but then Reinhardt definitely transferred his activities to the Deutsches Theater". When I became his assistant there the old house had been restored and provided with an impressive neo-classic façade. The house next door, a former dance hall, was turned into an intimate theatre, the Kammerspiel. In the floor above the theatre was Reinhardt's dramatic school. Behind both theatres lay a very large atelier which was used as workshops, storage for properties, costumes, etc. At the back a small river flowed between trees, the Panke. It was a piece of Old Berlin, one of the very few still surviving picturesque parts of an otherwise very sober urban scene.

When I began work in the autumn, Reinhardt's repertoire included Schiller's "Kabale und Liebe", Lessing's "Minna von Barnhelm", Kleist's "Das Kätchen von Heilbronn" and Shakespeare's "Merchant of Venice". Reinhardt then proposed to move "Midsummer-Night's Dream" from the Neues Theater to the Deutsches Theater and to stage it afresh. My job was to design the new costumes.

Immediately I explained my ideas of how Puck ought to be played and told Reinhardt how disappointed I had been with the female Puck in the Neues Theater. He listened to what I had to say and agreed at once, particularly to my proposal to get rid of the stupid tights. "They must be brown muscular legs, boy's legs," I insisted. Reinhardt nodded.

"Fine," he said. "But you're an artist; you've no idea how difficult it is to get a really talented youngster for a role like that. I haven't found one yet."[1]

And he sighed comically and passed his hand through his hair. It was a characteristic gesture of half-serious, half-humorous despair. Max Reinhardt was a great experimenter and he had to make his way against opposition, but nevertheless his was not a fighting nature. He was too fond of beautiful things. His was an artistic way of life and he had an enviable capacity for enjoyment. How often have I seen him at rehearsals smoking his cigar peacefully whilst everything around him was upside down! He would listen silently (he was not a man of

[1] He found one at last for his film version produced in Hollywood: the talented Mickey Rooney. The film itself was a failure.

many words) and apparently with amusement whilst his assistants disputed wildly, and then gave his summing up and judgement on the clashing opinions. He has often listened carefully to my views on this, and that and the other point in connection with some new staging—historic building styles for example, or costume—and at the end he has taken his cigar from his mouth and summed up in a few words, and he had always grasped the basic essentials.

It was only gradually that I got to know Reinhardt and his methods and ideas. He carefully avoided anything like didacticism and he preferred to let me work out things for myself. Felix Holländer, a first-rate dramaturgist, helped me a very great deal. My work also included co-operation with other designers and artists who worked for the Reinhardt theatres. For instance, right at the beginning of my activities there was the staging of Shakespeare's "Winter's Tale", a real titbit, but it had already been given to my colleague Emil Orlik before Reinhardt engaged me, so, whilst regretting that I couldn't do it on my own, I co-operated loyally with him, and that was not a bad thing either because I learnt a great deal in the process.

Opposite the iron door which led into my studio was another iron door which led over the attic floor to the tailor's workshop for the male actors. That was the place I visited first on my morning tour of inspection, and there I found the tailors busy repairing costumes or making new ones. After that my tour went through long, dusty corridors in which all sorts of old theatrical lumber was kept—and often left to moulder. As I had *carte blanche* to do what I liked with any of it, I examined it all very carefully. Nothing is more instructive than other people's errors. There were clumsy wooden halberds and spears, moth-eaten flags and banners, cardboard shields hanging on walls. Between broken-down and dilapidated old stage furniture were piles of fringed hangings, dusty and rotten with age; baskets and boxes of artificial flowers and garlands; and a gallery of stage portraits, mostly very ill-painted; pictures of bewigged men and palefaced women with powdered hair, and a whole series of crowned heads who stared at me with popping eyes. The portraits of saints struck me as particularly baleful. Then there was a row of thrones, including one upholstered in light blue satin and marked "Antony and Cleopatra". Behind this one was a clumsy cardboard sphinx with only one breast. And rows of noseless busts and armless figures stood dismally under an avenue of dusty palm trees. Beneath a collection of decorative chandeliers were suits of rusty armour on stands. Piles of ermine trimmed costumes bulged out of broken hampers. And to conclude the depressing scene was a glass coffin full of ancient top hats.

But not everything was so chaotic. There was our "collection of male costumes", for example. It went back over about fifty years, and there in long rows hung numbered kings, princes, heroes and characters of all ages and all periods. Old Wilke with his white beard had them all carefully noted down in his book, and he knew exactly what almost forgotten stars had worn them in just what roles and when. Poor old Wilke didn't

Old Wilke

like my morning visits at all. He knew that I had the right to use anything I found, to unpick old costumes and cut up old materials and use them for whatever purpose suggested itself, and he feared for his beloved collection.

On the floor below was our special pride, the newly-established ladies' tailoring workshop. At one time actresses had always provided their own costumes, and former managements had not attached much importance to the decorative whole. With Reinhardt that had changed; our actresses now had their costumes provided in the same way as the actors. The workshop was in charge of an elderly spinster named Fräulein Boheim. Like almost all the other members of the staff, she came from Austria. Reinhardt, himself an Austrian, got on much better with the Austrian temperament than with the harder and more vigorous Prussian character, and these Austrian craftsmen were more enterprising and self-reliant than their Prussian counterparts. At least 50 per cent. of the actors and actresses were Austrians too.

Although I was not Austrian, I had spent an important part of my youth in Vienna and in the related South-German atmosphere of Munich, and I fitted into the general atmosphere very well. I got on excellently with the employees and particularly with the property master, an Austrian from the Tyrol.

My friend, the Czech Ottewril, was in charge of the furniture room, and with his assistance I made a register in which every item was noted down, described, provided with a photo, and arranged according to period and style.

My tour of inspection always ended with the most important place of all, the holy of holies, the stage. At first I asked very few questions in order not to betray my ignorance, though passionate interest and instinctive understanding often replaced practical experience. It was the revolving stage used by Reinhardt which chiefly interested me, and I was determined to fathom all its secrets. Even the layman knows that a painted canvas scene in the background, supplemented by various dependent or upright pieces, represent the chief elements of stage scenery, together with various objects, such as steps and platforms, and various mechanical methods of raising and lowering scenery. This is the oldest system of stage-setting and it aims at producing an impression of reality in the minds of the viewers.

Pioneers, even before Reinhardt, had experimented with a symbolic system of stage decoration in which change of scene is indicated primarily by hangings of different colours supplemented by plastic walls, pillars and staircases, etc. Reinhardt occasionally used this system, but was very much opposed to painted scenery as old-fashioned and out of date and quite unworthy of a technically highly-developed age, though he made an exception in favour of farces and musicals, in which the décor had to be just as amusing as the content of the piece itself. For a classic repertoire he used only the revolving stage system.

The background of the 60-foot revolving table was a solidly

built semicircular cyclorama. This was faced with white plaster, and tiny lamps were let into it to produce the effect of stars at night. A gigantic lamp hanging over the stage illuminated the cyclorama (the horizon) and mechanically changeable sheets of coloured glass in several tiers made it possible to illuminate the cyclorama in any desired colour or combination of colours. Another lamp flung white clouds on to the cyclorama, and they could be made to remain motionless or to move across the sky-line at will. This apparatus became known in England later as the "Schwabe System".

The revolving platform was divided into various compart-ments, and separate scenes could be built up on each and turned towards the audience as required. The advantages of such a system were obvious: several scenes could be set up simultane-ously and there was no longer any need for the disturbing scene-shifters' pause. The lights went out for a second or two, the stage revolved, the lights flashed up again and the new scene was ready. In fact, if matters were carefully arranged there was often no need for the lights to go out at all. For instance, if at the end of a particular scene the actors had to go into another room, then as they walked through the door and into it so the stage turned with them and stopped when they were safely in the new setting and the illusion was preserved completely.

In time and with care it proved possible to link up almost all

Rehearsal on revolving stage

the scenes required in a particular piece, rooms, halls, galleries, courtyards and so on, so that the movement flowed on in an uninterrupted stream of action and, in addition, the set gave glimpses through the scene beyond and perspectives were formed. A curved interior superstructure could be made into an exterior with the necessary revolution and then it was the outer wall of a palace or a castle with the cyclorama in the background providing day or night atmosphere.

With the aid of inclined and curved platforms, it was possible to make rolling terrain covered with thick carpets of imitation turf which could be walked on by actors coming from all sides. The gradual rise of such terrain, often to quite a height, made the old-fashioned use of steps, which spoiled the illusion, unnecessary. Later on I succeeded in applying the same principle to the revolving stage, and in "Henry IV" our realistic battlefield, which could be walked on everywhere, extended even to the Falstaff alehouse in Eastcheap.

But when I first came to Reinhardt as an absolute tiro, the revolving stage technique was by no means so advanced. In principle it was all there, of course. The stage hands erected the scenery the night before, and when the revolving platform was empty the place for the props to be used in the next performance was already marked out in white chalk. Then new steps, platforms, banisters, walls, pillars, doors and window frames and what not were dragged along from the property rooms and set up, screwed, hammered and fixed into place. It was very much like building up a toy from the contents of a giant box of bricks. I worked hard and with enthusiasm for fifteen years to help improve and perfect the process.

If I had time I would often attend rehearsals. As a beginner in the theatre world, I assumed that at rehearsals one could get to know the theatre really thoroughly and from the inside. That was by no means the case: the actors spoke softly, almost in an undertone, and Reinhardt rarely said anything at all. He would sit there with his head resting in his hand, apparently taking very little notice of the proceedings at all, though from time to time he would rouse himself to say a few quiet words to an actor, and almost invariably they hit the nail squarely on the head.

But when comic scenes were rehearsed I have seen him laugh and laugh until he cried. He often said that he considered Shakespeare the greatest stage genius of all times, particularly because he almost always followed tragic scenes with comic ones. Very few dramatists after Shakespeare seemed to understand that after tragedy, bloodshed and slaughter the audience needed light relief. Reinhardt loved his clowns and he allowed them a good deal of freedom, regarding them as the direct descendants of the Merry Andrews and wags of the ancient fairs.

As an actor himself, Reinhardt knew the contents of the pieces he had acted in and not the contents of plays as such. The result was that he could approach the staging of a new piece without prejudice, without superfluous reminiscences and with no unconscious resistances. "Ignorance is bliss", and it was a wise principle. Reinhardt didn't care a damn that Bohemia hadn't a sea-coast, and he ignored the pedants who said that Shakespeare had made a mistake and that Bohemia would have to be turned into some unreal and ideal Arcadia. Reinhardt knew Bohemia well from his youth, and he saw Perdita, Mopsa, Dorcas and all the shepherds and shepherdesses in the delightful multi-coloured dresses of Czech peasants dancing on a village green. But after the first night of "The Winter's Tale" the critics fell on Reinhardt with almost one accord and tried to rend him limb from limb.

To understand just what Reinhardt meant to the German stage one must know something of the theatrical world before he arrived to turn it upside down. First of all the theatre was regarded as an educational institution rather than a means of amusement. At performances of the classics the audience was expected to do something for its culture rather than enjoy itself. There is, of course, every reason why the theatre should be an educational and cultural institution, but to regard it as nothing but that means to cripple it in a narrow tradition, and that was exactly what had happened. If anyone dared to deviate by one hair's-breadth from the old-established and long accepted traditions he was howled down and cast out. The worst and most reactionary band of all were the theatre critics, whose duty it should have been to encourage the healthy development of the theatre. Instead, they gave themselves the airs of despots and regarded themselves as the appointed defenders of the nation's literary traditions and treasures. At performances of Goethe, Schiller and Shakespeare the audience was expected to sit there humbly and listen to the words as though to a sermon in church addressed to the good of their souls. Leading theatres, like the Deutches Theater, were in the hands of literary men who carefully avoided all experiments and did their utmost to see that everything was done in exactly the same way as it had always been done before. The result was that when the classics were performed the audience saw what might be compared to blackened masterpieces in which all colour and life had been deadened by layer after layer of ancient varnish. And now imagine that overnight the dirt was cleaned away and the colours all shone in their pristine glory, and that a thing which had been dull and uninteresting before was now a delight to the eye.

That was more or less what happened when Reinhardt presented his staging of Kleist's "Kätchen von Heilbronn" and Shakespeare's "Merchant of Venice" and "The Winter's Tale". When he gave audiences something to see as well as something to hear, which, one would have thought, was exactly what the theatre was there for, the critics howled: "Sacrilege! Reinhardt distracts from the essential. Meretricious superficialities! A debasement of the classic spirit!" And so on. They seemed to regard his productions as a personal insult, as an attack on their supreme right to determine what should and what should not be done in the theatre, and they did their best to put him out of business, but the theatre public sided with Reinhardt, and the new movement progressed rapidly until Reinhardt's rivals, including even the State theatres, began to experiment in the hated and condemned *genre*.

Reinhardt was very little influenced by all the shouting. He just did not understand it when motives other than purely artistic ones were ascribed to him. How could light, colour and beauty do any harm to a play? He was convinced that they couldn't, and so he didn't care what the critics said. The battle has now long since been fought and won, and it was Reinhardt, not the critics, who won it.

There was one particularly valuable innovation Reinhardt was responsible for. He took every opportunity of giving his younger and unknown actors a chance of playing big roles. If one experiment proved unsuccessful he would try another one, and in this way he trained a new generation of young actors, many of whom subsequently became world-famous.

"Reinhardt showed me a painting by Edward Munch in his office to-day", I find noted in my diary. "It was a painting of a room in which the chief object was a large black leather armchair."

That was to be the scenery for Ibsen's play "Ghosts", with which the new Kammerspiele was to open. It was a typical Munch picture and there was very little else to indicate how the room was furnished. I pointed this out to Reinhardt.

"Maybe," he said, "but the heavy armchair tells you all you want to know. The dark colouring reflects the whole atmosphere of the drama. And then look at the walls: they're the colour of diseased gums. We must try to get that tone. It will put the actors in the right mood. Mimic needs space made up of form, light and, above all, colour to do itself justice."

The great psychological importance of colour—it was Reinhardt who put me on that track. Instinctively he always hit on the right thing, whether it was the colour of a costume, or even the material of which it had to be made. Iago in "Othello", for instance, he saw in green, "glistening like a reptile". Tybalt, the swashbuckler, was to have a costume like a fighting cock. Mercutio was to be as colourful as his speeches. In Schiller's "Don Carlos", which plays at the bigoted Catholic court of Phillip II, he demanded that the black and brown of the monastic habits should stand out against the cold white of bare interiors. His ideas on the costumes of Rosenkrantz and Guildenstern were original. They ought, he declared, to indicate that their wearers were interested in sports and physical culture in general. When I pointed out that they were, after all, gentlemen of the court of Denmark, he replied that really they were English, as English as the tradesmen in "A Midsummer-Night's Dream", or as Sir Toby Belch and Sir Andrew Aguecheek in "Twelfth Night".

Bernard Shaw's "Man and Superman" was my first attempt at a play. The *regisseur* (it was not Reinhardt) refused to let me try a modernistic experiment, and perhaps in view of the realism of the play he was right, but the result was not one which fills me with any particular pride when I look back on it. The next attempt was the "Liebes-König", which plays in mediæval Poland, and that went very much better. Once again Reinhardt was not the *regisseur*. I think he was waiting to see how I shaped before entrusting me with the artistic side of a play under his direction.

The "Liebes-König" did not have a long run, but my share in it was praised by a number of the critics, and from what Reinhardt said it was clear that he now considered that I had won my spurs. Throughout the fifteen years I worked with him his method of explaining his ideas to me was always the same. In the first discussion he would let me know in a few words what visual impressions he had received in reading the play, and what he considered to be the essential and striking characteristics. He never talked for long; all he had to say was said briefly and very much to the point. After that he let me do the talking. I would then carefully study the play, making innumerable sketches and trying out various ideas before I placed any definite plans before him.

I soon came to recognize that sketches were often misleading and therefore I began to build models, and that is the method I still use from the very beginning of a task. The plastic model of a stage scene is to the sketch as the reality to the dream. With paper, cardboard, paste and other materials, I began to manufacture my scenes, and then I found myself on much more solid ground. They were not always strictly accurate scale models, but at least they gave our stage technicians a much better and more tangible idea of what was required of them. Incidentally, Reinhardt himself drew excellently, and his carefully kept *regie* books are studded with stage sketches and scenes.

The next step was to see about whatever furniture was required, to find out what we already had and to superintend the making of anything we lacked. It was not long before I realized that real furniture, even when its style was correct, was no good on the stage; it always looked much too small for over life-size stage interiors. Our carpenters were excellent and therefore it was quite easy to have the pieces made larger than normal to suit the stage.

After that began the fascinating task of peopling my scenes and dressing my characters; seeing them in the setting I had created; watching them move and visualizing their costumes. First of all ideal forms were sketched, slim, elegant women and splendidly statuesque men. It is easy enough to clothe such types, but in practice the physical and other characteristics of actual players have to be coped with. And then there is the effect of the materials used. The scenic artist learns by experience that different materials exercise different effects. He knows that dark stuffs tend to slim down figures and that light stuffs tend to make them appear fuller. He will avoid dressing small persons in large-patterned or diagonally striped materials, and he will be very economical in the use of pure white. He will remember that blue is not a very intense colour in artificial light. And reds are really a danger sign for him; he knows that red can easily combine with other colours to make a garish show.

Our tailoring workshop not only carried out repairs, but made whatever was required, but before long it became pain- fully clear to me that although our tailors were good enough sewers, patchers and pressers they were really not "tailors" in the full sense. They were unable to interpret a sketch accurately or even to get the general feeling for it. All my detailed explanations, all the stress I laid on the characteristic features of the sketches were in vain. Our men were just incapable of independent intelligent work.

I went to our business manager, Reinhardt's brother Edmund, and explained my difficulties, and he promised to engage a really good tailor and cutter. However, before we got that far I found another way of settling the problem; one which saved the theatre money and myself a great deal of trouble. Quite by accident I came into contact with the proprietor of one of the leading theatrical-costume firms in Berlin, and from what he said in conversation it was clear that he regarded Reinhardt as a man who would win world fame. I got to work on him at once, and as a business man he realized that it would be a very good thing for him if the name of his firm appeared on our programmes. He offered us very favourable terms, and the bargain was concluded. After that as far as I was concerned the gates of heaven were opened wide.

I could let my fantasy roam at will and wallow in heavy brocades, fantasy patterned Lyons silks, satins, golds and every- thing the heart of a stage designer could wish for. Piles of materials of all sorts, embroideries, trimmings of all kinds, laces, metal weaves—it was all laid out before me like treasures in the "Arabian Nights". In addition, it was a big firm and it employed real experts, so that I could demand what I liked. After that our own workshop was entrusted only with very minor and unimportant tasks, primarily repairs and the making up of the old materials we already had in stock. Poor old Wilke's face always fell when he saw me coming: it probably meant that more of the treasures he so carefully guarded were to be unpicked and the material made up into something new; one day, perhaps, it would be an old Capulet cloak, another day a white senatorial toga. "The old order changeth, yielding place to new. . . ." But poor old Wilke had no interest in the new. All change for him was a change for the worse. He would sit perched in his corner wearing his faded old morning coat and looking the picture of misery. One morning he was found hanging in the gloom amidst his dusty and cob-webbed treasures. Decay he could stand, but not change; it was too much for him.

I have already mentioned that one of my first achievements was the abolition of Puck's tights, and I now continued my campaign against tights in general until some of our actresses began to feel that their morals were threatened, and trouble blew up. But fortunately there was Reinhardt's great authority behind me. The actors and actresses knew how much they owed him, and gradually I, too, succeeded in convincing them that I was open to reason and had no intention of bearing down all opposition by force. At the same time there is nothing more flattering for any woman than the knowledge that someone is honestly striving to present her physical attractions in the best possible light and setting. It soon became clear to me that amongst the many qualities a costume-designer must possess is a feeling for the personal psychology of his "victims". If he does, then having wisely and ostentatiously taken one step back he can afterwards venture to take two steps forward. There's nothing succeeds like success, and as the all-powerful Reinhardt never failed to be present at dress rehearsals, and as he invariably approved of what he saw, the game was won.

When I had been with Reinhardt for about a year my position was already secure enough to allow me to come into the open. A welcome opportunity arose with the production of the "Lysistrata" of Aristophanes. The erotic theme of the piece had naturally to be reflected in the costumes, and in designing them I had the charming Tanagra statues in mind. The material I proposed to use was transparent: gauze, muslin and so on, revealing more than it hid. There were about sixty women in the cast, including some of the leading actresses of the day. When I pointed out that for æsthetic and artistic reasons pink tights were out of the question there was determined resistance. "If we have to show our legs, then at least they must be covered," they declared. "We actresses have enough reproaches to bear as it is. We are always being accused of looseness." And they pointed out that at the State theatres even male singers in Wagnerian operas had to wear tights when their arms were supposed to be bare.

Reinhardt, who was completely on my side, used all his

powers of agreeable persuasion, but to no purpose, he even invited Adorée Villany, the famous nude dancer of the day, to give a private performance for the benefit of our actresses, but although leading critics were unanimous in praising the essential decency of her art, our actresses remained adamant.

"Lysistrata"

The "Lysistrata" rehearsals had already begun, and with his usual gesture, as though he were tearing his hair out, Max Reinhardt sighed in comic despair and said he thought we'd better give way. And then I came across a passage in the standard agreement signed by our actresses. It provided that if a piece required flesh-coloured tights the members of the company should provide silk-wove tights at their own expense. Now, silk-wove tights cost at least 80 marks a pair, a large sum for those days. The five leading actresses each received a letter pointing out their obligation and requesting them to provide themselves with the requisite silk-wove tights. After that I sat back and waited.

Miss A. arrived in my studio one morning.

"I've often been told what wonderful things there are in your studio," she said on entering. "Am I disturbing you?"

And whilst she praised my oil paintings to the skies she risked a glance or two at the "Lysistrata" figurines on the big designing table. I indicated the costume I had designed for her. "Light blue!" she exclaimed delightedly. "Suits me perfectly." And not a word was said about tights.

"I expect you could find an old pair of silk tights in stock," whispered Frau B. to me enticingly during a rehearsal.

"No, I'm afraid not," I replied with an innocent smile. "If you must have them, it means buying them new."

I showed her the sketch for her costume, and she, too, was delighted. "Perhaps it would be possible to make the slit at the side not quite so long? My husband thinks I might risk it." I knew what she meant: without tights.

The two most determined opponents of bare legs, Fräulein C. and Fräulein D., invited me to take tea with them in their dressing-room and to bring my sketches with me.

"Are the costumes very transparent?" they inquired uncertainly.

"Oh, not so bad," I replied soothingly. "There *are* more transparent materials."

They produced photos of antique Greek vases, but they had to admit that the costumes I had designed for them were very much more elegant, and in the end they gave way.

The fifth was Fräulein E., a plump and rather formidable person. She came storming into my studio one day. She was to play the role of the Spartan woman.

"I'm told that the others have all abjectly surrendered," she began. "Very well, I can't hold out on my own. Give me green instead of brown, my love, and I'll show all I've got."

We had won, because, obviously, once the stars had agreed the other actresses had to give way too. However, at the full-dress rehearsal there was still a certain amount of trouble. The scene was Athens; the stage rose in tiers to the Acropolis in the background. The women were grouped before it, fifty actresses in their more or less transparent white, yellow and green costumes with bare legs. Some of the girls were new, and one or two of them were enthusiastic amateurs delighted at the idea of playing with Reinhardt's company. These girls and some of the younger actresses had provided themselves with silk tights at their own expense. When it was pointed out to them that tights were not to be worn, there were scenes, tears and protests, appeals to modesty and reputations, and so on, whilst I did my best to soothe them and persuade them to take off their tights.

In the meantime, Reinhardt sat in his accustomed place obviously greatly enjoying himself. Then who should appear but Herr Glasenapp, the official Censor. In view of the daring nature of the piece, he had come earlier than usual. The preservation of public morality was in his hands. As it happened Herr Glasenapp was also a man of considerable insight and some depth of artistic feeling. The battle paused for a moment or two on his entry.

"Marvellous Acropolis, Herr Reinhardt", he declared appreciatively, and then he eyed the actresses grouped before it. "Pretty, 'pon my soul, pretty. But pity that some of the girls are wearing tights—it makes it so obvious that the other girls aren't."

The battle was not resumed; it was already won. If the keeper of public morals thought it was all right, then who else need complain? The same day a notice appeared on the board: "The Management announces that as from to-day the wearing of tights is discontinued at this theatre."

Talking of the Censor reminds me of another amusing episode in which this same Herr Glasenapp appears. It was some years later at a full-dress rehearsal of Goethe's "Faust", Part Two. Galathea is drawn in procession by hippocamps accompanied by nereids, tritons and so on. When I presented my sketches to Reinhardt for this fantastic procession he observed:

"As you know, Stern, the poet regarded Galathea as embodying the highest physical ideal; don't forget it."

When I tried to get further details out of him, all he would say was: "I've no doubt that as an artist you'll find the right solution."

"Don't forget Galathea as the highest ideal," he would remind me from time to time, and when I presented my sketches he would say, as though a trifle disappointed, "Is that how you see the ideal?"

After a while I stopped presenting him with sketches of beautiful goddesses and at the next mention of "the ideal" I merely nodded. When the first full-dress rehearsal came along the Censor, Herr Glasenapp, was sitting in the auditorium with Reinhardt, though not in an official capacity, because Goethe, as a classic, was not subject to the censorship. I was sitting a little distance away.

The classic Walpurgis Night began, and the procession of sea denizens moved slowly forward over the bottle-green sea. And there, at last, was Galathea, golden-haired and standing erect in an oyster shell surrounded by her court. I looked at Reinhardt. Would he approve? He smiled and nodded. Leaning

Galathea, "Faust," II

back, he listened to the praises lavished on our production by Herr Glasenapp.

"Honestly, I didn't think it would be possible to stage the second part of 'Faust', but you've done it splendidly. I almost had the impression that Galathea was naked. Wonderfully done."

"Oh, we had the tights specially woven for us in Paris; didn't we, Stern?" said Reinhardt, turning to me.

The Paris tights were, as you have probably already guessed, the lady's own skin as ever was.

It should be pointed out that Reinhardt never consciously played the role of innovator and iconoclast, and neither did I. When I became his costume and scenic designer he gave me no lectures on artistic principles and he did not urge me to combat the orthodox and traditional or to "release the theatre from its bonds", as the popular slogan went. The mere fact that I was a newcomer to the stage was apparently guarantee enough for him that I would avoid the rut. I did, and I think I can honestly say that I never let myself be swayed by anything I saw on other people's stages. In principle I wanted to rely on my own versatility and originality. Of course, I used text-books, visited art exhibitions and museums and used sketches I had made from life on my travels, but everything I took I saw with my own eyes and in my own way; I translated it, so to speak, into my own language.

Before doing "Twelfth Night" and thus opening up my period of collaboration with Reinhardt in the production of Shakespeare, I designed the scenes for Calderon's "Doctor of his own Honour", Goldoni's "Servant of Two Masters", Gogol's "Inspector-General" and other plays. When I came to design the costumes for "Twelfth Night", I chose Dalmatian costume—after all, modern Illyria is Dalmatia. In addition, the national costume for me there is still the so-called *fustanella*, which looks something like the starched skirts of a ballet dancer and is perhaps best known in Western Europe from the uniform of the Greek Royal Guards, a sort of half-male, half-female guise which was particularly well suited for Viola. The actress who took the part of Viola had fine, straight but very feminine legs, and she was delighted with the *fustanella* I designed for her in her role as a supposed man. The same dress was used for Sebastian and other male roles.

The play in this staging went through 122 performances in 1908 alone and was often repeated in the subsequent years in the same form. Thanks to its inherent wit and humour and to the fact that every leading role was in the hands of a first-class actor or actress, the play became almost as big a box-office success as "A Midsummer-Night's Dream".

"Twelfth Night" was followed by a Hungarian play, "The Teacher", by Alexander Brody, with realistic settings and real people. I knew the types from my early days, and the task was an easy one for me. What followed was something totally different, "Revolution in Krähwinkel", an old burlesque by the great Austrian comic, Johann Nestroy. 1848 was a year of revolution, men's minds were aroused and dissatisfactions came to a head. The inhabitants of Krähwinkel—something like the famous village of Gotham in Nottinghamshire—saw no reason why they shouldn't have their own private revolution, though they were not sure what for or against whom.

"As a cartoonist and caricaturist, you'll find plenty of room for your talents in Krähwinkel," Reinhardt said, and he gave me *carte blanche*. And it was as a caricaturist that I approached my task. Not only did I caricature all the characters, from the pompous mayor and his councillors down to the village gossips, but I also caricatured the scenes themselves, the rooms, the houses and the streets. Or perhaps parody is a better word than caricature. As I have already pointed out, Reinhardt wanted all the décor in his theatre to be plastic and three-dimensional, and furniture had to be solidly made of wood and to stand squarely on his revolving stage.

In Krähwinkel I used the revolving stage, of course, but I had everything built of the flimsiest lath, so that the usual deception we practised of presenting the audience with heavy solid furniture was deliberately avoided. Windows in Krähwinkel were not transparent, but just painted on the wall, and so was some of the furniture, whilst such furniture as had to be three-dimensional was made as primitively as possible and covered with stretched canvas. And each scene was framed in the traditional red proscenium curtain, or above it dangled yellow-gold fringes and bobbles. The general effect was that of a coloured children's theatre, and the décor certainly influenced the actors, who let themselves go and played the farce in rip-roaring fashion. But whilst Reinhardt was amused at my experiment he regarded the exaggeratedly old-fashioned scene-shifting stage settings as no more than the witty protest of a painter against the building-box system of the revolving stage.

Despite "Revolution in Krähwinkel" (which was performed over 100 times), the plastic method of approach remained, and was to remain for a good many years to come. The Acropolis in "Lysistrata" was a solid building set squarely on its tiered hill, and the settings in "Sumurum" were equally plastic. With "Sumurum" I come to the theatrical season 1909-10, and it was particularly important for both Reinhardt and me, because it was in this season that "Sumurum" made us both known abroad.

"It's easy enough to cook with the best of materials," says a proverb, "but the real cook is the cook who can cook with next to nothing." The management of the Reinhardt theatres was always reminding me of that proverb, particularly when new projects had to be financed. Private people invested money in our theatres, and although they were willing to let us experiment they liked to see a return for their money. When "Sumurum" came up for discussion I was expected to create the illusion of "Arabian Nights" riches, but as far as possible on the cheap. It was within such limits that I set out to prove my

capacities as an artist and to justify the flattering confidence
expressed in my ingenuity. The great success of the mimed
drama proved that I was a real cook, a cook who could cook
with—if not next to nothing, then at least with little.

"Sumurum", a pantomime musical, tells the story of the
dreamy young carpet-seller Nur-al-Din, who fell in love with
the dainty foot—it was all he could see—of one of the wives of
a powerful Sheik. The ladies of the harem smuggle him into the
palace in a great basket concealed under carpets. Parallel with
this goes another erotic drama in which the Sheik himself
kidnaps a lovely and seductive dancer from the booth of a
hunchbacked juggler, whose despair and jealousy drives him

"Sumurum"

to suicide. His two slaves find the body and panic at the thought
that they may be accused of having murdered their master, so
they hide the body in the same basket so that now the concealed
Nur-al-Din has a companion—the juggler's booth is next to the
carpet-seller's booth in the bazaar. Arriving in the harem, the
jealous cripple recovers and strangles the faithless dancer, whilst
in another room of the palace Nur-al-Din lies happily in the
arms of his inamorata. Dancing, juggling, acrobatic, fantastic,
grotesque, the supporting cast revolves wildly around the main
actors, whose language is that of gesture and whose movement
goes to the rhythm of the music.

I got many hints and much inspiration for my work on
"Sumurum" from an old book on the Near East which
appeared in 1860 and contained a great deal of information

concerning buildings, morals, customs and everyday things, but much more important than any reference book were the recollections of my childhood spent in the semi-Oriental atmosphere of my Roumanian home. There were the beautifully dressed Turkish women who sold us *rahat*, or Turkish delight. And then there were Tzatza Frunsa and Tzatza Sciopa, who sold us fruit pickled in vinegar. I recalled them clearly, sitting cross-legged on broad divans before their low-roofed, blue-painted house. Their dark hair was bound in white muslin shawls and they wore wide violet-coloured *scurticas* lined with fox pelt, and their toe-nails and the soles of their feet were dyed a deep red. At one time my home was still a province of the Sultan in Stambul. When I was twelve I can remember being in a Turkish town complete with bulbous-roofed mosque, pointed minaret and covered bazaar. The town was situated on Ada-Kalch, one of the islands in the Danube between Hungary, Roumania and Serbia. It had literally been forgotten in the Peace Treaty of 1877, when the defeated Turks had been compelled to surrender their Danubian possessions, and it had remained Turkish. In the bazaar there were fantastic Oriental eatables on sale, incredible sweetmeats and deep-black Mocha. There were dignified and turbaned Mullahs and Cadis to be seen, and, with a bit of luck, veiled women in flowing garments and harem trousers.

When the composer played us the music for "Sumurum" I imagined the architecture of the bazaar, the harem and the palace, glistening white just like the simple buildings on Ada-Kalch, and I subsequently had the satisfaction of hearing the critics describe my décor as "frozen music"; not very original, perhaps, but it showed that I had done what I set out to do. And against the white of the walls and arches I began to see my characters, some of them in white too, others in black and pink, sometimes even in green. I saw them as fantastically exaggerated silhouettes with touches of Samarkand, Bokhara and Malaya. Their headdress was to be Indian, the carefully wound turban. At about that time I made the acquaintance of a very dignified and amiable Hindu gentleman in the Ethnological Museum. He wore a beautifully wound turban, and he was good enough to instruct me in the art of winding this very becoming type of headgear, a task at which I soon became very proficient, with the result that all the male characters in "Sumurum" were provided with handsome turbans.

The "Damsels of the city", "the beloved with sugar lips", were a different problem. I gave them black turbans with small black veils, and the then current mode amongst the ladies of Berlin helped me to dress them. Big squares of batisk silk in brown, black, blue or violet with irregular circles or squares were very popular as decorative neckwear. Out of four such scarves I made an exiguous costume for the honey-lipped ladies of "Sumurum"—it was all they wore, and it received high praise as being both piquant and original. They went bare-footed and their only ornament consisted of wooden beads and ankle rings. This economy pleased our business management very much indeed. In fact, the only expensive costume, a sort of *bayadère* dress with a small jacket of green metallic material, was worn by the villainess of the piece, the faithless dancer. The tragic cripple was given a pierrot head; the other men were bronzed; the eunuchs had green skulls and faces.

"I come to you from far-off lands along the flowery road of life," declared Nur-al-Din in the spoken prologue of the piece, slowly mounting the inclined gangway decorated with flowers which led from the auditorium to the stage. This flowered gangway, of Japanese origin, served throughout the mime as an effective method of appearance.

Reinhardt's sworn enemies, the critics, naturally poured out their bile over this new outrage, but that did not prevent "Sumurum" from being a great success. Unprejudiced observers frankly admitted that the unfolding of the drama in mime without the spoken word was extraordinarily effective. Our actors and actresses mastered the new medium very rapidly and unexpected talents revealed themselves: extraordinary agility, rhythmic movement, dramatic clowning, acrobatic and ecstatic dancing. I came in for my share of praise, though "the magician of the Schumannstrasse", as Reinhardt was called (both the Deutsches Theater and the Kammerspiel were in the Schumannstrasse), was anxiously exhorted not to neglect his sacred duty: language, he was told, was the highest and most valuable of all means of expression; not movement, not the dance and not the rhythmic undulations of graceful female bodies.

With "Sumurum" Reinhardt found himself for the first time in a position to extend his art to the great circle of audiences outside Germany. In "Sumurum" the word had been replaced by music and mime, and they were universally understandable. And so thought Sir Oswald Stoll. He saw "Sumurum" and the contract was signed. "Sumurum" went to the London Coliseum.

Forty years ago it was the custom in London for anyone who was at all anyone to wear a top-hat and frock coat "in Town". It was no use our trying to stand out against this sartorial tyranny, so when we went to London top-hats we wore. Reinhardt with a sigh, because it meant having his hair cut. However, the wonderful oysters and juicy beefsteaks at Scott's consoled him in great measure for the innumerable times he knocked his top-hat off against the doors of hansom cabs and so on.

In Berlin I had caused exact scale models of all our scenery for "Sumurum" to be made and Sir Oswald Stoll had promised us that they should be copied exactly "down to the inch" for the revolving stage of the Coliseum. At the fixed time there it was all set up for us to see and ready for the first performance: the curved roof of the bazaar, the juggler's booth, the palace, the two storied harem hall with its galleries and winding stairs. It all rolled round before us accurately and noiselessly. Sir Oswald was there with his staff waiting for our praise at the good job they had done. But Reinhardt, who spoke no English, turned to me.

"A catastrophe", he said bluntly. "Tell him it just won't do. We're not playing in it."

Although the décor was accurate enough in everything else, it had been coloured with motives from the Alhambra, and the scenery was now red, gold, yellow, blue and heaven knows what other colours of the rainbow.

I did my best to make it clear to Sir Oswald that in our view motley was the enemy of colour, and that the white background was an essential feature of the production.

"The London public expects its Orient to be colourful," objected Sir Oswald. "That's in accordance with its taste."

I translated this.

"Tell him it's not in accordance with mine," said Reinhardt laconically. "It's got to be altered."

"But we've only got twelve hours to the first performance," declared Sir Oswald, who by this time was beginning to get very worried. "It can't be changed in that time."

"It can," I said. "Give me half-a-dozen men, and I'll get it done in time."

And I did and, when the story became known, the Press gave me the nickname of "Mr. Black and White". My six painters completely hid all Sir Oswald's Oriental glory under white paint, and the stage itself was painted black. Sir Oswald and his men were very doubtful about it all, but the house at the first night ("Sumurum" was played twice daily, with a so-called matinée in the afternoon) was enthusiastic. The audience recognized that they were faced with something new and unusual. The characters moved, ran, danced and mimed like sharply defined silhouettes against the white background of the décor. Every costume and every gesture was stressed to the utmost by the contrast. The so-called "procession scene", in which the whole company defiled against a white wall, was particularly effective and it always produced long rolls of applause from delighted audiences. The reason for this was that the colours of the costumes, which were carefully chosen and ordered, combined in a logical harmony against the white of the wall to produce a most striking effect. There was only one scene in which I had made the background pink rather than white, and that was the outer wall of the palace, whose arched doors were guarded by green-faced eunuchs. This, too, was written down to me as a touch of decorative genius.

Literally overnight Reinhardt and I became famous in London as the most daring and successful of stage innovators. Even to-day, forty years later, I still occasionally meet older playgoers who saw "Sumurum" and still remember the striking impression it created.

Success, of course, leads to success, and C. B. Cochran, far-seeing as always, appeared on the scene and proposed that Reinhardt should stage a pageant at the Olympia. Reinhardt agreed and the result was Vollmöller's "Miracle".

"Sumurum." Procession Scene

CHAPTER VII

"EXTENDING THE LIMITS OF THE STAGE"

"*SPRENGUNG DES BÜHNENRAHMENS*" was a favourite slogan at that time; it meant breaking down and extending the physical limits of the stage, extending the action beyond the footlights. I have already mentioned the Japanese gangway decorated with flowers in "Sumurum". This was one example of what was meant. But even earlier, in the summer of 1909, when our company was playing in Munich, Reinhardt attempted to produce "Œdipus Rex" without the usual stage. Opposite the theatre was a large hall with an orchestral platform at one end. Around this platform were tiers of seats forming a semicircle and leaving a place in the centre without seats. Thus the arrangement was similar to that of a classical theatre, whilst the platform was similar to the *Skene* on which the actors faced the audience against an unchanging background. As in the classical theatre, this hall also had no curtain and no proscenium arch.

"Œdipus Rex" plays before the palace of Œdipus, and that we indicated merely by a high screen with the suggestion of an entrance. Platform and orchestra were connected by steps. Above and beyond the seats were the stage lights. That was our complete theatre. It turned out that we were able to obtain impressive effects without a normal stage, without scenery and without the usual curtain. The players were in a raised position; they always faced the audience and addressed them directly, and this emphasized the effect of language. In addition, the spotlights could pick out exactly what was necessary as the action proceeded: heads here, torsos there, the gesticulating arms of the chorus in the orchestra, whilst the audience, sitting around in a semicircle, had the impression of taking a part in the performance themselves.

The experiment was highly successful, and it was repeated later with "Orestes" and "Everyman". This was the first practical step to the so-called breaking down of the physical limits of the stage. The second was the use of the flowery gangway I have described in "Sumurum". When we saw the lay-out of Olympia in London, we realized at once that a further step could now be taken. The hall was long and wide and its two sides and one end had rising tiers of seats. The other end was without seating accommodation and there were a number of large openings which permitted the entry of riders and guns at tournaments.

Our mimed drama was to be staged in the centre of the enormous hall, because that was the only place where there was any chance of its being seen by the audience. However, the staging was altogether simple. When our mimed drama gradually took shape and we began to realize more clearly the dramatic content of our pageant, we found that we needed a raised platform of some considerable size in the centre of Olympia, but only for certain scenes, so we had a large platform built which could be mechanically raised and lowered.

The "Miracle" was a sort of Mystery or Morality Play with a half-secular, half-religious content such as was performed in the Middle Ages. At first such plays were given in churches, but later they were transferred to the market-place. From the beginning I worked together with Reinhardt and the author, Carl Vollmöller, as they went through every phase of the action together. And whilst they noted down, very sketchily at first, what was to take place, I began to draw the characters. What I sketched seemed alive to me, real persons who moved and had their own being, but as soon as the two decided that the scene we had just worked out must be altered for this or that reason, or perhaps abandoned altogether, my figures seemed to sink back into the paper, lose their depth and become nothing but lines on paper again.

But whatever changes were made in the course of our preparatory work—and there were many—one thing remained: the action took place in a great church, and so I built a cardboard model of a vast nave with tiers of seats and set down a few scale model figures in it. It was already quite clear from these models how very, very small our actors would look to the spectators, and that we should therefore have to do our utmost to make each actor immediately recognizable by stressing his visual characteristics.

In that enormous cathedral we had to make it clear to the audience at once who it was and what he was doing. The spectator had to grasp immediately why the nun fell victim to temptation and danced from lover to lover, dragging one after the other into the abyss. Her favours, her love meant destruction;

her dance was the dance of death. In order to reinforce this action psychologically we had to stress visual phantasy to the utmost.

The gothic style of the fifteenth century, the so-called flamboyant period, offered great decorative possibilities. First of all there was the hall of Olympia itself; that had to be turned into a church interior with pointed arches decorated with masses of tracery soaring upwards. Improbable and fantastically involved arabesques curled into flowers, leaves and fruit which, on closer examination, proved to be grotesquely distorted masks. And the costumes were as fantastic as the architecture, like something out of a feverish dream. The actresses wore enormously high steeple hats. The actors wore massive headgear from which stiff folds of cloth shot out like flames. And the leg-of-mutton sleeves were fantastic, more like balloons, whilst the trains of the women were tremendously long and ornate. To add to the fantasy there was a vast amount of scalloping which hung down magnificently rounded, pointed, jagged, from every seam. And on their feet these men and women, dressed like Harlequins and parakeets, wore boots and shoes with excessively long pointed toes.

And then in contrast to this over-dressing was the revelation described in the text of bosom, belly, leg and thigh. The fashion was devilish, grotesque and mocking, recklessly extravagant and exaggerated. It grinned, so to speak; it mocked; it stuck out its tongue at the prudish. And the colours were dazzling. The scallops and hangings twisted and twirled in the dance of life like the flames of hell. Without exaggeration, this reckless and exaggerated method of costuming the piece helped our actors to appear larger than life.

Because of the size of the hall, I had all the props manufactured much larger than usual: crucifixes, baldachins and banners for the processions, crossbows, halberds, pikes and two-handed swords for the huntsmen and their pages, cannon after drawings by Albrecht Dürer, and so on.

As we already knew who our main actors were to be, I was able to take their appearance into consideration from the start. The famous comic actor Max Pallenberg was to play the infernal tempter, the wandering street-player. We were already very good friends and it did not take us long to come to an agreement. The female leading roles in "The Miracle" are the Madonna and the Nun. For the former role Mme. Carmi was to come from Florence, the authentic land of beautiful Madonnas. She was classically beautiful and very slim. Although she was not a professional actress she proved to be an ideal figure for the role of the wonder-working picture which comes to life when the situation calls for a miracle.

Humperdinck was the composer of the music, and it was in his house that I first met Mlle. Natasha Trouhanova, our frivolous Nun, late of the Imperial Opera House at Petersburg and of the Opéra Comique and the Châtelet in Paris. She was of a very different type to our Madonna, Mme. Carmi. She "made an appearance", disappeared behind a screen and then appeared again, striking a seductive pose—in nothing but a cloud of perfume.

Old Humperdinck, who was well into the sixties, was highly embarassed by the performance. He seized the ornate covering from the grand piano, wrapped it round the astonished lady, observing that, after all, she was to play the part of a nun, and pushed her in a fatherly way behind the screen, where she exchanged the piano cover for her own clothes, burst out again, kissed and embraced us both and was gone. There was no doubt about her temperament, and it was real, not assumed to fit a role. Later on in London we were to discover that she was not only an excellent dancer, but a fine actress and mimic as well. Hardly had she left when in came Frau Humperdinck, looking rather forbidding, to open all the windows and let out the sinful smell of patchouli.

"This is the tale of the beautiful nun whose life was one of joys and sorrows", as the blurb put it. "She heard the world calling and she heeded its call, tasted its sweets and tasted its bitterness. Then she went back to her sanctuary different, but the same. . . ."

The procession winds into the enormous cathedral through the open doors. In the centre, still hidden in a sort of tabernacle, stands the wonder-working Madonna. The priests, the nuns and the people fall to their knees all around. In rows at the foot of the tabernacle are the stretchers of those who have come to seek a cure. The doors of the tabernacle open to reveal the Madonna carrying the babe in her arms and wearing a costly crown and a flowing mantle studded with jewels. All is silent, and then suddenly there is an outburst of joy. One of the lame men awaiting a cure has risen from his stretcher. Once again the Madonna has worked a miracle. A great hymn of praise and jubilation rises, accompanied by the pealing of the organ and the tolling of the bells. Everyone is singing. Gradually the cathedral empties and the sound of the singing fades away in the distance. The doors of the cathedral are still wide open.

"*The Miracle,*" *I. Before play starts, curtain or tabernacle hides Madonna*
"*The Miracle,*" *II. Curtain or tabernacle up. Madonna visible*

The nuns have filed out through a side entrance. One nun, however, has remained behind, and she kneels in prayer before the Madonna as though she has been left there to keep vigil.

Through the open doors of the cathedral appears the figure of the fantastically-garbed street player with his pipe. His playing has drawn a band of happy children in his wake. The praying nun raises her head at the sound of the piping, and then she is irresistibly drawn to it. Lost in a dream, she dances. In the twilight the figure of a knight on horseback appears framed in the cathedral portals. Sitting motionless on his white charger, he watches the nun, and when she sees him she returns his gaze with admiration. At that moment she is surprised by the Abbess. The doors of the cathedral are closed, the nun is rebuked for her levity and exhorted to do penance. Darkness falls and a single spotlight now illuminates the Madonna and the nun once again kneeling before her in prayer.

But again the enticing piping sounds, again the nun is caught in the conflict, and she appeals to the Madonna to help her. Struggling desperately against the pull of the life outside, she commits the sacrilege of mounting the throne of the Madonna, of plucking at her jewelled cloak. But the statue remains motionless, and in her despair the nun seizes the Babe, which disappears into nothingness at her touch. At that moment the great doors of the cathedral swing open again and the young knight rides in whilst the piping swells triumphantly. The nun throws off her grey garb, the badge of her order, and in a simple white under-robe she stands there with arms outstretched. The knight lifts her into the saddle before him and rides out into the night.

And now the miracle takes place. Slowly the statue comes to life; the jewelled mantle slips from her shoulders and she takes the crown from her head. In a long white robe she descends the steps into the nave, where she lifts the nun's robe from the stone flags and puts it on. Then she kneels before the tabernacle in the same attitude of prayer as the nun.

The Abbess enters and to her horror she discovers the disappearance of the Madonna. She calls her nuns and they flutter around searching the cathedral like a flock of frightened birds. Then the Abbess sees the kneeling figure. At first, because of the habit she thinks it is the nun, but then she discovers that it is the Madonna herself who has taken the place of the run-away. All bow down in reverence before this strange miracle.

The throne of the Madonna has disappeared. The wide-open doors of the cathedral reveal a rural landscape. The knight is lying in the grass and his lover is dancing before him. The procession of the robber baron then comes on the scene, magnificently and colourfully costumed, with crossbowmen, esquires, pages and bearers carrying the game that has been killed in the hunt. The robber baron sees the nun and is immediately enamoured of her. In the ensuing conflict the knight, her first lover, is killed and she is carried off by a new lover.

The platform now rises silently from the depths of the nave and on it there is a drunken orgy of the robber baron and his followers in which the run-away nun dances. In the middle of this scene the prince appears with his gay and splendid following. He, too, is immediately enamoured of the nun and the tragedy is repeated. The robber baron is killed and the prince carries off the nun.

The scene continues, but this time with the prince and his friends. The nun, fantastically and luxuriously garbed, dances with a supporting company of attendant women, all splendidly dressed. The prince and his feather-brained friends compel the nun to take part in a comic parody of her wedding. In the middle of it the king appears in person. In the resultant fighting both prince and king are killed.

The people are now stirred up; they regard the nun as a witch responsible for bringing so much suffering on their country. She is seized and brought before the judge—the demoniac strolling player in disguise—who sentences her to death. But the executioner falls victim to her charms. She is enabled to flee and then falls into the hands of a band of licentious, irregular soldiery who are marauding through the countryside.

The landscape before the cathedral is covered in deep snow. A procession of mercenaries on horse and foot, dragging their cannon, plods past. The rear is brought up by women camp-followers, and the last of them carries a baby in her arms. It is the ragged, exhausted nun. She collapses in the snow and the soldiery marches on. Then in the uncanny light of the moon and to the growing tones of the devil's piping, shrill and mocking, a different procession passes the body of the nun: the long line of her lovers, the men who have perished of her charms.

In the cathedral the doors of the tabernacle are open and the throne of the Madonna is once again in its place, and on the throne lie the jewel-studded cloak and the crown. The Madonna kneels before the altar in her nun's garb, picked out by the spotlight. Slowly she rises, discards the robe and goes up the steps of the altar where she dons the crown and the blue cloak again and then becomes motionless—a statue as at the beginning. Now the doors of the cathedral slowly and silently open and through the twilight comes the nun, bowed with sorrow and repentance, and carrying the dead baby, which she lays at the foot of the Madonna. Once again a miracle takes place: the Madonna rises and takes the babe into her arms. The bells begin to toll, the nuns file in praying aloud, and a choir of angels celebrates the new miracle amidst a shower of shining roses.

Our job was to put on that ephemeral airy-fairy confection of sugar candy in the great hall of Olympia. When we first saw it, the place looked like a railway station of iron girders and glass full of motor cars. We were not daunted, but we had less than a month to do the job—three and a half weeks to be exact. And when you consider that we were trying out something which was completely new and that we had nothing to go on, it will be understandable that we regarded our job as something in the nature of a miracle itself—at least, as a daring and risky venture. A piece like "The Miracle" presents no difficulties for an ordinary stage, even a fairly primitive one without any very great degree of modern technical means, but we were faced with a very different situation: to stage a fairy story realistically and convincingly in a railway terminus.

Fortunately, seating accommodation in rows and rising in tiers as though in an amphitheatre was available and easily set up, but everything else, the vast floor space, the wide curve of the roof—in short, everything still visible of the great iron-and-glass hall after the seating was arranged—cried aloud for decorative treatment. At one side a wall had to be erected to represent the inside end of the cathedral, and it was in this wall that the great doors—a hundred feet high—opened to give on to the countryside consisting of a series of planes offering room for 1,800 people and strong enough for horses to prance on. In the centre of Olympia, i.e. in the centre of the cathedral nave, a large pit had to be dug to contain the lifting mechanism for the platform. And high in the curved roof the limelights had to be built in. All this raised no insuperable technical problems, and our chief difficulty was shortage of time. However, we succeeded in getting everything ready, quite literally at the last moment, on December 23rd, the day of the first perform-ance.

The great hall with its curved roof was turned into the interior of a gigantic cathedral, chiefly with plaster, and this plastering was a dreadful ordeal for all the rest of us. Plaster dust was everywhere; every hole and corner and every nook and cranny, including people's eyes, noses, mouths and ears, was full of it. We sat down in it; we walked in it; we got smeared all over in it; we rehearsed in it; we despaired in it. We had no time to wait until the plastering, the digging and the hammering was over. Everything had to go forward at once, and every minute was precious.

If "The Miracle" had been just another play to be performed on just another stage, our job would have been easy, but it wasn't. For example, the distances were much greater than those usually reckoned with on a stage. We had to note the time taken by actors or groups of actors in going here and there, and work out the length of the musical accompaniment required, and so on. It must have looked quite funny to an outsider: bands, troops, swarms of women in ordinary street clothing, destined to be nuns on the night, traipsed tragically up and down the chaotic plaster-smeared hall, gesturing

D

dramatically. Processions of men and boys singing hymns staggered over mounds of freshly dug earth thrown up from the excavation below. "Nuns to the left," someone would shriek. "Get a move on, huntsmen," someone else. And in one

"The Miracle." Rehearsal at Olympia

corner of it all two pianists hammered away desperately on an old piano smothered with white plaster dust in a despairing attempt to make the accompaniment heard above the din, whilst old man Humperdinck in a floppy felt hat, a fur-trimmed overcoat and button-boots, also smothered in plaster dust, beat time with his umbrella. And somewhere or the other there was Reinhardt, the ultimate controller of all this chaos, sitting tearing out his hair in his usual comic despair and dimly wondering whether something worth while would come out of it "on the night".

And as for me, I never had a moment to spare: I discussed the painting of the transparent stained-glass windows of the cathedral with the scene painters; I made sketches for the modellers who were doing the plaster masking; and whatever I did or was doing there was always a constantly replenished line of people waiting to pounce on me the moment they spotted an opportunity with questions, questions, questions. And on top of all this there was the costuming; that was my job, too, and off I would be hauled to solve some problem, hurrying through the apparently never-ending corridors of Olympia, some of which had been turned into dressing-rooms for the 1,800 actors and actresses taking part. Cases and cases, baskets and baskets of costumes and other things arrived, many of them containing mysterious garments whose significance was known only to me and had to be explained to the dressers. Once the costumes had been sorted out more or less into their groups, "Court Ladies", "Soldiers", "Knights", "Courtesans", "Pages" and so on, there was all the trying on to be supervised when the actors and actresses came to dress for their parts, and all the innumerable questions to be answered: "In what scene do the soldiers become citizens? . . . In which hunting scenes? . . . What clothes do the nuns wear when they're dancers?" And so on, and so on.

And perhaps when I would find a seat in the always over-crowded restaurant to swallow a bite of lunch, my old friend C. B. Cochran would come up to discuss, say, the question of the horsemen with me. Our horsemen—and they were all picked men—had to ride dressed from head to foot in shining armour. There were over a dozen of them, and they had to practice riding in such a get-up—and so did the horses.

Incidentally, the question of the horses gave us quite a lot of trouble. I wanted really big, heavy horses which looked capable of carrying a knight in full armour, and I wanted them dappled. As we couldn't get any in London, we went into the country where a circus was wintering. There we saw all sorts of horses running around in paddocks and nibbling the grass, and we were assured that under the mud and dung with which they were plastered they were really dappled. But when we finally got them to Olympia and had them groomed and curried there wasn't a dappled horse amongst the lot of them. As an experienced publicity man, Cochran made capital out of our trouble, and there were immediately articles in the newspaper: "Ernest Stern paints the horses for the coming Olympia Show." And it was quite true: I had literally to paint them.

When we came to rehearse with our knights, they found it quite impossible to keep their seats as soon as the horses broke into a trot, and down they would come with an enormous clatter. In their armour they had to stand upright in the stirrups, and modern saddles were no use, so we had to have special saddles made for them. With the horses and their riders galloping along and the excited clamour of a pack of hounds in full cry for the hunting scenes, the grotesque chaos and bedlam at Olympia reached its peak.

"Uncanny to see what I invented walk around on its own", says a note in my diary for December 26th. "In the rooms and corridors outside the gothic cathedral of Olympia I meet the mediæval men and women I sketched, but now they are flesh and blood. Suddenly I am faced with a bishop in the full pomp of his canonicals. Michael Pacher first painted you in 1457, I thought. And there are groups of mediæval burghers in their fur-tipped and decorated costumes and hats. They, too, came from the paintings of the old Tyrolean master. The knight in armour who rides towards me owes his existence to a statue of St. George by the old master, Hans Multscher. The cut and the material of their long, trailing dresses and their billowing coloured veils and their high, pointed hats, cause the women unconsciously to strike attitudes such as Master Froissart has immortalized in his minatures."

There are many details I can well remember in connection with "The Miracle" without referring to my diary. The fantastically clothed mediæval mercenaries with their slashed sleeves and doublets playing cards. The flag-wavers who marched into the cathedral at the head of our troops. They practised zealously under teachers specially imported from Switzerland, where flag-waving is still treated as an art. They would wave their brilliantly striped flags around, toss them into the air, and catch them as they fell, very much like a drum-major does with his mace. And there was the schoolroom where the children engaged in "The Miracle" had their lessons during the day, already costumed for their parts. Call-boys would speed through the endless corridors on bicycles calling the individual groups into action, and then perhaps 150 women would hasten towards the stage—if such it can be called—their white, grey and black habits flowing rhythmically as they walked, many of them carrying their sandals—an unaccustomed form of footwear—in their hands.

" 'The Miracle' is not only a triumph of stagecraft, it is also an artistic work of deep significance" was a fair example of the praise the critics gave to our work.

When I first came to England in 1905, to get married, I knew very little English, but on my second visit (with Reinhardt and "Sumurum") I spoke much better English, because in the meantime I had read a good many modern English novels and so on, chiefly through the invaluable Tauchnitz volumes. Arnold Bennett, Meredith, Thomas Hardy, Conan Doyle and H. G. Wells in particular were well known to me. I had also read a good deal about the work of Inigo Jones, Sir Christopher

London, 1905

Wren and the Adams brothers, and when I visited St. James's and Lambeth I made copious notes for future scenic inspiration in Shakespearean productions. I went with Reinhardt to see Granville Barker's production of "The Winter's Tale" at the Savoy. We also saw a delightful production of Maeterlinck's "Blue Bird", Beerbohm Tree as Wolsey, and Bourchier as Henry VIII. Reinhardt was so impressed by Bourchier's performance that in all seriousness he suggested that Bourchier should learn German and come to Berlin to play for him.

Something that we found very agreeable and exhilarating about London was the fact that an evening at the theatre was taken seriously and treated as an occasion.

"In London people go to the theatre to enjoy themselves in style," sighed Reinhardt enviously. "The ladies are *décolleté* and wearing their jewellery, and their escorts are all in white ties and tails. As they have all previously dined in peace, their digestions are in order and they are not disagreeably critical. How I envy producers who have such a contented public! In Berlin the men must rush from their offices to get to the theatres before seven o'clock, and then they grouse and grumble about everything because they're hungry. Their bellies come before their minds. And whereas in the interval the Englishman has a quiet drink, the German rushes to the buffet to swallow hot-dogs or a ham sandwich with perhaps a glass of beer, if he can get one in the crush."

"Returning from the land of eccentricity, Reinhardt is more eccentric than ever, and so are his artists." "To turn Shake-speare's comedy 'The Taming of the Shrew' into a piece of clowning verges on madness." "After 'Œdipus Rex' in a circus it is quite natural that the circus should conquer the stage." "Every moment one expected Petruchio to make his Katherina jump through a hoop." "Grace, humour, poetry—where are they in this production of 'The Taming of the Shrew'".

Reinhardt replied that for one thing, unlike Shakespeare's other comedies, there was very little poetry in "The Taming of the Shrew"; and that for another there was no disputing the drastic methods adopted by Petruchio to tame his Katherina. The piece was less a comedy than a farce, hard tack for primi-tive tastes, and thus to play it as a piece of barnstorming was right. After all, argued Reinhardt, for whom was the piece intended? For Christopher Sly, the drunken tinker. It was not high comedy, but typical low comedy, a rumbustious farce. Only so interpreted did Petruchio's coarse brutalities become at all tolerable. When, as was often the case, the prologue with Christopher Sly was omitted and the main play given straight, Petruchio was a disgusting brute.

"Before an alehouse on a heath" read the stage directions for Scene I. A timbered Elizabethan alehouse from which the drunken Christopher Sly—now sleeping off the effects of his drink in a ditch—had obviously been thrown. Lords in Eliza-bethan riding dress arrive with servants and huntsmen. In the next scene we find Sly, now awake, in the great hall of a Lord's house, a splendid hall with galleries, pillars, stairway and a monumental fireplace. The doors of the hall open and the members of the troupe of strolling players enter, pushing their cart, which they then unload, setting up their gaily-painted and primitive props. Red, violet-and-yellow-painted houses and

interiors with all sorts of cases and boxes as furniture indicate
the various scenes of the comedy. The fact that the galleries and
the pillars of the hall are still visible does not trouble Christopher Sly in the least, or that the great stairs are used by
Petruchio, Gremio and the others as the action demands. He
is used to such primitive and extemporized scenes from the
fair-grounds, and he knows that the players are clowns,
dancers, acrobats and jugglers all in one, that they are dressed
in exaggerated clothing and that they disguise themselves for
their parts in big hats, false beards and false noses. In
order to stress this wheels within wheels I put "the players" in
"The Taming of the Shrew" into the striking and colourful
costumes of the clowns, harlequins, columbines and pantaloons
of the Italian *Commedia dell' Arte*, after the engravings of the
great French master, Callot.

London, 1910

CHAPTER VIII

THE PLAYERS

IN THE BURG THEATER in Vienna there was a painting on the ceiling of the foyer entitled "The Thespian Cart". According to tradition, the Greek poet, Thespis of Icaria, who lived in the sixth century B.C., founded the tragedy, and Horace tells us that he trained a band of players and went round with them from place to place, carrying the props, etc., on a cart. The painting in question shows a primitive ox-cart loaded with the various stage paraphernalia. The figures around the cart seem to be learning their roles and declaiming their parts as they walk.

Reinhardt regarded these former troops of strolling players as ideal representatives of the acting profession. In his opinion, the ordered and respectable life led by modern actors was not at all in accordance with their profession. A man who had a permanent home, paid rent and rates and even had the right to vote—"What's Hecuba to him or he to Hecuba that he should weep for her?" An actor with a bank balance was incapable of interpreting profound dramatic feelings.

"Look at So-and-So up there in the spotlight with his crown and his ermine mantle," Reinhardt said to me one day at a dress rehearsal as we sat in the auditorium. "He just puts the things on without a second thought and takes them off again when the scene is over. That crown and mantle don't belong to him. They're just props. 'Every inch a king!' I don't think! Now, when a fellow trailed around with his fellow vagabonds from place to place, trudging along by the side of their cart loaded up with their primitive props, tramping through snow and rain with boots that let water, he wore his royal mantle all the time for the simple reason that he hadn't got an overcoat, and he folded it round him with an air on the stage and off. He must have felt himself a king all the time and not merely when he stalked around the village stage declaiming his lines."

Reinhardt believed that a light-hearted, free-and-easy life was the only one for the player. One day he would have money for a first-class meal; the next he could afford only a pickled herring. But in his fantasy the pickled herring was Scotch

salmon and his glass of schnaps a vintage Tokay. One night
he would sleep in a real bed, and the next night in a barn with
the stars peeping between the rafters. A vagabond in ragged
trousers and without a penny to bless himself with during the
day would be transformed to a hero in the romantic glow of the
tallow footlights at night.

Reinhardt also much preferred the born actors, those whose
parents had been actors before them. We had a number of
them in our company. During the day and off the stage they
were chiefly remarkable for their ignorance and their bad
manners, but in the evening in the footlights they really were
transformed; every step, every gesture, every word was perfect.
Reinhardt had not much time for the educated well-read and
academically well-trained actors. In his opinion, their literary
knowledge was so much ballast, a hindrance to be flung aside
if possible, because it made them self-conscious; although they
might be more or less talented, their acting remained purely
formal.

I once showed Reinhardt a reproduction of Hogarth's
"Actresses dressing in a Barn". He was not in the least impressed by the humour and satire of the thing; he was enthused
by the reality of it, and he felt quite certain that in the romantic
period of vagabondage of that sort actresses must have been
very much better players than they were to-day. For him there
were three categories of actresses—apart from all those who
merely thought themselves actresses: those who could at least
be relied upon not to spoil anything; those who were actresses
all the time, both on the stage and off, and were therefore
always convincing; and, finally, the born geniuses, known to
Reinhardt as the "venomous reptiles".

My particular relation to the players was as their costume-
designer, and I must say that I got on very much better with
actresses than with actors. A woman has a natural feeling for
the unusual, the original. No one reproaches a woman for her
vanity. We regard it as natural and we are even prepared to
make all sorts of concessions to it. But men—at least, male
actors—are just as vain, and I had a great deal of trouble with
them. The difficulty was greatest where "historical" costumes
were concerned. They all, even the most intelligent of them,
wanted to show their legs. And if their legs were not particularly well shaped, they were quite prepared to adopt all
sorts of little devices to improve matters. They all hated long

costumes which covered their legs. It made them look old, they complained, and they were all terribly anxious not to disturb the fond illusions of their female fans.

If a historical piece played in the seventeenth, eighteenth or nineteenth century in which male legs were in fashion, then our actors sighed with relief. And if the period demanded long and flowing robes which covered the nether limbs—"curtains", as such costumes were contemptuously called—they would often counteract their effect by splitting them up the side or by inelegantly pulling them up and sticking mantle or toga into their belts, with complete indifference to the exigencies of style and costume.

Colour was another thing which constantly caused trouble between me and our male leads. Even before I came to Reinhardt, I attached a great deal of value to colour and texture as important psychological factors in a role. In addition, if the general picture was to be artistic and harmonious, the colours adopted for the various roles had to be chosen with a view to the whole and to the contrast with other roles. But it was often very difficult to persuade actors of all this; all they were interested in was whether or not, in their opinion, the colour I had given them suited their own style of beauty.

But it was not always so easy with the ladies either. When I first came to the theatre the crinoline was avoided as far as possible because it was supposed to hamper free and graceful movement. It was used only to obtain grotesque or comic effects. However, I was untouched by theatrical tradition, and right at the beginning I put a number of actresses into crinolines in Gogol's "Inspector-General", and I followed it up by doing the same with all forty actresses of "Revolution in Krähwinkel". The many voluminous and highly coloured crinolines brought together on the stage created a striking decorative effect and the scene was compared with an aviary of exotic birds. Fortunately our Viennese dressmakers knew how to make the complicated understructure of the crinoline so that it was elastic in wear, and our actresses soon discovered that once they had learnt a trick or two they could move very gracefully in their crinolines. The ban was broken, and when a little later I proposed to use Velasquez crinolines in the staging of Calderon's "The Doctor of His Own Honour", there was no objection at all, and I used the same Spanish fashion for the female roles in Schiller's "Don Carlos".

The famous tragic actress Adele Sandrock of the Vienna Burg Theater came to Berlin to play for Reinhardt. Her first role with us was to be as the Princess Eboli in Schiller's "Don Carlos", which was one of our repertory pieces. She was introduced to the crinoline of her predecessor in the role. It was made of green brocade with gold embroidery and was in perfect condition. Adele regarded the costume balefully and then ordered her dresser to produce whoever was responsible for costuming the show. I appeared in her dressing-room as the delinquent.

She looked at me for a moment or two in silence, her unusually bright eyes shining menacingly.

"*Mein Herr*," she began in her deep and beautiful voice—which incidentally had brought her in the nickname of "Frau General"—"am I to assume that this is the costume you intend me to wear in the role of the Princess Eboli?"

And she pointed dramatically to the lovely crinoline lying over a chair. I confirmed that such was, in fact, the case.

"And are you aware, *mein Herr*," she continued tragically, "that the role of the Princess Eboli requires that she should fall to her knees in the greatest emotion, and that she should then even faint? If I did anything of the sort in this dress I should expose my legs to a no doubt appreciative audience, but instead of sympathy I should provoke ridicule and laughter."

When I pointed out that our previous Princess Eboli had been able to fall to her knees and faint in that very same dress without embarrassment or difficulty she shook her exceptionally fair curls at me to underline her doubt: "I'll believe that when I see it; not before," she declared.

"And you shall see it right now, Fräulein Sandrock," I exclaimed. "There are just a few tricks to learn and the dress is tamed for good." And with that I took off my jacket, got into the dress and demonstrated how it could be managed, and how she could kneel down and collapse in a faint, all with the utmost decency and elegance.

"I must say you do it very well," she admitted generously, and when she tried the frock on herself under my tuition it was impossible for her to deny that she could move around in it freely and play her role with grace and dignity. After that Adele Sandrock and I were firm friends.

A few evenings later I visited her in her dressing-room.

"Welcome!" she cried with a queenly gesture. "As you see,

I wear your instrument of torture with ease. I really *have* accustomed myself to wearing it.

"So completely," she added, in a sepulchral aside, "that even a natural urge could be satisfactorily attended to in the smallest of chambers."

It was a long long time ago that I tamed the great Adele to wear the crinoline, but as recently as 1947 the same trouble occurred again.

"The design is charming," admitted a well-known English actress, "but you might as well put me in a barrel as in a crinoline if you want me to move."

"On the contrary, Miss ——, you would move as gracefully as a lily on its stem."

At first the lovely creature was not to be persuaded, and there were tears in her eyes as she pleaded with me to design her a different costume, but I had to explain to her, with regret, that the Empress Elizabeth of Austria, whom she was to impersonate in "The Bird Seller", would have to appear, as usual, in a crinoline. In the end, of course, all went well.

As a result of my preoccupation with the stage, and of my close observation of actors on the stage, I soon noticed the difference in their attitude when they had to play a piece in modern dress and when they played in historical, and therefore unusual, clothing. In the one they moved naturally and easily, but in the other, although it was part of their job to wear the clothing of other days on the stage, they were stiff and self-conscious. Quite naturally, an actor would go to put his hand in his pocket without thinking, only to find that there was no pocket; his hands would then wander off somewhere else and his arms would hang hopelessly. If he couldn't do what he normally did with his hands he didn't know what to do with them. I therefore proposed to Reinhardt that he should costume his actors as soon as possible in order to get them used to it, and that even in the very first rehearsals, when the costumes would, of course, not be ready, they should wear something or the other quite different from their everyday wear: a short tunic, a flowing robe, a belted or unbelted garment. For a variety of reasons, it proved impracticable to carry out my proposals, but at least I was able to introduce such rehearsal garb for the young student actors in Reinhardt's dramatic school.

Just as Schiller's Maria Stuart, Elizabeth and Leicester,

Goethe's Tasso or Shakespeare's Cæsar are not supposed to be exact portraits of the historical personalities they represent on the stage, so it would be absurd for the costume-designer always to make their costumes an exact replica of whatever was worn in their own day, copying pedantically from old pictures or statues. Stage costumes representing a particular historical period should pick out and underline the characteristic features or any particular historical style; that is all. In some cases it may be the task of the costume designer not merely to underline but even to exaggerate the sartorial characteristics of a period. The stiff ruffs and the hip padding of the Elizabethan period determined the carriage of the men and women of the day. The same was true of the Roman toga. Shylock in a long *caftan* moves differently from Gratiano in a short tunic. And it is not only the clothing as such which determines by its material, its cut and its form how a man and woman moves, but also articles which a person may carry constantly with him—for instance a sword at his belt—which determine certain movements and attitudes.

Goethe, who was himself a producer at the Weimar Theatre, recognized this, and he is reported to have said to his actors: "If you are going to play in shoes to-morrow, don't rehearse in boots to-day." The logic of this should be clear at once; obviously a man, or woman, will move differently in boots or shoes than in slippers or sandals. In Stanislavsky's production of "Tsar Ivan Fedorovitch" the courtiers wore old-Russian costumes with very high, stiff collars and very long sleeves of a stove-pipe shape which covered their hands altogether when they held them to their sides. The stiff collars compelled them to adopt a carriage of the head which indicated subordination to the Tsar. The excessively long sleeves made them push back their cuffs as soon as they had to do anything with their hands. In reply to my inquiries, I was told that this gesture had been deliberately aimed at as typical of the Russian costume and period in question, and that Stanislavsky's group wore those long-sleeved costumes from the very early rehearsals on.

Stanislavsky's Moscow Arts Theatre was a great success in Berlin. Although I did not understand a word, I found myself following what happened on the stage in "Tsar Ivan Fedorovitch" almost breathlessly. It was a gala performance, with Kaiser Wilhelm II in Russian uniform in the royal box. His applause at the end of each act (I don't know whether he understood Russian) provoked the not very large audience to storms of applause. It was good box-office, and from that evening on the Russians played to full houses, particularly as the critics now showed more interest in the performances.

None of the Berlin Theatres, with the exception of the Royal Opera House and the Theatre Royal (Königliches Schauspiel-haus) had ever been honoured with the Royal Presence. Our Deutsches Theater would have welcomed a royal visit, but although the crown Prince and his brothers August Wilhelm and Eitel Friedrich often came to our performances and were well disposed towards Reinhardt, they were unable to persuade their father to visit a Reinhardt performance. The Kaiser is credited with the witty observation that as he was himself a theatre-owner it would be bad business on his part to take his custom to his competitors.

But an opportunity did arise of showing the Kaiser an example of Reinhardt's theatrical art without his visiting Reinhardt's theatre. The Crown Prince was in residence in the Bellevue Palace in the Tiergarten and we were to give a per-formance there at a formal evening reception in the presence of the Kaiser. I had to supervise the erection of a stage complete with curtain and lighting arrangements. The play we were giving was Lessing's "Minna von Barnhelm". Despite its very definitely Prussian spirit and background, this piece, written in 1763, is a delightful comedy. The scenes are simple and consist of nothing but the entrance hall of a provincial inn and a room giving off it, in which Fräulein von Barnhelm lives. In view of the provisional and primitive character of the stage, which naturally had no special technical equipment, I had to design a very simple décor. I had light canvas scenery made which could be used on both sides, so that merely by turning it round it could serve for the one scene or the other. The requisite furniture in the rococo style of the period was available in the palace.

The theme of the piece is the essential decency, good nature, selflessness and uprightness of the profession of arms. It is not over-sentimental and it really is humorous. The male lead is Major von Tellheim, who has been cashiered after the Seven Years' War and is now practically penniless. His former Sergeant, Werner, and his batman, Just, are both typical rep-resentatives of the Frederician soldiery, trained in the hard school and accustomed to iron discipline. The female lead is the rich Minna von Barnhelm, who is temporarily staying at the inn, together with her maid, Franziska. Supporting characters are an inquisitive innkeeper and the amiable adventurer, Riccaut de la Marinière, one of the many Frenchmen in Prussian service at that time. In him Lessing created a real character, the happy-go-lucky, likeable cardsharper. His favourite phrase, *"Corriger la fortune"*, has become a byword.

The uniforms of Tellheim, Werner, Just and Riccaut were replicas of the illustrations in the famous book of the Frederician Army done by Adolf Menzel. The costumes and the hairdressing of Minna and Franziska I took from the contemporary engravings of Daniel Chodowiecky. Minna was dressed in the crinoline type of frock with panniers standing out at the side, and it needed a considerable degree of natural grace and

A character in "Minna von Barnhelm"

acquired skill to manage it elegantly between the furniture. Else Heims, the actress who played the part of Minna, was a tall and exceptionally attractive woman who had both in full measure.

On the day before the reception, the stage was completed and I was checking everything, including the rise and fall of the curtain, when Prince Eitel Fritz came to me and asked me whether there was anything I still required. I replied that as far as the stage was concerned everything was now ready. He then pointed to the corners which had been created to the right and left of the stage between the newly-erected proscenium and walls of the great Empire banqueting hall.

"They look rather bare, don't you think?" he said. "What can be done to take away the empty look?"

"Oh, perhaps vases of flowers or candelabra, or statues, something in the style of the Frederician epoch," I replied.

The prince nodded his head once or twice and then went off. Although the stage was ready, there was still plenty for me to do, and I forgot all about the minor problem of the corners. The great evening came and the illustrious gathering, the Kaiser, the princes and the whole brilliant court assembly, was present, the gentlemen in uniform or evening dress, decorated with their orders, the ladies in beautiful and elaborate evening gowns. Everyone seemed to enjoy the performance greatly, although as good Prussians they had known "Minna von Barnhelm" inside out from their earliest youth as part of their literary curriculum. The performance itself was absolutely first-class, and the actors and actresses were the finest in the country. I had caused imperceptible spy-holes to be made in the proscenium walls, and Reinhardt on the left and I on the right used them to survey our unusual audience. The Kaiser in particular seemed highly pleased with the performance of Else Heims as "Minna" and I could see him gesticulating with his right hand (the left was crippled) as he talked to his neighbours.

In the pause after the first act, Reinhardt asked me what had been put into the empty corners between the proscenium and the walls. I said that as far as I knew nothing had been put there, but he insisted that there was something there. Thereupon I went to my spy-hole and when I looked as far to the right as I could I thought I could see something or other, but I couldn't make out what. The solution of the mystery was revealed when the adjutant of the Crown Prince came on to the stage during the interval. After he had inquired whether everything was going according to plan, he remarked:

"That was a very good idea of His Royal Highness Prince Eitel Fritz to put two of the 'Beanstalks' in the empty corners, don't you think, Director Reinhardt?"

The "Beanstalks" was a popular nickname for the men of the Potsdam Regiment of Guards, who were all exceptionally tall men and still wore the historical uniform of the Frederician epoch with the high plated helmet which made them look even taller—"*Langen Kerls*" was the actual German expression.

"The Beanstalks," echoed Reinhardt at a loss.

"Yes, the Beanstalks. The two sentries who have been placed in the corners standing at attention. Wonderfully suitable. Authentically Frederician, Majesty thinks."

And with that he clicked his heels, saluted and departed, leaving us speechless. Living soldiers at attention on either side of the stage throughout the two-and-a-half-hour performance! We were horrified, and hastily we dashed to our spy-holes and anxiously examined as much of the soldiers as we could see. The news went round and the actors nervously squinted to the sides. As Prussian Guardsmen, the two were probably used to standing absolutely still for hours on end, but it upset us. We theatrical people are too imaginative perhaps, but after all, even Prussian soldiers are human, and all the things that might happen to upset the apple-cart crowded in on us. In the circumstances, our actors stood the test well, but even the most patriotic and monarchist amongst them had to admit to their indignant colleagues that to use human beings as statues in this fashion whiffed a little of mediæval despotism.

We all breathed a sigh of relief when the performance was safely and satisfactorily at an end. Reinhardt and Else Heims (who, incidentally, was not only our leading actress, but also Reinhardt's wife) were honoured by an invitation to take supper at the royal table. The rest of us were served at small tables elsewhere. The supper was excellent, but unfortunately it was taken at the gallop, the pacemaker being the Kaiser himself, who was, of course, served first and who ate like lightning and gave no thought to the poor wretches who were served last and often saw their plates whisked away the moment they had been placed before them. At table the Kaiser questioned Else Heims with great interest about what it was like to wear a crinoline. But our production of "Minna von Barnhelm" at the Schloss Bellevue remained the one and only Reinhardt performance the Kaiser ever consented to see, and he could never be persuaded to visit the Deutches Theater.

To revert to my favourite idea of making the actors and actresses wear their costumes right from the beginning of the rehearsals, I succeeded in doing this on only one occasion, and that was for Reinhardt's production of Heinrich von Kleist's "Penthesilea". The theme of the play is the saga of the Amazonian queen, Penthesilea, who was, so the legend says, slain by Achilles before Troy, who was then much affected by her beauty. Kleist takes the legend and links it up with the indeterminate manner of the death of Achilles, making Penthesilea, mad with love, kill Achilles and then herself. It is a piece which is very rarely played and for a long time it was regarded as a reading play impossible to stage. The constantly changing scenes and the wild battles between Greek warriors and raving Amazons seemed to set the producer an impossible task. However, when the proposal was mooted at the Deutsches Theater and I studied the script, I could find nothing particularly difficult in the constant change scene. In fact, Heinrich von Kleist might have had the revolving stage in mind; there was nothing technically impossible in his demands. I was confident that I could make the figures of the Amazons convincing and that, if I were given a free hand, I could even satisfactorily solve the always difficult and embarrassing problem of staging mock battles. Reinhardt was on holiday and our performance was to be produced by Felix Hollander, a highly intelligent and capable man, who gave me permission to do as I liked.

I have said that the scenes changed constantly, but really this is not the case; what happens is that the same battlefield is seen from various points, something which is very easy to do with scenery built up on a revolving stage. The action takes place in part whilst the characters are walking, running or climbing rocks, and the stage directions mention a valley and a bridge. Our revolving stage was 60 feet across, and on this I had two hills built up, one higher than the other. Between them lay the valley mentioned in the stage directions, whilst the bridge, a primitive stone structure, crossed it from one hill

"Penthesilea" with ground-plan,

to the other. Inclined surfaces and more or less curved platforms smoothed out with upholstery gave us a terrain which could be used from all sides without the necessity for stairs or steps, and this was covered either with brown earth-like carpet or grass. The only two trees were two three-dimensional cypresses near the stream in the valley. The multi-shaped and contoured hills, the varying levels of the stage and the rocks allowed us to obtain a much more picturesque grouping of our actors than would have been possible on a flat stage. We had not to bother about the usual clumsy side-by-side position of actors on the flat. When our Amazons and Greeks stood on the mounds their silhouettes appeared impressively on the cyclorama at the rear.

The simplicity of this décor would naturally rivet the attention of the audience all the more on the appearance of the actors, and my task was therefore to costume our Amazons and Greeks as effectively as possible. It was easy enough with the men. We had quite a number of good-looking, well-developed young actors and, in addition, we had the male pupils of our dramatic school to draw on if necessary. I also approached an athletic association, who promised the co-operation of its members. The problem of the Amazons was another kettle of fish entirely, but it had to be solved because they represented an essential—the essential—part of the play. The great danger was that we might find ourselves drifting into the ridiculous operatic tradition. In "Penthesilea" on the whole the men get the worst of it in battle with the Amazons, and in order to convey this with some conviction it was necessary that our actresses should be able to handle arms convincingly and that they should, in addition, look the part physically.

Kleist spoke of his Amazons as helmeted and armoured, as fierce women clothed in snakeskin, whose favourite weapon was the bow and arrow. Amazons with their bows and arrows are often to be found on Greek vases dressed in a sort of Phrygian garb with caps and close-fitting trousers, but when our stage was set and I began to try out one or two ideas in the actual scenery, I discovered that the ornamental Phrygian garb was not in the least suitable. It was quite clear to me by this time that this army of women would have to consist of big, strong Junoesque types unless they were to look ridiculous. Their role as warriors was to be shown by characteristic but economically used indications. I designed leather kilt-like skirts studded with small plates of copper and iron, simple helmets, battle-axes and spears, and light shields made of covered wickerwork. Their bows were 5 ft. long and the arrows 3 feet long, and each Amazon had a dozen of them carried in a big leather quiver slung at her side. These bowmen, or rather bowwomen, were the only ones who wore the Phrygian cap, which I had made of leather.

Of course, I presented all my sketches, drafts and proposals to Felix Hollander, and he invariably declared himself in agreement with everything. Then I explained to him that if our Amazon army was to look at all real it would have to be carefully trained first. At this he merely shrugged his shoulders.

"I gave you *carte blanche* from the beginning," he pointed out. "How you manage it all is entirely your business, my friend."

We needed fifty women. For the minor roles we had quite enough amongst our own company, and I took a dozen others from the school. The rest were obtained by our manager for walking-on parts, and many of them were artists' models. Some of them belonged, in fact, to a sort of Amazonian society; they lived in the open air all the time and wore the sort of clothing recommended by Isadora Duncan—incidentally, their group was a forerunner of the later nudist camps.

The costumes and props I had ordered were soon ready and we were able to begin training our Amazons. In particular, the broken nature of the terrain had to be taken into account. They had not only to go or run up often quite steep inclines, but everything had to be done æsthetically. Once one group had climbed up a slope it had to wait in a deliberately arranged pose for the next and combine with it in a harmoniously planned ensemble. Another thing which had to be carefully practised was a scene in which the female warriors fled in panic down a hillside. Despite the chaos of flight, the movement had to conform to a certain prearranged order, and so on.

There was another very important reason why our Amazons had to be very carefully rehearsed in standing, walking and running; they were to go barefooted. Walking, running and even standing in bare feet is not easy for those who are not used to it, and even otherwise graceful people can look clumsy and awkward. Our women sighed and grumbled and found me a hard taskmaster, but they were willing. Even standing still had to be practised. I wanted statuesque and yet easy poses, and very few people naturally fall into the "classic-academic" pose when they stand. In this position the main weight of the body is carried on one leg whilst the other is slightly bent at the knee and the sole of the foot does not rest squarely on the ground. It is unnecessary for me to stress the serene beauty of this pose; it will be well known to all who have given a second glance to the antique statuary in our museums.

In Kleist's play there were constant fights between Greek warriors and Amazons. Now, the pantomimic antics of fighting with sword and spear always look ridiculous on the stage. I circumvented this difficulty by exploiting the advantages of our terrain. If, for example, the Greeks were to get the better of the fighting, then I saw to it that they were in the more favoured strategic position from the start, i.e. that they were on the hill and could push back the attacking Amazons with a wall of Greek shields. Or from their position on the heights the women drove the men down into the depths, where the battle was represented by the clash of arms, the flight of arrows, and the dust of conflict, etc. Groups of Amazonian archers discharging their arrows from the hills made a very effective picture. One end of the 5-foot-high bow was planted on the ground and held in position with the toes of the left foot, and the spanning of the bowstring and the release of the arrow by slim but muscular women made impressive silhouettes against the cycloramic background.

Naturally, the young actors who played the role of Greek warriors also had to have a certain amount of training. I dressed them in breast- and back-plates made of hammered copper, and under it they wore short linen tunics. The visors of their helmets covered their faces like masks. In addition to their weapons, they all carried large round shields which were decorated with various classic emblems actually taken from ancient shields. These shields were the only touch of colour in the whole scene; everything else, weapons, costumes and so on, was sprayed a light brown. Achilles, Odysseus, Diomedes and all the other Greeks were bronzed, whilst the Amazons were of a darker brown. The legendary nature of the theme permitted me to replace what is usually known as realistic lighting with something more fantastic. I allowed the lighting to be guided completely by the individual scene and my lights were concentrated on the essential whilst everything else remained in a picturesque twilight.

The main figure in the play was, of course, Penthesilea, played by a tall, slim young woman who had studied all her movements, as I had urged her to, in front of a mirror whilst in costume for her part. The wonderful grace of her movements and the natural and elegant poses she adopted did much to make the production a success.

Often during the course of the play the Amazon Queen calls for her wild dogs, and at last we took the poet at his word. A pack of great dogs strained forward at the leash, excited by the wild shouting of the women, and did much to give us an effective and impressive finale.

Sporadic high-lights spring up; they sparkle colourfully; they are greeted with admiring "Oh's" and "Ah's", and then they die out and are forgotten. In theatrical life they are particularly frequent.

"To use a colloquial phrase, Herr Ernest Stern has let himself go over 'Turandot'. The imagination which dressed 'The Miracle' in all its pomp for us, now riots in the court of the Emperor Altoun at Pekin at a period unspecified. We are warned not to take the costumes as archæologically exact. . . . They are grotesque; they are splendid; they are sumptuous; they are ravishingly delicate. They are monstrous; they are hideous; they are marvellously beautiful. They make you laugh; they make you dream. They seem to be the very spirit of old China, with all the pomp and circumstance and absurdity—these robes and tufts and comical hats; these crowns and swords and battle-axes, these stuffs and embroideries and funny shoes; these pigtails and whiskers, and lanterns and trousers—Herr Stern has certainly let himself go."

That is a quotation from a criticism of the production of "Turandot" at the St. James's Theatre under the management of Sir George Alexander in 1913. This "Turandot" was the old rococo comedy of Gozzi, whose stuff was turned into an opera a century later by Puccini. The critic was right: both in costume and décor I had "let myself go". The piece had first been produced with my décor and costumes by Reinhardt in the Deutsches Theater in Berlin, where Sir George Alexander had seen it and ordered, that very same evening, an exact copy of everything for a London production.

I superintended the making of it all down to the last detail, as ordered, then it was sent off by train and ship to London, all the props and innumerable baskets containing the costumes, and I went off with it. But no one knows when a book is going to be a best-seller or a play a box-office success. A success in one country is not necessarily a success in another. No one has ever been able to analyse the thing satisfactorily. In any case, despite the fact that I had really "let myself go" and despite all the lavish praise of the critics, "Turandot, Princess of China" was not destined for a long life at St. James's Theatre.

And how often it was like that! Looking through the old programmes of our two theatres was often like looking through a family album of the dear departed. How many plays had I worked on with enthusiasm, determined to create master-pieces? And what remained? In the best case a few faded photographs. That was the fate of both "Terakoya" and "Kimiko", two original Japanese plays. I managed to obtain real Japanese kimonos wonderfully embroidered for these two plays. The male actors wore real Japanese armour of beautiful workmanship. A Japanese assisted us to give the actors authentic Japanese poses and movements. And the end result —two flops.

And there were others: "Good King Dagobert", by André Rivoire, "The Cloister", by Verhaeren, "Bankban", a Hun-garian piece which we also produced in Budapest. And all that was left of them was the record of their existence, a drawing or two in an old sketch-book, a word or two in an old diary. . . .

CHAPTER IX

PLASTIC OR PAINTED DÉCOR

COVENT GARDEN SPARKLED. The ladies were *décolleté* and bejewelled, and their escorts were resplendent in white tie and tails. The delightful old theatre was a worthy frame for a performance of Diaghilev's ballet.

Reinhardt and I were amongst the audience; it was the first time we had seen the Russians dance. They performed "Cleopatra", Debussy's "L'Après-midi d'un Faune" and Rimsky-Korsakov's "Sheherazade". Reinhardt was entranced. He described the experience as memorable and declared that both costumes and décor represented the utmost pitch of perfection. Needless to say, I agreed with him. Here was indisputable proof of how much more effective the painted canvas was than the three-dimensional décor of the revolving stage. I at once took advantage of Reinhardt's admiration and enthusiasm to try to convert him to my point of view, and I hammered it home that the light and shade was produced purely by painting, that the whole magnificence was nothing but lath and canvas painted!

With some caution, I even hinted at the practical advantages of such scenery: it could be taken down and packed flat. But this side of the question had to be merely hinted at and overlaid again and again by praise of the highly artistic aspect, because when Reinhardt was planning a new production—wholly artist that he was—he allowed no considerations of a strictly practical or economic nature to affect him. Once he had made his decisions, he left it to his brother Edmund, his business manager, to find ways and means of putting them into execution. And, shrugging his shoulders and heaving deep sighs of despair, Edmund would find the money somehow.

Now, this question of plastic, three-dimensional scenery was financially important. Edmund Reinhardt was constantly being called upon to raise money for the manufacture of new three-dimensional props for our revolving stage. And because our stock of these things steadily increased, it meant that we required more and more storage space and thus storage charges increased. In addition, we were a repertory theatre, which meant that we never had long runs and thus our requirements were always changing, with the result that there were constantly recurring charges for the transport of heavy props to and from the theatre and the warehouses.

In view of the many practical disadvantages of the style of décor we used and the many great artistic advantages of the two-dimensional, painted type of stage scenery, I was delighted to hear Reinhardt describe the painted scenery of the Russians as representing the utmost pitch of perfection. In my mind's eye, I could already see us adopting the same system for our production of the classics; I could already see Lear and Cæsar against fantastic and magnificent painted backcloths, so when we got back to Berlin I treated Reinhardt to a practical demonstration in an attempt to clinch the matter. I put two columns on the stage. One was plastic and three-dimensional, complete with capital and base, and perfectly made. The other was an exact copy, but painted and its contours silhouetted. This painted pillar was provided with light and shadow to make it appear plastic, and the light and shade did not disappear when it was illuminated. When the plastic column was lighted from one angle only, it, of course, also had light and shade, but when it was lighted from all sides, all light and shade disappeared and the plastic column looked two-dimensional, whilst the painted two-dimensional column looked plastic and realistic. My little demonstration showed quite clearly that in stage lighting, which must come from all sides, plastic, three-dimensional scenery no longer looked plastic, whilst painted, two-dimensional scenery looked plastic.

Unfortunately, Reinhardt's first impression waned and he proved a backslider. For fifteen years I tried to convince him, but without success. Later I was to use painted décor on a large scale, but not for him. At least I had the enormous satisfaction of observing his astonishment when I presented him with a tremendous and impressive baroque hall and informed him that it consisted of nothing but paint on a canvas background. At first he refused to believe it, but when I had convinced him he generously expressed his admiration.

Before the First World War, when the world seemed young to me, and new theatres were still being built all over Germany, I was often approached by their architects and asked what technical system I would advise, and I always gave the same answer: "None in particular, and all of them in general. Build a huge stage as broad and as deep and as high as possible, and then the space at the producer's disposal will enable him to adapt whatever system he considers best for the particular piece he is staging." But that was a counsel of perfection, and I have never seen it put into practice.

The modernist "arts and crafts" movement was particularly active in Munich. German graphic artists avoided all the wild and superficial ornamentation which flourished around what the Paris Exhibition of 1900 propagated as *Art Nouveau*, and on the whole—though there were exceptions—good results were obtained. The artists who turned their attention to this new movement, including a number of painters, were soon joined by architects, and they all aimed at developing a new and reasonable style for the new age. Even the State began to interest itself in what was going on. Bavaria, with her magnificent alpine scenery and her wonderful old towns, had always been a land for tourists, and now the authorities decided to add a new attraction in the shape of an "Arts and Crafts" Exhibition, and the centre of this ambitious venture was to be a theatre!

An excellent auditorium was built with seats in tiers all around, so that each seat offered an uninterrupted view of the stage. There was no circle or gallery and no boxes, and the decorations had been kept down to an absolute minimum. The front of the stage was 30 feet across. Behind the footlights was a sort of platform about 12 feet deep, flanked on the right and left by a kind of tower in which there were openings to allow entrance to the stage platform. There was no entrance at the rear, because it ended in a so-called pit of the same length as the stage. At the back of the stage, beyond the pit, was a very high wall of white plaster. Thus when an actor came on to the stage either from the left or the right he had an area of 30 feet by 12 feet at his disposal. He was picked out sharply against the white wall at the back, which was lighted from the "pit" and from the flies. He could himself be illuminated from the front and from the sides without any shadow being thrown on to the white background. For the audience he appeared as a silhouette, or in relief, and from this came the name of this particular type of stage principle: "The Relief Theatre". There was no scenery in the ordinary sense, but a few pilasters, columns and hangings were used to indicate interiors, etc. Exteriors were indicated merely by the empty stage. Everything,

every mood and all decorative effects, was obtained exclusively by lighting and by the colour and the character of the
costumes.

The direction of this theatre during the exhibition was in the
hands of a group of Munich artists and architects. "Faust"
was produced, "The Birds" of Aristophanes, and a number of
other pieces. The good citizens of Munich were very proud of
their innovation and they were quite sure that it was going to
conquer the world, as the local Press assured them. But when
the exhibition was over none of the various theatrical companies was anxious to play on the "relief" stage, because it
was a condition of performance that the "relief" principle
should be strictly adhered to. However, Reinhardt was
passionately interested in all theatrical experiments and he
finally decided to risk a short season. He took his own company
with him, accepted the co-operation of a number of Munich
scenic artists in the production of one or two pieces, but
insisted that "Lysistrata", "Sumurum" and, in particular,
Shakespeare's "Comedy of Errors" should be played in his
own fashion.

For "The Comedy of Errors" I disguised the side towers of
the stage as stylized houses. A bridge was constructed and
spanned the stage platform from end to end in a single arc,
leaving sufficient room for a kind of apron stage in front of it.
The words of one of the critics give a fair idea of our interpretation:

"Comedy of Errors"

"Shakespeare's 'Comedy of Errors' must be handled as though by a puppet master, and that is how Reinhardt does handle it. It must be treated like a ball, tossed into the air, caught again and tossed up anew. Perhaps Reinhardt even overdoes the acrobatics and gives us a handspring and a cartwheel too many, and occasionally he abuses the scenic possibilities—but how wittily and ingeniously he does it all! Right across the stage is an arched bridge and through its arch we see the ships anchored in the harbour, and quite intentionally they give the effect of pretty playthings. The action takes place partly on the bridge and partly on the apron stage before it. It is thus two-tiered, and Reinhardt's actors, who are also climbers, boxers, wrestlers and sprinters, are able to let themselves go like youngsters in a playground."

The "Relief Stage" theory of my Munich colleagues—incidentally, they always regarded me as one of them, and to a certain extent they were right, because I obtained the greater part of my artistic education and training amongst them—did not meet with any great success. In the following summer I went with Reinhardt to Munich to produce Offenbach's "La belle Hélène", but we needed more room than the stage platform of the Relief Theatre afforded, so we covered over the "pit" at the back and thus enlarged the acting area and, with some difficulty, we constructed an inclined ramp up to the stage from the auditorium—our Japanese gangway of flowers.

Our leading comic actor was Max Pallenberg, and he cracked his jokes in Viennese dialect. As Menelaus in "La belle Hélène" he was superbly droll. He was one of those rare comic artists who could extemporize adroitly and wittily, and his humorous asides on current political and other events were extraordinarily apt. At the same time he was a real artist with a true feeling for style and he managed to get the most out of everything, including whatever costume it was he happened to be wearing.

But what made our production of "La belle Hélène" particularly attractive was a perfectly trained troop of eight English dance-girls. This was a sensational innovation for operetta. I can remember how our people stood around and stared at the charming girls when they first came on the stage to rehearse. Everyone had wondered when it became known that we were engaging a troop of English dance girls, because, of course, English women are tall and bony, with prominent teeth, red hair and big feet—just as, of course, all German women are fat, frumpish and graceless. But these girls were slim, elegant and lovely, and everybody was astonished, particularly as the troops of dance girls who occasionally appeared at music-halls and elsewhere on the Continent before the First World War were always regarded as American. And when, in addition, it was discovered that Ethel, Eileen, Irene and Pat and all the others were happy, good-natured girls who laughed and giggled like their contemporaries of all other nations, our people took them to their hearts at once and our theatre did good business.

These girls, or "Djierls", as they were called in Munich, remained in Germany up to the outbreak of the war, and after the war they returned in increasing numbers. After "La belle Hélène" they played in our production of Offenbach's "Orpheus in the Underworld", and then in Knobloch's "Kismet" at the Münchner Theater, which was not produced by Reinhardt, but for which I did the costumes and décor.

After every Berlin theatre season my wife and I used to spend the summer at the Ammersee in Upper Bavaria, accompanied by our Berlin servant-girl and our fox terrier, Flip, in a half-dilapidated, picturesque house beautifully situated on the ridge of a hill overlooking a lake lined with willows. The big veranda was studio and living-room together, and from its many windows there was a wonderful view over the whole lake, the woods of fir trees and the hills sloping down to it and the gigantic chain of Alps in the south.

It was on this veranda that I sat and worked on the designs for the next Richard Strauss opera. It was "Ariadne auf Naxos", and it was to be performed as the play within the play in Molière's "Le Bourgeois Gentilhomme". The first performance of a work by Strauss was already a big occasion in the theatrical world in Germany, and this time the Royal Wurtemberg Opera House in Stuttgart was to have the honour of staging it. The libretto of "Ariadne" had been written by Hugo von Hofmannsthal, the Austrian poet, who also wrote the libretto for the "Rosenkavalier". The theme of "Ariadne" is mythological and it abounds in delightful and charming anachronisms. The scene is in a grotto in a palm grove. Ariadne and Bacchus (as a young man) sing, and the supporting cast consists of various nymphs and a number of familiar figures, such as Zerbinetta, Harlequin, Truffaldino and others from the *Commedia dell' Arte*. Jourdain, the *Bourgeois Gentilhomme*, is a spectator of the opera—like Christopher Sly in "The Taming of the Shrew".

The wishes of Strauss with regard to his opera were, of course, law for the management of the Stuttgart Royal Opera House, and absolutely first-class operatic and orchestral personnel were engaged in Berlin, Dresden and Vienna. Strauss, on the advice of Hofmannsthal, demanded that Max Reinhardt should be engaged as producer and that his company should perform the Molière play. Reinhardt, supported by both Strauss and Hofmannsthal, wanted to bring his own scenic artist and costume-designer with him, and finally this was agreed to. At the time I had no idea what difficulties had to be ironed out and what obstinate resistance had first to be overcome before an official letter arrived from Stuttgart confirming my engagement, or I might have declined with thanks, scenting the difficulties still to come.

The music publishers instructed me to complete a portfolio containing the designs, not only of the scenery for both pieces but also for all the furniture and other properties to be used. I was to make all my drawings to a certain size and to deliver them ready for reproduction. After that all theatres producing "Ariadne" were to play it together with "Le Bourgeois Gentilhomme" and present it exactly according to the designs in the portfolio. The position of Strauss in Germany was so strong that such dictatorial conditions were possible. Incidentally, I handed the printed reproductions to the Victoria and Albert Museum a long time ago.

Now, I had seen a certain number of Molière's plays produced by the Comédie Française, and whilst the acting was superb, the production, both with regard to the scenery and the costumes, was very disappointing. I had a copy of that most valuable work, "La Mode au XVII Siécle", according to contemporary engravings in the collection of Emile Liez, and, in addition, Hofmannsthal had very valuable architectural and theatrical material concerning the period in his collection. There was thus no particular reason for me to go to Paris for my work, as had at first been suggested. I could work very well where I was, particularly as Strauss lived only about an hour's motor-car journey away, and I felt that the strains of his music would help me to catch the spirit of the piece much better than all the undoubted treasures of the "Musée des Arts Décoratives" in Paris.

I have already expressed my view that the scenic artist must rely more on his own imagination and feeling than on the authentic material of any particular fashion period, but the more I studied my task the clearer it became to me that "Le Bourgeois Gentilhomme" was a social and moral satire abounding textually in drastic persiflage of a particular epoch, and I therefore decided that the costumes in our production of it must be characteristic of the period around 1700. At the same time, I argued, my operatic types must look as French society of 1700 would have expected its mythological figures to look on the stage.

Having come to this conclusion, I wrote to both Reinhardt and Hofmannsthal setting out my views. Reinhardt merely replied that I could do what I liked, but Hofmannsthal wrote expressing complete agreement with my views. There was nothing pedantic, as far as he could see, in my plan to put a whole epoch on to the stage with all its stylistic exaggerations.

Thus encouraged, I set to work. "La Mode au XVII Siécle", with all its wonderful engravings, is almost a complete text-book of illustrations for Molière's piece. Practically all the characters are there: the Dancing Master, the Hairdresser, the Fencing Master, aristocratic and bourgeois ladies and gentlemen, their lackeys, and so on. The list of illustrations reads like a list of characters from the play. My glass-enclosed veranda was an ideal studio, and very soon the 15-inch figures began to accumulate. And when I felt I needed spiritual refreshment, I went over to Strauss and listened to the "Ariadne" music. The work went with such a swing that within five weeks I had all my designs finished. Three weeks before the date fixed for the first night everything had arrived in Stuttgart.

When I went to the Opera House to examine the scenery I found Jourdain's living-room, the dining-room and the island of Naxos all ready set up on the runners. The experienced property master praised the technical efficiency and the manufacture which was accurate to a fraction of an inch. Then half-a-dozen gentlemen introduced themselves formally and began to examine the scenery. Not a word was said and in the end I was handed a letter couched in typical officialese requesting me to present myself for an interview with His Excellency the Director of the Royal Opera House the following morning.

A little startled and with some misgiving, I returned to our hotel, to be greeted in the hall by our comic, Viktor Arnold, who was playing the role of Jourdain:

"You've just come from the Royal Opera House," he exclaimed. "I can read it off the end of your nose. So it's started, has it?" And he let off a long, rolling, whistling laugh and waved his short, thick arms like a penguin's flippers. "They don't like us here, my boy, and you'll soon find it out, all of us, you, me, everybody, not forgetting our famous Master Reinhardt.

"Ariadne," opera by Richard Strauss

Theatrical art from Berlin! Dear oh dear, laddie, they don't like it."

We all knew Viktor as a malicious old cynic and pessimist, but how right he was this time! The following day I presented myself "in a neat and well-washed condition", as German call-up notices always say and my letter barely omitted saying, and met His Excellency on the stage. After a few coldly formal words of thanks for my efforts, His Excellency adjusted his monocle and began an examination which revealed a complete innocence of all artistic understanding. For example, he wanted to know why the walls of Monsieur Jourdain's living-room were cream coloured and why his dining-room was decorated only with a few pilasters; why the furniture was not more delicate, and so on. When I pointed out that it was a question of the period in which the piece played he merely shook his head doubtfully, and when I said that the walls had been kept just cream coloured in order to show off the costumes to better advantage, he exclaimed:

"The costumes! Oh, they're quite a chapter on their own. But let us keep to the scenery for the moment," and he indicated the palms for the Isle of Naxos scene: "I have been in the tropics myself," he informed me, "and I know what palms look like. Why have you given them such strangely contorted shapes and garlanded them with flowers? And some of the leaves have been painted pink. Didn't you consider that we should have to use the palms for other plays as well?"

No, I certainly hadn't considered that, and I pointed out that they had been designed specially for "Ariadne" and with nothing else in mind.

"But we wanted to use them for 'A Midsummer Night's Dream'," he said reproachfully.

Even the fact that I had designed the costumes in the fashion of Molière's day was regarded as an entirely superfluous experiment. Why hadn't I designed the costumes in the rococo period as usual? Louis Quatorze costumes were really an expensive luxury for a theatre with a regularly changing programme.

And so it went on. Like master, like man. Encouraged by the disapproval of the All Highest, his subordinates began a general campaign of complaints and grumbles; nothing was right. The wood from which the Berlin manufacturers had made the stage furniture was allegedly of inferior quality; the upholstery was poor, the tables and chairs were much too heavy, and so on. And the costume department was worst of all; they grumbled at the quality of the materials used; they grumbled at the cutting; they even grumbled at the way the buttons were sewn on. But at last they went too far and I had them on the hip.

One morning I was invited into the office to meet a collection of men and women obviously under the chairmanship of a portly gentleman with a massive beard and an air of great dignity and severity. At a sign from him, Monsieur Jourdain's gala coat was laid out before me on the table. It was a most expensive and luxurious garment, liberally embroidered with gold thread and decorated with a striking pattern of flowers. With solemn finger, the bearded one pointed to these flowers.

E

"*Mein Herr*," he began, "I take it that you failed to notice that the flowers on this coat have been embroidered upside down. Instead of pointing upwards, as they should, they point down."

"No," I agreed, suppressing my delight as best I could. "I did notice it."

For a moment there was an embarrassed pause whilst they all looked at each other. Then the bearded one continued his catechism:

"Are we really to assume, *mein Herr*, that you noticed the error, and that you nevertheless . . . that you nevertheless . . ."

The shocking conclusion seemed to rob him of words so I sprang to his assistance:

"That I knowingly let it pass. Yes, that's quite true. By the way, is there a copy of the script available?"

There was icy silence until the script was produced. When it arrived, I turned up the requisite page and handed him the script.

"Would you care to read what Monsieur Jourdain says to his tailor and what his tailor says in reply. Here it is in Scene Five of Act Two. And would you please read it out loud, so that everyone else can hear it."

A little subdued he began to read the text I had indicated:

"Monsieur Jourdain: 'What's this. Your flowers are upside down. Look, their heads are pointing downwards.'

"The Tailor: 'You didn't say that you wanted them pointing upwards.'

"Monsieur Jourdain: 'Good Heavens! Is it necessary to say things like that?'

"The Tailor: 'Certainly it is. All persons of quality wear them pointing downwards.'

"Monsieur Jourdain: 'All persons of quality wear their flowers upside down, you say?'

"The Tailor: 'Certainly, sir.'

"Monsieur Jourdain: 'Oh well, that's a different matter.'

"The Tailor: 'If you wish it, I can make them point upwards.'

"Monsieur Jourdain: 'Oh no, no, no . . . not at all.' "

After which there was deathly silence and I left the room.

None of them dared to approach Strauss himself, or Hofmannsthal, for Hofmannsthal was an aristocrat, but failing that they could vent their spleen on the unwanted guest from

Berlin, and, in fact, as he was not used to opera he certainly made minor mistakes here and there, and that was the longed-for opportunity for a certain Herr M. N., the permanent operatic producer attached to the Opera House. Forth he would then rush, spouting musical technicalities, in order to give the interloper from Berlin, the man who knew it all better, an unkind lesson. Big and fat as beseemed a former Wagnerian singer, he would trample on to the stage with a confident and superior air, take off his coat and roll up his sleeves demonstratively, as though now he'd show the interloper just how it was to be done.

And Herr M. N. did not even wait for my unimportant errors; he was adept at tripping me up and organizing a little sabotage here and there. Viktor Arnold, the keen-eyed and mistrustful, observed the proceedings from the ringside, and it was not long before he discovered beyond a doubt that Herr M. N. and his friends were deliberately provoking operatic technical difficulties.

It would take too long to enumerate all the tricks, all the passive resistance, all the difficulties which were deliberately placed in my way at every step. It was very difficult for me to keep up my interest and enthusiasm in face of this deliberately malicious opposition, but at last my purgatory came to an end. I stayed on to see the première, but before the final aria of Ariadne had died away I was on my way out with my grip, making direct for the station.

After my flight from Stuttgart, my disagreeable job done, I met Reinhardt in Paris together with Carl Vollmöller, the author of "The Miracle", and Maria Carmi, who had played the role of the Madonna. Together we went off to London, where we produced "Venetian Nights", a mimed drama, on a revolving stage specially built for the purpose at the Palace Theatre. This time the former Madonna played the part of a rich and beautiful Venetian lady. In its original form, the adventurous affairs of the lady met with the disapproval of the Lord Chamberlain, Lord Sandhurst, and we had to alter a good deal before he finally let it pass. All our efforts proved in vain; the piece was not a success.

From London we returned to Berlin and began preparations for producing a whole cycle of Shakespearian plays in connection with the three hundredth anniversary of Shakespeare's death.

A winter trip

CHAPTER X

A WINTER TRIP

THE COUNTRYSIDE LAY DEEP under snow. Hill after hill rose gently round and white against the dark green of the pine woods which stretched far away to the horizon. The wooded expanse rose higher and higher. Here and there were snow-covered hills, isolated at first and then in lines, until finally they rose majestically into the clouds to form the tremendous ridges of the Alps.

I had worked hard on the staging of "Romeo and Juliet" and "The Merchant of Venice", and the costumes and décor had been something quite new and untried before. It had taken a good deal out of me and now I was tired and needed a rest. I was on my way to Italy, to Naples and Pompeii, for a holiday.

"What about a little inspiration for Julius Cæsar whilst you're in Rome," Reinhardt said before I went. It was a good idea. So far I had tried my hand only on Shaw's "Androcles and the Lion", and the idea of doing "Julius Cæsar" attracted me.

When the train ran into the main station of Munich, I remembered that the Christmas market would be on, because in a few days it would be Christmas, and there were always wonderful things on show and for sale. I forgot my fatigue, and I stayed in Munich for twenty-four hours and went to the market, where I bought Christmas angels of shining, coloured paper and a series of carved and decorated animals for the Holy Crib. That sort of thing came natural to Munich; decorative art was in the very air.

I remember when on one occasion I was invited to celebrate Christmas with friends in Munich. In Germany the main celebration, including the distribution of presents, takes place on Christmas Eve, and not on the morning of Christmas Day, as here. There were three children in the family and they had dressed themselves up as the "Three Kings", making their costumes and their crowns. The crowns in particular were real works of art: they were beautifully done, with many points, and openwork as delicate as gold filigree or lace. After the presents had been distributed and the children had sung, we all sat down to our Christmas dinner. The children kept on their lovely crowns, and suddenly their mother, who had been admiring and praising them still, gave an exclamation of horror.

"Paul!" she cried to the eldest, a ten-year-old boy. "Where do those crowns come from. Don't say they're the lace from my best knickers!"

But that was just what they were. Paul had taken his mother's best lace-trimmed knickers (which were very modern and popular in those days), cut off the lace, dipped it in paste, let it harden and had then fashioned it into the crowns and gilded it. Mama's best knickers were ruined, but the result was impressive. That's the sort of thing I mean when I say that practical artistry was in the very air in Munich.

After visiting the Christmas market, I continued my journey through the snowy countryside. My train ran into North Tyrol between two chains of Alps and on into Italy where I awoke as we were travelling through Tuscany. It was grey rainy weather, but Florence was still Florence whatever the weather, and so I was not unduly depressed.

"The 'Monna Lisa' has been found," was the first thing I heard on arriving at my hotel. "It is being exhibited at the Uffizi before it goes back to the Louvre, but only for one day. The 'Monna Lisa!' 'La Gioconda'. Leonardo da Vinci's greatest work!"

Leonardo's "Monna Lisa" had been stolen some years before, and all efforts to recover it had failed. And now, after all hope had been abandoned, it seemed to have turned up. The Italians

—who certainly have style—exhibited the long-lost painting in the Uffizi Gallery and invited the citizens of Florence to come and see it. Naturally, I took advantage of the opportunity, and what I saw there was like a pilgrimage to the holy places. An endless procession of men and women passed slowly before the masterpiece, which was guarded by carabinieri in gala uniform—a fitting touch! The atmosphere was like that in church; everyone walked silently and almost on tiptoe and spoke in whispers, and the men took off their hats.

The same day I sent a telegram to my Russian painter friend, Sch——, in Paris: "She has been found! Congratulations!"

When I first went to Paris, in 1900, I lived with Sch——. He made his living by copying the "Monna Lisa." The thing had become not only his occupation, but his aim in life, and he devoted himself utterly to it. Imagine his dismay, therefore, when one night the "Monna Lisa" disappeared from her accustomed place in the Salon Carée! It was more than dismay; it was despair. Every day he would go to the Louvre and stare unhappily at the square of red wall where the "Monna Lisa" had once hung. The attendants knew him well, of course, and he was known to them as "Monsieur Monna Lisa". They now began to treat him as though he were a mourner who had lost his lover. I met him again after the First World War. He was still engaged in making copies of his beloved "Monna Lisa", but in the meantime he had become old, bowed and white-haired.

"When I asked her where she was and what she was doing in all those long years she spent in Italy, she just gives a mysterious smile," he complained.

Even at that time it had become popular to reproach the Italians rather contemptuously with living on their brilliant past. The great masterpieces of former times were their heritage, and now they lolled back, did nothing, and lived on the interest, it was said. I must say that my visits to Italy gave me no such impression of the Italian people. The citizens of Florence lived with their buildings as something real and alive, not as the dead husks of the past. The Ponte Vecchio, the Loggia dei Lanzi, the Santa Maria del Fiore were as alive to them as Piccadilly Circus to the Londoner or the Grand Boulevards to the Parisian, and the same was true of their famous painting and sculptures. As a visitor, I walked amongst it all in constant exaltation, and every familiar building, sculpture and picture that I saw was an old friend.

In one respect I was privileged. I knew Maria Carmi's brother, Gigli, who owned a café and was at the same time a well-read and highly cultured man who spoke several languages. Thanks to him, I got to know the town of the Medicis much better than any ordinary visitor with the traditional guide-book could possibly have done.

Although it was December, the weather was fine and quite warm and the shops in the arcades of the Piazza had drawn down their great linen blinds. A small crowd had collected before one of these blinds on which was written in blue lettering "Hairdresser". The assembled people were intent on a pair of feet encased in patent leather button boots with cloth sides, which obviously belonged to a customer sitting quite close to the blind and being attended to by the hairdresser. A small group of German tourists led by a guide was amongst the throng and the guide now informed them in a solemn voice that they were about to witness something sensational. "Now. Now," he cried, as the feet in the cloth-sided patent-leather button boots moved. Their owner was rising to his feet. "He is having his hair and beard curled and pomaded," the guide explained in an awed voice. "This he does every day at this shop."

"Who does?" asked the somewhat mystified Germans.

"Gabriele," the Italian whispered. "Gabriele."

"Gabriele who?" persisted the Germans.

"Gabriele d'Annunzio," returned their guide in horror. As though there could be any other Gabriele! "*Si, si,*" he ejaculated in triumph, "here he comes: Gabriele d'Annunzio! Italy's greatest living poet."

In those days d'Annunzio played a big role in Italy's public life. His books and his plays were beginning to be known abroad, and he was, in addition, a man of forceful character and impetuous temperament—after the First World War and after the Treaty of Versailles he seized Fiume off his own bat and incorporated the town into Italian territory. There was a rumour, much exaggerated, no doubt, about d'Annunzio and Reinhardt. The Italian poet had written a silent drama, "St. Sebastian", which was staged in Paris with Ida Rubinstein in the leading role. It was then offered to Reinhardt for production in Germany, but Reinhardt rejected it. This, it was said, mortally offended d'Annunzio, who ever after that hated Germany and all things German, and it was thanks to his influence that Italy subsequently refused to play her part in the Triple Alliance and even entered the war on the side of the Entente. *Si non e vero e ben trovato!*

On the journey to Rome I read the play "Ovid" of the Roumanian writer, Alexandrii. By chance it had been sent on to me in Florence and it came into my hands just when I was about to study the history of ancient Rome. To outsiders the connection between ancient Rome and modern Roumania will not be obvious, but it is nevertheless a connection of which the Roumanians are—or at least were—very proud, and Ovid is a name which links Roumania with Rome. Ovid was banished to the Black Sea town of Tomis, which, it is claimed, is the present-day Constanta. And, of course, Dacia was a Roman province under the Emperor Trajan, whose legions were thus stationed on what is now Roumanian territory. Present-day Roumanians feel themselves the lineal descendants of the old Romans, and, in fact, the many Latinisms in the Roumanian tongue suggest a one-time close association with the Roman Empire.

The book had been sent to me because the Roumanian National Theatre in Bucharest proposed to stage it, and I was invited to design the scenery. However, despite this new reason for staying some time in Rome, I did not do so, but went on to Naples, where I had ordered a room with a view on to the sea and Vesuvius. It was not until the following morning that I discovered that although I could look out over the sea, I could not see Vesuvius. Annoyed at this, I called the manager to complain. Thereupon he invited me to enter the bathroom and sit in the bath, which, somewhat mystified, I did. Then he pushed open a small window in the larger, frosted window of the bathroom and exclaimed dramatically:

"Ecco il bellissimo Vesuvio, Signore!"

It was perfectly true: seated in my bath with that small window open I could see the contour of Vesuvius and watch the smoke gently curling from its crater.

I had lunched the day before in Rome, and something or the other I had eaten had disagreed with me. I had no energy, and certainly not enough to quarrel, and so I let it go at that. During the day I sketched ships, buildings, palm trees and streets, and I envied the Neapolitans for their masterly indolence. Before the famous Aquarium, I remembered that I had a letter of introduction to a young Russo-German who worked in the institute. I was made very welcome and I was particularly thankful to him that in my present mood he made no attempt to persuade me to marvel at the fantastic wonders of the sea moving around in their numerous glass tanks. Instead, he talked about the catches and the trade of the aquarium with the underwater denizens of the Bay of Naples. I had fasted that day believing that to be the best way of dealing with a disturbed digestion, but I accepted his invitation to take supper with him.

After that I visited a "Fantochi Theatre," where Pipistrello, Pepenapa and Columbine jerked and twitched amusingly and addressed each other in Neapolitan dialect. I could not, of course, understand a word, but from the delighted reaction of the audience I felt sure that their lines were highly seasoned. When it grew dark I rejoined my young friend of the Aquarium. I had ordered *Pollo arosto* in the Trattoria and I had visions of fresh lobster just out of the sea. My young friend took off his jacket, rolled up his sleeve, and picked a lobster out of one of the glass tanks, and that we had for our supper, and a very good supper it was. What came afterwards was not so good, and it upset my digestion once again.

We passed through a small square enclosed by tall, gloomy houses and lighted only by the windows and the open door of a tavern. Suddenly there was a terrific hubbub of noise and a troop of shrieking women and cursing men poured out into the street fighting. Suddenly one fellow smashed a bottle down on to the head of another, and in a split second I saw for the first time in my life a face covered with blood. Unfortunately, I can still see it; it has pursued me.

On the way to the museum in which I proposed to study the excavated finds from Herculaneum and Pompeii and make sketches I fell in with crowds of people going to the Cathedral for Christmas Mass. That promised to be more interesting than any archæology, so I joined them.

The Church of Rome is a brilliant producer; a *regisseur* could learn his business from the church. No one knows how to exploit the suggestion of colour better than the Catholic Church. Against a packed brown, grey and black mass of kneeling monks and nuns stood out a row of priests clad in violet cassocks. The next group, situated a little higher up, was clad in purple, and the next beyond that in vermilion red. Above them again were priests in yellow and white, like an illuminated cloud. And over all throned the bishop in his golden robes. Incense swirled up into the vaulted roof far away above our heads and the yellow flames of a thousand candles flickered lambently. Accompanied by the deep tones of the organ were the ecstatic treble voices of boys. The impression was tremendous, overpowering.

I almost ran back to my hotel afterwards to get it all down as far as I possibly could on paper. "What a pity I hadn't this before!", I thought. I could have used it for "The Miracle".

The next day I visited Pompeii. I had bought myself a green eye-shield such as tennis players and others sometimes use against the sun. My idea was that if I wore it at a certain angle

Pompeii. Studying

I should be able to walk around Pompeii almost as though it had never been destroyed, because in most streets the ruins of the walls are still standing up to a height of 12 feet and more. In this way I should be able to take in the preserved flags of the streets, the wells, and the doors of shops and houses. And in my imagination—a very lively one, as befits my profession—I peopled the streets with the Romans of old, men, women and children, as they passed through the streets about their business. I could see them standing at the counters of shops discussing their purchases, worshipping in the well-preserved Temple of Isis, sitting in the amphitheatre watching the games. It is one thing to study the architectural treatise of Vitruvius and quite another to see the buildings standing tangible and plastic in the bright sunlight.

On the evening before I left Naples I went to see a performance of Boito's "Mephistopheles" in the San Carlo Opera House, and I was delighted to note that my Italian colleagues had not lost the art of painting the décor on canvas.

CHAPTER XI

THE WORLD COLLAPSES

"On Sundays, holidays, there's naught I take delight in,
Like gossiping of war and war's array,
When down in Turkey far away,
The foreign people are a'fighting.
One at the window sits with glass and friends,
And sees all sorts of ships go down the river gliding:
And blesses then as home he wends
At night, our peace abiding."

Thus "Another Citizen" in Goethe's "Faust", Part One, Scene II, "Before the City Gate". And that was more or less the case with me when I discussed the situation with my painter friend in the summer of 1914. His house, like mine, was on the Ammersee, and we sat at his open window with filled glasses in our hands watching the sailing boats slide peacefully over the lake. And "down in Turkey far away" lay Sarayevo—at least, it had once been Turkey. Despite many indications to the contrary, we were both optimistically convinced that we lived in an enlightened world, a world which would, in the last resort, settle its political differences in a civilized fashion by international conferences, and so we refused to let ourselves be unduly alarmed by the increasingly frequent rumours of war.

And after that consoling conversation, I went back to my own romantically situated house. But when I looked down from my hill into the valley it seemed to me that the peasants were harvesting their grain earlier than usual. They seemed in a much greater hurry to get it safely into their barns, and the swaying, jolting hay-wains seemed impatient to finish their journeying. In the village ale-house the men were silent and their faces over their beer mugs were serious. The peasant woman who brought me my milk did not chatter so loudly and cheerfully as usual. The village teacher no longer seemed anxious to indulge in one of his favourite discussions about art; he would nod silently and return to his paper.

But I still ignored all these signs and went on with my painting until one morning, long before I expected him, the village carpenter appeared with a wooden case I had ordered for my paintings, declaring that he had done it as a rush job for me before he left the village to rejoin his regiment.

The sound of the nails being hammered into the case as he closed it up with my pictures inside sounded like the hollow blows of doom on the coffin of peace.

War was duly declared, and I hurried back to Berlin where I found the theatrical world in a panic. What would happen now? Would we be permitted to go on playing? And if we did, would the audiences still come? Would actors be called up? Our Austrians had already gone. For myself there was no immediate fear; I was a Roumanian, and Roumania was neutral.

As far as we were concerned the situation was not long in clarifying itself. All theatres were soon playing to packed houses. People wanted distraction, and the authorities declared that the theatrical and amusement industries represented work of national importance; it was essential that morale should be kept high on the home front whilst the soldiers were away in the field. We continued our Shakespeare cycle and looked around for new productions. "Life is earnest; art is joyful", says Schiller in the prologue to his Wallenstein trilogy, and I concentrated my attention so much on the new designs for "Wallenstein's Camp" that I quite forgot the war. "Wallenstein's Camp" is laid before the walls of the Bohemian town of Pilsen, and it is full of many different uniforms, Croats, Hungarian mercenaries, Butler's dragoons, female camp-followers and other colourful types—just the thing for me. The great French artist Callot was an eyewitness of the Thirty Years' War, and he has left us graphic pictures of the scenes, and as for the background, I knew Bohemia and its woods very well from my visits to the Sudete areas.

The second part of the trilogy is "The Piccolomini" and the third part "The Death of Wallenstein". There was a good deal of baroque scenery to be designed and—a special titbit for the scenic artist—Wallenstein's astrological observatory: the inside of a round tower with mysterious machinery and the "Seven Colossal Figures representing the Planets", each in its own niche and uncannily lighted—as Schiller says in his stage directions. I was fully taken up with this work, but from time to time I was called back to reality to observe the careworn faces of those around me and listen to the pessimistic views of so many, Reinhardt included.

Generally speaking, the Russian bear was regarded with a good deal of contempt in Germany, particularly since the Russian defeat by the Japanese in 1905, but at the same time people did not forget that "The Little Father" had enormous masses at his disposal, and that made up for a good deal. What did the loss of 100,000 men mean to him? He had millions in reserve; as masses were mowed down, so he could push more and more masses into the fighting line. German victories were being reported from the eastern front, but people realized that they were no more than advanced-post skirmishes; Russia needed time to mobilize her vast resources, and then the steam-roller would begin to move.

The general war psychosis began to count its victims. The famous Capuchin speech comes in "Wallenstein's Camp", in which the monk inveighs against the godless, reckless soldiery and even denounces Wallenstein himself. The role of the Capuchin monk was played by Viktor Arnold (the same actor

"The Terrible Horseman"

who had taken the part of Monsieur Jourdain). He was a fine actor both in comic and serious parts.

> " 'Tis a time of misery, groans and tears!
> Portentous the face of the heavens appears!
> And forth from the clouds behold blood red,
> The Lord's war-mantle is downward spread—
> Whilst the comet is thrust as a threatening rod
> From the window of Heaven by the hand of God,
> The world is but one vast house of woe,
> The Ark of the Church rides a bloody flow. . . ."

Up to this point Arnold dutifully followed Schiller's text, but then one evening he burst out with an interpolation of his own:

> "And terrible horsemen wielding the knout,
> Burst over the frontiers in endless hordes
> to kill, and kill and kill."

They were his last words as an actor, and having shrieked them at the audience he collapsed on the stage. Down came the curtain and as his colleagues carried him off he babbled of Cossacks. "They're coming! They're coming! They're on us!" He was taken to a mental home, where he succeeded in evading observation long enough to cut his throat with a piece of jagged glass. On a grey and miserable day we assembled around his open grave. The coffin was lowered into it and as the first clods of earth fell with a hollow thud on to the wood his widow rushed forward hysterically shouting, "Viktor, Viktor, don't leave me alone!" and sprang into the open grave.

As the theatre had been officially pronounced as service to the Fatherland, it also had to provide cheerful and amusing matter to keep the public spirits up; laughter helps to overcome a good many things. And so we decided to stage Raimund's farce, "The Mountain King and the Misanthrope". Reinhardt and I therefore set off for the Alps to obtain local colour for the production and steep ourselves in the comic ghost world of the Alpine fairy story. But when we got there it was all so marvellous and exhilarating that we wasted no time on the piece, but set ourselves to enjoy the magnificent scenery, the fir trees laden with snow, the gleaming landscape, the sparkling sky. As two complete tiros, we spent more time sliding on the seats of our breeches than on our skis, but we enjoyed every minute of it and returned to Berlin and work thoroughly at one with the atmosphere of the snow fable.

It did not take us long to come to an agreement. We gave the piece a new title, "The Crackpot", modernized it without materially altering the trend of the piece—namely, the transformation of the misanthrope into a philanthropist. The actors clambered over hills thickly covered with convincing snow, whilst equally convincing icicles hung down from friendly fir trees. Astrologus, the Mountain King, wore a long robe of snow and a crown of inverted icicles and his beard glistened with ice and snow. It was a lively affair, and it went with a swing with

Scene from "The Crackpot"

dancing, snowballing and acrobatics, and a chorus whose heads emerged from the snow crowned with small fir tree hats. "Crackpot" was first staged in the New Year of 1915.

Unlike Hitler's Third Reich in the Second World War, Hohenzollern Germany in the first was very anxious to remind the neutrals that she was a country of eminent cultural attainments, and to this end the Government subsidized operatic and theatrical companies to tour neutral countries. Our company was one of them. We went to Scandinavia, and our programme included Goethe's "Faust", a number of Strindberg's plays and several Shakespearian productions. In this way, in particular, the world was to learn that Great Britain's enemy honoured

Great Britain's greatest poet despite the war. We had a transportable revolving stage built, and that, together with a shipload of props, was transported over the Baltic at Government expense. We went to Sweden via Denmark, and whilst we were in Copenhagen we were invited to a magnificent lunch by Danish authors, led by the world-famous critic, Georg Brandes. I must confess that I didn't pay a great deal of attention to the flattering speeches which were delivered—in any case, they were more for Reinhardt and his works than for Germany's cultural achievements as such—the greater part of my attention being taken up by the wonderful food, which by that time had become a great rarity in wartime Berlin.

Press and public in Stockholm received our performances in the Opera House with enthusiasm, and I had no cause to be dissatisfied with my share of the praise. At this time Reinhardt was planning to put a long-cherished wish into execution—namely to form his own theatrical ballet company—and he thought he would be able to find more suitable recruits in Scandinavia than in Germany. The management of the Opera House placed a suitable hall at our disposal and Reinhardt and I interviewed innumerable dancers who were anxious to join his company.

One of them was a slim and very beautiful young woman who appeared in a fantastic Oriental costume and performed a wild and whirling dance, at the end of which there was very little of her costume left. I pointed out that as remarkable as her dancing undoubtedly was, what we actually wanted was the classical "on the points" dance. She didn't seem in the least put out or even very much interested, but began a conversation (she spoke fluent German) which had nothing to do with dancing. She was full of praise for Germany, praise which was so excessive as to be a trifle embarrassing, and above all she wanted to know what was happening in Germany at the moment. She was a little too importunate, and very firmly I brought the interview to a close.

We were staying in a first class hotel, in which, as is usual in Sweden, there was female service in the baths. These female attendants, all well past the canonical age, not only kept the rooms spotlessly clean, but they also rubbed down the bathers, massaged them and dried them most carefully and efficiently. We were not used to this sort of thing, of course, but we soon grew accustomed to it, and the service was, in fact, the last word in discretion and comfort. At the same time, not a word was spoken, particularly as none of us understood Swedish. The baths department was not very well lit and in addition there was the steam, so that we hardly noticed the various faces of the women who attended us.

However, one morning I was sitting in my bath as usual when I suddenly noticed that the hands of the woman attending to me were not the usual short, solid, muscular hands, but slim, elegant and well-manicured. Astonished, I looked up at the woman's face and found it young and beautiful. Seeing my astonished and rather horrified look, she whispered:

"It's all right. We know each other already."

As though that explained and put everything right! It was the importunate young woman who had shown such great interest in what was going on inside Germany. Somehow or the other—probably by a little bribery—she had managed to take the place of one of the usual attendants. It was perfectly clear that she was a spy. We had been told that Stockholm was full of them, and our experience confirmed it. I didn't know quite what to do. Throw her out? That would have created a scandal, so I just put up with it and parried her never-ending questions about the situation in Germany, until such time as I could escape from her attentions. This was a rather daring trick to get into touch with a German; the other methods were less sensational. Extremely polite and friendly gentlemen would get into touch with us in the hall or bar of the hotel. It was, of course, very easy for them to strike up an acquaintance with us, because we never knew whether their friendship was real, just that of hospitable Swedes anxious to make the visitor feel that he was amongst friends, or assumed, until the tenor of their questions made it obvious. Even the waiters, almost all of whom spoke excellent German, seemed to be in the game. They were all very attentive, and whilst inquiring as to how we liked the food, particularly the Swedish specialities, they would ask adroit questions about the food situation in Germany.

Towards the end of our stay we were invited to a "Goose Banquet" by Harriet Bosse, the widow of Strindberg. The menu at such a banquet is quite ingenious; almost everything is made of some part or parts of this highly savoury bird. Then we packed our things and went off to Oslo, which in those days was still called Christiana. Although the sympathies of the Norwegians were definitely with the Entente, they received us very well, and they greatly appreciated and highly praised our art. For Reinhardt this visit to Oslo was chiefly valuable for the fact that in the persons of Frau Gydda Christensen and her daughter, Lillebil, he found just the right people for his ballet plans.

By this time I was already an "enemy alien" in Germany, because my own country, Roumania, had joined the Entente. However, the German authorities had put me into the "unobjectionable class", particularly as my work was recognized as valuable for the war effort, though I was supposed to be under police surveillance, and I had to report to them regularly but it was only a formality.

Before we left Germany, in order to show the neutrals that, despite the clash of arms and all Germany's great military efficiency, she was still the land of Goethe and Schiller, we had arranged that the Deutsches Theater should carry on as usual in our absence, and Reinhardt had staged a production of Schiller's "Maria Stuart", undoubtedly one of his best and most popular plays. Schiller creates Mortimer as a fiery and passionate young supporter of Mary Queen of Scots. Elizabeth is shown as bitterly jealous of Leicester, whose feelings for the Scottish Queen she more than suspects. There is a grand scene in which the two queens meet as women. Elizabeth rejects Mary's attempts at conciliation and accuses her of plotting with England's enemies. When Elizabeth then goes on to accuse Mary of immorality, Mary pays her back spiritedly in her own coin and points out that "the Virgin Queen" can hardly have inherited either honesty or virtue from her mother, Anne Boleyn. Schiller the historian allows Schiller the playwright a good deal of licence in his treatment of the stuff for his tragedy. In one scene Mary is shown bitterly repentant for her share in the murder of her husband. Her majordomo, Melville, is a secret priest (according to Schiller), having been ordained by the Pope himself, so that at the last moment Mary receives the *viaticum* and the consolations of the Church, which the brutal Burleigh had refused her. Schiller describes her on her way to the gallows as follows:

"Enter Mary in white and sumptuously arrayed as though for a festival. Hanging from a necklace of small beads at her throat is an *Agnus Dei*. A rosary swings from her girdle. She holds a crucifix in one hand and there is a diadem of precious stones in her hair. Her long black veil is thrown back."

We preferred to put Mary in the typical Stuart hood rather than let her wear the diadem, but apart from that she was just as Schiller described. In striking contrast to her ladies-in-waiting, who were all dressed in black and all in tears, she went serenely to her death in gloomy Fotheringay Castle. Elizabeth

"Maria Stuart," by Schiller

we presented always in the stiff pomp of the period, with a tremendous ruff and costumes of gold brocade decorated with pearls against the background of her throne room. All the interiors of the piece I had designed in the Tudor style.

When we returned from Scandinavia, we followed "The Taming of the Shrew" in our Shakespearian cycle with "Macbeth". Neither Reinhardt nor I saw any virtue in the experiment of playing Shakespeare in modern dress, as had already been done in England, and "Macbeth" in particular was set against a gloomy, mysterious and uncanny background, with swirling mists and fantastic figures, witches and ghosts. Primitive people succumb to the influence of Hecate, the goddess of night and magic, and evil thoughts proliferate and lead to cruelty and murder. When I think of "Macbeth" I always recall a performance I saw some fifteen years after the period I am discussing. It was in New York, and the cast was all Negro. They were dressed rather strangely in Regency costumes, and although, in fact, their performance was not very good, there was one thing about the production which made a deep impression on me, and that was the psychological and emotional atmosphere. They had, so to speak, translated the sombre magic of the north into their own idiom, into their own voodoo sorcery, and the uncanny manifestations of this secret cult pervaded the whole production. In the witches' scenes the Negro witches shrieked, sang and danced in much the same fashion as their European counterparts, but the effect of the whole was greatly enhanced by the insistent and thrilling throb of African drums. The nerve-titillating effect of this jungle throbbing has often been described in the tales of returned travellers; in this Negro theatre I experienced its hair-raising effect for myself, and I found its introduction into "Macbeth" a touch of genius, but one which was perhaps almost a matter of course to the Negro producer. When Macbeth and Lady Macbeth planned the murder, their plottings were accompanied by the background throbbing of the drums. It merged naturally into the knocking on the door: "Wake Duncan with thy knocking! I would thou couldst!" Sometimes the throbbing was subdued, like the insistent echo of a guilty conscience, like a steady pulse beat; sometimes louder and more insistent, according to whether it conveyed the memory of past horrors or the suggestion of new horrible deeds to come.

I chose the kilt and tartan as the primitive dress of the Highlanders to costume our production, and the scenery consisted of a number of movable towers, which could readily be set up in any position on the stage, and with the help of walls, buttresses, steps and archways any required space could be created. Placed at the back and sides, the scenery formed the background for a rolling, treeless heather-covered landscape with changing clouds. Constantly changing lights, a spot light here and there as required, and the blue flicker of lightning heightened the general effect. The wind whistled, moaned or growled. And in this atmosphere—there were already technical possibilities for the production of all these effects, and the sound specialist was already a well-known technician back stage—I set my barbarian Scotsmen, and as I sketched them my mind dwelt on the hoarse croak of ravens, the shrill call of seagulls, piercing whistles and loud shrieks. On primitive basic sounds, so to speak, and into this atmosphere, the primitive musical instrument of the Scottish highlands and their savage inhabitants, the bagpipe, fitted perfectly.

Reinhardt greatly approved of the bagpipes, particularly in the banqueting scene. It was not difficult to obtain bagpipes, but very difficult to find anyone who could play them. In fact, at first it was impossible, and then it occurred to one or the other of us that there must be bagpipe players amongst the Scottish prisoners of war. We put the case to the military authorities, who immediately showed themselves very helpful, and so we found our bagpipe-player, a giant of a Highlander with red hair and intensely blue eyes. He had never heard of either Macbeth or Shakespeare, but that didn't matter; he could play the bagpipes. But would he? I explained to him that he would be allowed to leave the camp and even earn money for himself, and all he would have to do would be to play his pipes.

"Where would I have to play them?" he inquired suspiciously.

"Behind the scenes of a theatre in Berlin," I explained. "Every night. To give the piece we're playing the right atmosphere; it plays in Scotland, you see."

He shook his head obstinately:

"I'll be damned if I'll play the pipes for a bloody lot of Boches," he declared uncompromisingly.

In the summer of 1916 Reinhardt sent for me. He was staying on the island of Hiddensee off the Baltic coast and he wanted to discuss a new project. He was taking on a third theatre in addition to the two we already had, and he wanted to open the new one with a production of "The Tempest". I went by train to Stralsund and took the small steamer which plies across the narrow, shallow arm of sea between the coast and Hiddensee, which is flat and sandy and forms part of a chain of islands in front of the coast.

"I see this Hiddensee as Bermuda," Reinhardt explained. "The proper scene for Caliban, Ariel and Prospero. A little imagination and you can turn this waste of sand into a tropical island easily, don't you think, Stern?"

That was the only indication he gave me of his idea for the décor of "The Tempest", and, as usual, he left the rest to me. The fact that we were surrounded by the sea on a comparatively small island was enough for the main inspiration in his opinion, and that was true, because although there were no picturesque cliffs and rocks or bays and promontories, we were surrounded by the main scenic principle, the sea with its constantly changing moods, sometimes calm and sparkling in the sun, sometimes grey and threatening with great clouds rolling across it, and sometimes lashed into a fury of tossing waves and flying spume. The few houses I just ignored. Part of the island was grazing land, and every day I watched the cattle being driven over at low tide to feed. Busily I sketched them and the women, who waded with bare thighs, through the low water with them. To me it was a mythical scene, the procession of Amphitrite accompanied by screaming, wheeling seagulls.

In the villa which Reinhardt had taken for the summer the food was excellent. "Enter several strange shapes, bringing in a banquet; they dance about it with gentle actions of salutation; and inviting the King, etc., to eat, they depart." And that happened without a hitch twice a day, for Reinhardt's Viennese cook and her local assistant, the wife of a fisherman, could be described without exaggeration as "strange shapes", and the table they prepared for us was truly worthy of a king and his guests.

Our latest theatre was equipped with a so-called drum stage, i.e. the revolving stage was a sort of drum 6 feet deep which could be raised or lowered at will. When it sank away out of sight it left a cavity about 60 feet across, and over this cavity our ship rolled and swayed splendidly on a lively sea. And when in the middle of the tempest Gonzalo exclaims, "Now would I give a thousand furlongs of sea for an acre of barren ground, long heath, brown furze, anything. The wills above be done! But I would fain die a dry death," the ship disappeared in a thick cloud and our island rose from the depths. Its gentle, regular undulations were covered with strangely shaped brown and yellow rocks and unreal reddish vegetation of cactus type. Our "Mary Stuart" was now a slim and boyish Ariel all in blue. Caliban was that unforgettable actor, Rudolf Schildkraut. By nature he was sturdy and broad-shouldered, with powerful arms and legs, a head like a bull and great staring eyes. In short he needed very little titivation to make him the "savage and deformed slave" he had to play, but I provided him with a certain amount of fishy, jellylike additions to heighten the impression.

The war had not been on for two years, but already we were beginning to experience considerable difficulties because of the shortage of materials of all kinds, and it was only because we were specially favoured by the authorities that we managed to obtain even a part of what we required for our constant series of new productions. Again and again we were faced with the necessity of finding substitutes for material which was no longer obtainable.

When we returned from our Scandinavian tour, I was charged with scouring Copenhagen in an attempt to obtain silk for our costumes. At the same time I was to visit a ballet school and report back to Reinhardt. I had already seen their work, and I had promised the principal of the school to report back favourably to Reinhardt on the performance of her delightful girls when I was urged to stay to watch them in a performance of the Dance of the Seven Veils from the Strauss-Wilde "Salome". The solo dancer was a dark, Junoesque type very effectively costumed in Babylonian-Assyrian style, with long, close-fitting trousers. Her hands, arms and bare feet were bejewelled. She also wore a strange cloak which she could alter with extraordinary adroitness seven times during the course of her dance.

The thing that interested me much more than her dancing, good though it was, was the fact that she had made this extraordinary costume herself, and that her real profession was that of costumier. On going into this side of the matter, I decided to engage the girl, not as dancer, but to take charge of our ladies' costume department. A few days later she followed me to Berlin and started her new job. I had made no mistake. Anzi, as she came to called, was a jewel, and all the more precious in the difficult circumstances of wartime because her ingenuity was extraordinary and she could make up the most marvellous things almost out of nothing.

She settled herself in a little room partitioned off from the main ladies' tailoring department, and there she worked her magic day in and day out. Her real name was Georgina Winckler, and her father was a South German and her mother a Dane. Our actresses gave her the nickname of "Anzi" because her constant litany when they went to visit her in connection with their costumes was "Undress!", "Dress!", "*Ausziehen!*", "*Anziehen!*", hence "Anzi".

Anzi took her work seriously and did it like an artist. When she said "Undress!" she meant it. Underwear got in her way; it was the human body she was interested in. Our actresses soon got used to her and her ways, and they submitted willingly and all the more readily when they realized that Anzi was a genius. Her predecessor, a Viennese, had certainly been a capable woman, but not a genius, and when substitute materials had to be used—and very often invented before they could be used—she was out of her depth. Anzi revelled in it. Of her Goethe's axiom, *"In der Beschränkung zeigt sich erst der Meister"*, was certainly true.

Anzi was a characteristic product of the environment from which she came. She had been born into the circus, and she had been used to hard physical effort from early youth. In addition, she had all the thoroughness and the earnestness which marks the trick rider, the acrobat and all the other circus performers, whose life and limb depend on their care and preparations. She had travelled around with circuses and was used to inventing costumes out of little or nothing. Thanks to this early experience and a natural gift, her ingenuity would find a satisfactory solution to problems before which other people wrung their hands helplessly. You can often meet such types in the theatre world; after their wanderings they are cast up behind the scenes to work in some capacity or the other with tremendous efficiency.

Anzi's small workroom was furnished with a large cutting-out table, a large cheval mirror and a sofa which was always

Anzi trying out costumes

piled high with costumes and materials of all sorts. A powerful lamp cast its light on to the table even during the day as her large but well-shaped and capable hands tirelessly manipulated the heavy cutting-out shears. She always wore a sort of overall of her own invention which was so made that a movement or two would open it here or there to allow her to try on whatever it was she happened to be making.

"A theatrical cutter has got to be her own dummy," she would say, and she tried on everything: Iris, Ceres, Juno and the nymphs, often forgetting that she had practically nothing on underneath her overall. "Enter Ariel, like a harpy; claps his wings upon the table . . ." say the stage directions in Act III, Scene 3. I had sketched the harpy with wings instead of with arms, and bird's claws on the feet, and in a second sketch I had covered the claws with feathers in view of the difficulty we were having in getting things. Anzi made the wings excellently and she was unwilling to give up the claws. I found her sitting on her table fitting pieces of rubber tubing to her own toes and using curved pieces of celluloid as claws. Her experimenting was successful, and Ariel as the harpy had claws.

We had been using Russian Jewish prisoners of war (because as Jews they spoke Yiddish and therefore understood German) as stage-hands, but the wives of our called-up stage-hands came round in a body and declared that they could do the work just as well and had first claim. They were taken on, and under the direction of one or two experienced older stage hands who were beyond military age they proved reasonably satisfactory. The chief difficulty was their clothing, and in particular their long skirts—no one had ever heard of women wearing slacks in those days—so they asked for something or other more suitable to wear. The management turned to me in the matter—and I turned to Anzi. Anzi had come up against the same problem herself and solved it, as usual, excellently. One morning she appeared in trousered overalls all in one piece and of a material tastefully decorated with exotic flowers and garlands. The shape and style was just what was wanted for the women stage hands, though her own effort was a real work of art and might have come out of a fashion book. She had made it out of some old linen which had once served as a background scene for a tropical forest.

Having nothing else to do at the time, Anzi then set to work to make similar garments for them all. One by one they were completed, and one and all they were just as decorative and elegant as her own—though the wearers were not. It was typical of Anzi's thoroughness and her feeling for style that she had not been content merely to take any old material and cut it up as it came; instead, she had carefully pieced it out and made up the overalls so that the pattern of the stuff, whatever it was, became an integral part of the garment. After that our stage-hands were a gay lot. One of them wore multicoloured overalls like a Harlequin; another had blue with a sickle moon

Female stage hands, Berlin, 1917-18

and stars, the moon neatly in the middle of her back; another was decorated with heraldic emblems, and another one had heads of satyrs and fauns all over her rather plump person, and when she moved around their faces seemed to grin and smirk realistically.

We were busy at this time with preparations for our own ballet company. Reinhardt was not thinking of the ballet as the Russians do, as a thing in itself, as the chief thing in fact; his idea was for the dance as part and parcel of the mimed drama. We first made one or two experiments—for instance, we produced the minor ballet "The Two Shepherdesses", with music from the French composer Lully, in a play by Molière, and when that proved satisfactory we started on something much more ambitious: a ballet mime entitled "The Green

Flute". In the fairyland of China lived an old magician with
six arms and six legs named Wu, and Wu lived on the blood of
youths and maidens. His sister, the old witch Ho, used to catch
gallant young princes and delicate young princesses for her
brother and bring them to him like flies to the web of the spider.
One of them was the lovely princess Fay-yen of the land of
Thse. One night the magic strains of a flute are heard, the
bars of Fay-yen's golden cage fall apart and she dances out to
freedom. By the bank of a river she sinks to the ground exhausted by her flight, and on the other bank appears Sing-ling,
Prince of Thsu. It is he who plays the magic flute, but even the
flute isn't magic enough to ford the river and allow the two to
come together, and whilst the princess Fay-yen is still longingly
extending her arms to the prince, who is just as longingly
extending his on the other side, the wicked witch Ho appears
to recapture her and take her back to Wu. In despair at the
tragedy he is unable to prevent Sing-ling hurls his magic flute
into the river and plunges after it himself. But at this moment
the benevolent spirit of the place, the river goddess, rises from
the depths, saves the drowning Sing-ling, charms a ship into
existence, gives him his magic flute and puts him on board to
sail after his beloved.

In the meantime Wu, the old magician, has been rejuvenated.
Casting aside his surplus arms and legs, he dances to win the
heart of the Princess Fay-yen, who, however, spurns him and
is determined to die if she can't have her lover Sing-ling. At
that moment she hears the magic tones again—but Wu hears
them too and immediately turns himself into a terrible storm
to sink the ship bearing Prince Sing-ling. But the magic flute
is stronger than Wu's storm and Prince Sing-ling advances to
cut through Wu's golden web with his sword. Unfortunately, he drops his flute and is rendered vulnerable. Wu, who
has done another quick change and is now a terrible dragon,
seizes him and is about to kill him when the river goddess
appears from her watery lair and restores the flute to Sing-ling.
Its magic tones cause the dragon Wu to flee into a nearby
cavern, where he is very properly reduced first to a heap of gold
and then to ashes, after which Prince Sing-ling carries off his
beloved Fay-yen to his palace.

The author of this airy trifle—"A Dance-Play" as Reinhardt
finally decided to christen it—was Hofmannsthal, who read it
out to us in the presence of the actors who were to play Wu

and Ho, Princess Fay-yen and Prince Sing-ling. Now and again this or that motif from the accompanying music was played for us; it was all Mozart and taken from "Les petits Riens". The final music was Mozart's Turkish March, to the strains of which Prince Sing-ling bore his Princess home in triumph, followed by all the other princesses and princes who had been freed from the clutches of Wo and Wu.

"Chinoiserie," said Hofmannsthal. "Of course," I replied; "eighteenth-century China. Rococo! Chinese dignitaries with powdered wigs. And rococo cliffs, and gaily convoluted clouds. And many roofed fantastic pagodas. . . ."

Reinhardt interrupted me:

"All very fine and large, Stern; too fine and large for three-dimensional scenery. That's what you mean, isn't it?"

I nodded delightedly. Yes, that was just what I meant. It couldn't possibly be done three-dimensionally in wartime.

"Right," said Reinhardt. "You shall have it your way this time. Painted décor only."

I could have danced around for joy. Apart from all other considerations, I was convinced that only painting could properly represent the elegant dream world of Louis Quinze. "The Green Flute" called for an anachronistic China filled with people who were only disguised as Chinese. And the music of Mozart demanded that the trees, cliffs, clouds and waterfalls should be just as much rococo as Asiatic.

I have not previously mentioned that for me melody translates itself into line and form. In fact I have often tried to sketch to rhythmic inspiration. "The Green Flute" was just the thing for me. The principle in this special case was clear: the actors and dancers would have to be an integral part of their surroundings more than ever before, and their surroundings again should be them and of them as closely and intimately as possible.

And what about the colour? The title itself was a certain indication, but that applied only to the flute. It would have to be of an outstanding, shining green that dominated the scene whenever it appeared. Gold was also mentioned; the cages were of gold, Wu's web was of gold, and the defeated Wu himself was turned into a heap of gold. Happily I plunged into the work of sketching and designing, only to find with bitter disappointment that everything I did was unsatisfactory, banal, useless. . . .

When that happens there is only one thing to do—as my
master in Munich had taught me years before—nothing.
Abandoning the work I went out. Stopping with very little
interest before the shop window of an old junk-seller I suddenly
saw a grotesque and horrible face framed in a dirty old shawl.
The nose was hooked over almost to the bony chin, the skin
was shrunken and in many folds, the eyes were bleared and
the mouth was toothless. Bony hands like claws scrabbled in the
window moving this and that article around.

"My goodness!" I thought. "Wu's sister, Ho."

I have often found in life that unexpectedly a solution for
a seemingly insoluble problem turns up "by accident", and so
it was this time. I watched the clawlike hands with horrid
fascination as they made room in the window for new items of
junk, and then they pushed forward a small lacquered tray on
which there were a number of long glass beads. As it happened,
these glass beads were of a particularly intense green and the
background of the tablet was black. The tablet itself was a very
poor imitation of a Chinese work of art, painted with mountains, clouds, trees, flying birds and bridges by an unskilful
hand, but for me the green beads on the black and gold of the
tablet represented just the colour scheme I had been looking
for. I pushed open the door of the junk-shop and went inside.
The old witch was mistrustful and probably thought she was
parting with a treasure unawares, but I secured the wretched
tray with its green glass beads and hurried back to the studio
with my inspiration.

"Have we got any black hangings in stock?" I asked the
property master.

"Piles of it," he replied nonchalantly, "both cloth and
velvet. The stuff's in the way; I'd like to get rid of it."

We found we could paint on it with gold and silver-bronze,
and the golden cliffs with the many-storied decorative pagoda
looked as though they had been embroidered. Seen through
veils, the effect was dreamlike. Hangings of black velvet are
just the thing to create an impression of nothingness, and so I
hung it all around the stage and created a sort of limitless
vacuum within which I could set up or hang my painted
scenery as I chose. When the light went up, it concentrated
itself on the painting in gold and silver-bronze and the impression was one of cliffs, rocks, trees, pagoda and clouds in
filigree materializing out of nothing against a black background.

And then silently other mountains and other clouds became visible to the audience by the simple trick of lowering them from the flies. Here and there the bronze contours were kept vague by black veils which hung before them. All that was necessary to heighten an impression was to withdraw the veils or intensify the lighting, or both, and then the landscape appeared, almost glimmered on the sight. The background of the river scene showed jagged mountains down which a silver waterfall plunged into the depths to lose itself in grottos from which the river emerged over the stage, which was also black, and came up to the footlights, separating Princess Fay-yen and her disconsolate lover Prince Sing-ling. The realistic flowing river was produced by an equally simple trick: a long broad piece of velvet was painted with silver undulating lines; at the near end there was a sort of slide under the velvet and two crawling youngsters pushed the silver water forwards, their movements increasing the impression of tumbling water.

On principle I avoided the use of mechanical aids as far as possible and, where necessary, I helped myself out with the naïve tricks of the authentic Chinese theatre. For example, the ship magically conjured up by the river goddess was only a shallow prop in the form of a junk. Sing-ling held it under his left arm and rowed with the right, moving along behind waves erected for the purpose. I also borrowed the idea of the dragon into which Wu transformed himself from the way in which the Chinese still produced such monsters on their own stage. Boys were concealed in the great horned and pop-eyed skull of the beast, and in the many articulated parts of the body. This animal was also covered with black velvet painted with golden scales. When the dragon moved the legs of the boys were visible and it progressed like a centipede.

The only three-dimensional props used in "The Green Flute" were the golden cages in which Wu imprisoned his victims, and the long arched bridge over which Prince Sing-ling led his beloved Princess Fay-yen and all the other released prisoners away to safety. The procession contrasted like a silhouette against the silver mountains in the background, on which the decorative pagoda with its silver whorls jutted into golden clouds.

All the costumes fitted into the general style of the scenery. Fay-yen wore a black pagoda-like, full-skirted dress embroidered with golden flowerets. On her black silk wig sat a miniature pagoda as a hat. Prince Sing-ling with his Green Flute was in black and gold trousers and a tailed wig. The sorcerer Wu was played by Ernst Matray, a slightly built young Hungarian, a mimic genius and a wonderful acrobatic dancer.

"The Green Flute." Ballet Costumes

His obstinate Hungarian accent unfortunately made it impossible to use him as a straight actor. He first came into notice as a servant of Petruchio in "The Taming of the Shrew" when he fell down a flight of steps, throwing a whole series of somersaults with extraordinary grace and ending on his feet as light as a feather. Reinhardt was delighted, as he was with any perfect performance no matter what its nature, and after that Mattray was one of his favourites. Mattray's performance as the wicked Wu finally established his reputation. His make-up as Wu was impressive and his hair stood out stiffly in all directions. At first he had six arms and six legs, and this effect was achieved by two lads who were concealed with him in his costume, their arms and legs only appearing. Mattray trained them marvellously and the effect was really that of a crab and extraordinarily convincing. Wu's final defeat and destruction by the magic flute was represented in a whole series of astonishing leaps and acrobatic contortions. In this scene Mattray was at his best and the performance demonstrated convincingly what a dramatic effect acrobatics could achieve.

The part of Wu's sister, the witch Ho, was played by a man who subsequently became world-famous in a very different fashion, Ernst Lubitsch. He was a pupil of the great comic actor, Viktor Arnold, whose tragic suicide I have already described. Lubitsch, black-haired, rather undersized and very droll, played many roles for us, including Launcelot Gobbo in "The Merchant of Venice", Peto in Henry IV, and so on. Towards the end of the war he was already playing film roles and then he began to make comic films of his own, and this brought him to the notice of the bigger film companies and he was given more important work. After the war Americans founded a film company and he became its manager. In 1921, when my contract with Reinhardt expired, I went to Lubitsch as his Art Director.

Whilst the final rehearsals of "The Green Flute" were still taking place Reinhardt decided to stage Georg Büchner's play "The Death of Danton", whose theme is the conflict between Danton, Camille Desmoulins and their friends and Robespierre. The action takes place in the Convention, before the Revolutionary Tribunal, at the Conciergerie and in the streets and squares of Paris in 1793. When I read the play my impression was of dramatic, tragic and fantastic scenes which flamed up for a short space and then disappeared. The chaos of the revolution struck me as a terrible storm to the accompaniment of the constant rolling of thunder, sometimes near, sometimes in the distance, the scene lit up with flashes of lightning, the passionate actors in the drama appearing for a while as though in the spotlight and then fading into the background. In one respect my work on "The Green Flute" helped me here because it struck me forcibly that "lighting" was the solution for the problem of staging "Danton" just as it had been for the fantastic Chinese fairy tale. The revolving stage was quite out of the question, and fortunately Reinhardt agreed with me that "Danton" required a special system of décor and I was allowed to carry out my own ideas on the subject.

"Reinhardt undertook the daring experiment of producing a famous realistic piece whilst abandoning realism in the scenery and presenting the visual aspect of the great revolutionary drama chiefly as human bodies and lighting effects. The stage was a neutral construction which was neither obviously interior nor exterior and therefore served as both. To the right and left of it great pillars reared up into the flies. The changing background of the play was represented very simply by various coloured hangings, and steps, on which the members of the Convention or of the Revolutionary Tribunal sat. At the

F

same time these steps served to represent the front of the Palais de Justice up which the turbulent masses raced to storm the building. Here and there railings were used, a wall with book-shelves, a barred prison window. Perhaps two or three times throughout the play, not more, a sombre silhouette of old Paris appeared in the distance. All this would change, merge and disappear in a moment or two. The thing that constantly remained was the two columns at either side of the stage, and they were constantly treated as an integral part of the play and drawn into the action. It was in this framework that the tragedy of Danton was allowed to unroll—from the beginning of the play, which showed him in lighter mood at the gaming table, or with his head resting in a woman's lap, right until the last when a ray of moonlight austerely picked out the guillotine in the background. The two columns appeared as rocky banks between which the stream rolled, sometimes calm, sometimes tumultuous, carrying the action to its inevitable end. . . . The impression of a tremendous plenitude and variety of life, the impression of passionate movement, was obtained by lighting up only one small part of the stage at a time whilst the rest remained in gloom. Only individuals or small groups were picked out in the spotlight whilst the masses always remained in semi-darkness, or even in complete darkness. But they were always there and they could be heard murmuring, speaking, shouting. Out of the darkness an upraised arm would catch the light, and in this way thousands seemed to be where hundreds were in fact. This principle of the rapid play of light and darkness was maintained throughout. Scenes would flash up for a second or two. Lights would go out, darkness would persist for a fraction, and then lights would go up elsewhere, and this rapid and often abrupt change reinforced the rhythm of the piece. The last words of one scene were still being spoken when the first words of the next would sound and the light change to it. The sound of singing, the whistling of "The Marseillaise", the tramping of many feet, booing, the echo of a speech being delivered somewhere, applause from out of the darkness. A lamp-post lights up and the mob is seen hanging an aristocrat. Half-naked furies in colourful rags dance "La Car-magnole". And already the light turns to a peaceful room in which Danton is resting in the arms of a *grisette*. And because whatever is the important thing for the moment is suddenly illuminated out of the darkness in a fiery or ghostly white light, the producer is able to stress the main figures of the play and their action to the utmost: Danton, the People's Tribune; the young Desmoulins; the sea-green Robespierre; St. Just with the fair-haired, girlish head and the heart of ice—they appear for a

Scene from "Danton's Death"

moment or two and disappear again. And at the end the slim Lucille who has lost her Desmoulins leans exhausted against the guillotine. A short and deeply moving moment in the cold light of the moon".[1]

My name is nowhere mentioned in all this, but, in fact, it was I who had tried something completely new, namely, to paint with light, to stress only the essentials. Fortunately, in Germany the scenic artist does the lighting and not the producer as in England, and that is because, after all, it is part and parcel of the scene and can make or mar it.

[1] Heinz Herold, "Reinhardt und seine Bühne".

CHAPTER XII

REVOLUTION, 1919

Fantastic Indian buildings surround a paved courtyard. A gigantic figure of a goddess with many arms sitting with crossed legs on a proportionately enormous lotus flower is being pushed forward on rollers by sweating, half-naked slaves. A powerful female with very little on holds a scourge in each hand and urges forward the panting slaves with loud shrieks and blows.

Suddenly the exotic scene is interrupted by a dominant male bass speaking in Berlin dialect:

"That'll do, boys and girls. Time to go home. Pack it up!"

The female slave-driver turns round in astonishment towards the intruder, who proves to be a man in civilian clothes and a hard felt hat, who looks most incongruous in the courtyard of our Indian temple.

"Who the devil are you?" she exclaims indignantly. "Get out. You're interrupting the take."

He is not in the least disturbed, and once again he begins to shout at the slaves, who have straightened their backs and now stand around open-mouthed.

"All over. Pack it up. Go home now." And taking the astonished slave-driver by the hand he leads her out of our Indian magic to the window of the film studio and drags back the curtain. Against a background of factory buildings and smoke-stacks, a long procession of men carrying red flags and banners is visible slowly moving forward to some unknown objective.

It was November 9th, 1918. The revolution had begun with a general down-tools, which was, apparently, to include film studios as well. All the film workers left the studio, followed by the cameramen and their assistants. I had designed and built the Indian temple. The slaves were Russian prisoners of war made up as Indians. The women slave-driver was not only the female star of the film, but also the producer and financial backer. We left her behind sitting on the steps of my Indian temple and looking the picture of misery. If her bosom had been larger, she might well have served as the symbol of Germania mourning over the ruin of her land.

In the streets I joined the tremendous throng winding its way into town. Here and there Army lorries full of soldiers appeared, but they wore red armlets and were obviously making revolution too. There was no singing or shouting, and no excited shouts or fiery speeches. After "The Death of Danton", I was a bit disappointed with this silent and very orderly revolution as a spectacle and an experience, and I made my way to Unter den Linden and the official quarters, where I hoped to witness exciting revolutionary scenes. I was all prepared with sketch book and pencils to record it for posterity. But I hung around in front of the royal palace and saw nothing of any interest except a soldier with a rifle stopping a car in which a lieutenant was seated. Producing his Army jack-knife from his pocket, the soldier very carefully cut off the white-faced lieutenant's

"Revolution in Berlin," 1919

epaulettes and then let him drive on. Neither said a word that I heard and a disinterested crowd watched the scene equally wordlessly.

There were rumours, of course: officers were said to have barricaded themselves in the Zeughaus, a sort of military museum, and, naturally, they might be expected to open fire on the people at any moment. But nothing happened and the

crowds just hung around as I did. Then suddenly one or two
people began to run and the urge to do the same spread rapidly
until everyone was running madly in all directions—except
me and I was too busy sketching. Many of them fell down very
satisfactorily in their haste and others fell over them, but as
nothing happened and there was no sound of shooting or any
other unusual noise, calm was restored again. It had been a
false alarm and a panic without reason. But at least before the
monument to Kaiser Wilhelm der Grosse, always referred to
popularly as "Willy in the Lion's Den", because of the lions
amongst the supporting group, I was to witness a typical scene
of Berlin revolutionary ardour. Two rather fat women from
east Berlin, apparently up west for the revolution, stopped in
front of the statue, looked up at the petrified monarch, directed
a stream of rather vulgar witticisms and abuse at him, and then,
to demonstrate their contempt, they both turned round, flung
their skirts up over their backs and obscenely exposed their fat
rumps to his stony indifference.

There was nothing very exciting throughout the revolution,
but I persisted in my efforts, and I did manage to set down a
number of unusual if not dramatic scenes, and I found a first-
class publisher prepared to issue my bag as a portfolio of
lithographs under the promising title, "Revolution in Berlin".

As an enemy alien, I didn't know quite what to do, but when
the time came for me to report myself I decided to go round to
the police station as usual. There I was received by a disinterested and cynical official who declared:

"Sir, the German Reich whose enemy you were now no longer
exists, so you can't be its enemy any more. Good morning to you."

The new republican form of government established itself
without any obvious convulsions. A few leaflets were distributed,
a few speeches were delivered, soldiers or sailors occupied a
number of Government buildings, but beyond the disappearance of the old Hohenzollern emblems nothing seemed to
change much, though the liberal and social-democratic newspapers published triumphant articles on the new order.
But the average German citizen, never very well informed
politically, remained rather indifferent to the change, though
many were inclined to ask dimly: "What! Revolution! Is that
allowed?" Many of course, preferred to howl with the pack
whatever the howl was, and they promptly donned red armlets
and hurried along with the rest for fear of missing something.

The same sort of people went over in the same way to Hitler later on.

The "Independent Socialists", although their leaders were in the new republican Government, were not altogether satisfied with the situation, and the extremists, the "Spartakists",

"Revolution in Berlin," 1919

wanted a real revolution, and they became more and more active, with the result that sporadic shootings took place here and there. We lived quite close to two railway stations at the time and they seemed to be a centre for disturbances. Our nights were often disturbed by the sound of shots, and on one occasion extremist elements even climbed on to our roof and began to fire at something or the other from there—to our great discomfort. The disturbances culminated in the so-called "Spartakist revolt" with the occupation of the newspaper quarter, and in particular the building of the social-democratic "Vorwaerts", by the Spartakists, soon to be better known as Communists. The Social-Democratic Government brought in regular troops and artillery and soon crushed the rising.

Quite a lot of people felt themselves endangered who probably weren't in the least, and one of them was the Kaiser's son, Prince August Wilhelm, known as "Auwi", who stayed for a time, hidden from God knows what terrible dangers, in Reinhardt's house. In the meantime we lived only for the day and enjoyed a number of minor luxuries, such as imported oranges and Dutch chocolate, which we had gone without during the war.

One of the good things the republican Government did was to abolish the theatre censorship. One of the formerly forbidden plays we considered was Frank Wedekind's "Pandora's Box". Reinhardt made no mistake about Wedekind's talents, but he finally decided not to produce the piece himself, so an empty theatre was leased and the piece was produced with actors from his company. It was a tremendous box-office success. Wedekind's heroine, Lulu, ends up as a prostitute in London and falls victim to Jack the Ripper. At every performance there

"Orestes," Tragic Chorus

were protests and shouts, but always packed houses. I did a series of twelve lithographs depicting scenes from the play and they were published in a portfolio which sold very well— whether on account of my art or the theme I can't say, though I suspect the latter.

In the general catastrophe and chaos which was post-war Germany, Reinhardt's project of turning the old Circus Schumann into a theatre—"The Theatre of the Five Thousand"—still went on, and in November 1919 the new building, afterwards called "Das Grosse Schauspielhaus", was formally opened with the "Orestes" of Æschylus. The stage was very large, and it extended forward into the old circus arena, giving the layout a classic note. It was, of course, provided with a revolving platform, a built-in cyclorama and the last word in modern lighting technique. I designed a sort of troglodyte architecture for the play.

The next play to be staged there was Shakespeare's "Hamlet". It had been a very easy matter to fit the old Greek classic into the new theatre, but "Hamlet" was a different kettle of fish altogether and our production was an experiment from almost every point of view. Between the stage and the arena was provision for a broad platform, which could serve as a sort of apron stage on which Hamlet could deliver his monologues. The difficulty was that the size of the theatre and the distances were so great as to be intimidating. Goethe once summed up the Hamlet tragedy by calling it "a great deed laid on a soul not big enough to support it". And our problem was how to represent the psychological and spiritual aspect of the Hamlet figure in such an enormous space. Reinhardt was full of enthusiasm and optimism; it was my job to provide the background and ambient for him.

I designed some very simple articulated walls which could easily be moved around. Pushed together, they framed interiors; pushed apart, they made a framework for exteriors. The background was given by the curved cycloramic horizon with its moving cloud effects. A wall and a terrace was enough for the ghost, and we made the graveyard scene quite impressive with one or two monumental mausoleums. All that remained was the problem of the costumes. But it was a very real problem in view of the circumstances in which the actors had to play, partly on the apron stage and partly in the arena. It was quite clear that the usual historical costumes, even if stylized, would be quite unsuitable. Both Reinhardt and I had been in close touch with earlier attempts to play "Hamlet" in modern dress, but we were instinctively repelled by the idea of staging it with actors in stove-pipe trousers, boiled shirts and stiff collars. We agreed that I should continue to study the problem during the rehearsals, which all took place in the Grosses Schauspielhaus. At the same time we experimented with newly-installed lighting as the actors rehearsed their parts.

Alexander Moissi was playing Hamlet and during the rehearsals he wore a dark cloak-like garment with a fur collar and on his head was a fur hat—the November days were almost wintry. I found that in this get-up his gestures looked very impressive in the limelight. And there was another thing:

Leaning on the balustrade which surrounded the arena were a number of men in hats and coats. Their silhouettes remained visible whilst the actors were reciting their lines and doing their business, but far from proving disturbing it seemed to heighten the illusion, primarily, of course, because Hamlet was dressed in more or less the same style as themselves. I then decided that our "Hamlet" should be played in modern dress after all—but with a difference, because it was clear to me that I could use only certain articles of modern clothing, those that gave a neutral effect, so to speak. The sight of Moissi's fur hat reminded me of Hamlet's lines in Act I, Scene 4, when he declares: "The air bites shrewdly; it is very cold." These lines have often been cited to show that "Hamlet" is supposed to play in winter and there has been much discussion on the point. I didn't care which side was right; Moissi's fur collar and fur hat settled the problem for me. With fur-trimmed garments I had a possibility of obtaining decorative effects even with modern clothing. The awkward problem of the stove-pipe trousers remained. And then I spotted one of our stage-hands returned from the wars with his calves in puttees. That

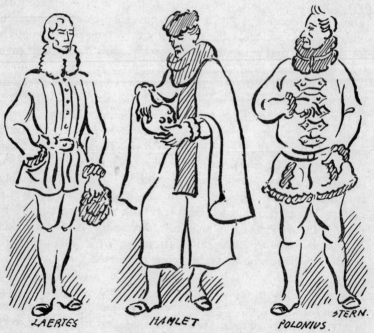

Modern costumes for "Hamlet"

was far more æsthetic than trousers, so I decided that my male actors should wear high gaiters, and they appeared in long, loose coats, voluminous capes, loose jerkins and high gaiters. The effect was timeless rather than modern. Together with fur trimming, there was no doubt that the general impression was picturesque. Fur trimmings for the royal pair was more or less professional *de rigeur*, and fur trimmings helped to make the ladies even more attractive. An astonishing and very welcome revelation was the grace and ease with which our male actors moved in this clothing. It was more or less what they were used to wearing and so there was none of the sawing and strutting complained of by Hamlet himself in his advice to the players.

The ghost and all characters of a military nature I put into steel helmets of the German Army type, a particularly impressive headgear of austere nobility.

"Julius Cæsar" followed and then "Everyman" and "Der weisse Heiland" by Gerhardt Hauptmann. I designed the scenery and costumes for this latter piece, but Reinhardt did not produce it. I was particularly interested in it because the action took place in Mexico and the characters were Aztecs. By this time the arena had been abandoned as an extension of the stage and filled in with seats and made part of the auditorium. Reinhardt's original idea in projecting the "Grosses Schauspielhaus" was that promising young playwrights should have a chance to come before the public in this "Theatre of the Five Thousand" with quite new productions, but his idea was never carried out. The economic climate of the post-war era proved icy, and there was no encouragement to take chances. In addition, the film was proving a very powerful rival to the theatre in more ways than one. There was nothing in the usual contracts of actors and actresses to prevent them from working, often at the same time, for the films, and the result was that rehearsals suffered by the absence of actors who were away in the studios during the day. Some actors even gave up the stage altogether and devoted themselves entirely to the films. The dollar was again almighty. Reinhardt abandoned the direction of his two Berlin theatres and went to Vienna and Salzburg. My contract with him expired in 1921 and although I could have renewed it with his successors I preferred not to do so; I went out of my blue-painted office and my studio for the last time and became a free-lance.

A happy domestic event took place at the same time as this

new departure in my life. After sixteen years of marriage a
child was born to us, a daughter. The doctor who attended my
wife let me know pointedly enough that he was very fond of
watercolours. In this way I secured a reduction of several
thousand inflation marks in his fee. We moved into a large
studio and adjoining flat in the so-called "Old West" of Berlin

"Kismet"

and once again the world appeared to me in rosy colours. In
fact, my optimism soon proved to be well founded and there
were plenty of operettas which required scenery and costumes
which needed designing, and, in addition, there was work in
the new medium, the films. Then, quite unexpectedly came an
offer from London asking me if I would care to undertake the
staging of a revival of Knoblauch's "Kismet". As I have
already mentioned, I did the scenery and costumes for a
production in Munich in 1913 at the Künstler-Theatre, and I
had invented an "Orient" all my own. I had seen Oscar
Asche's production at the Garrick, and whilst I had no ambition
to do anything better, I did want to do something different.
Where he went in for Moorish Arabian I went in for Persian-
Bokharan. Where he built Baghdad I decided to have Samarkand. His characters were Mussulmen from Cairo or Damascus;
my characters came from farther east, from the Caspian.

For economy's sake, the scenery and the costumes were made
in Germany, and when everything was ready I went off to
England with some misgivings. Although my passport assured

everyone that I was Roumanian, my name sounded German. The piece was produced in the New-Oxford, which, of course, no longer exists to-day, and there were, in fact, one or two disturbances and protests. But the critics were kind to me and all went well in the end.

"Ernest Stern, formerly designer and right-hand man to Reinhardt, is the most distinguished scenic artist in Germany, where the level of theatrical production is extraordinarily high," wrote one of them. "His designs for 'Kismet'—both in scenery and dresses—are of very remarkable beauty. . . . And there is no more reason why we should object to German décor for 'Kismet' than to German music for 'Lilac Time'. 'Kismet' is not great drama, but then, it is not intended to be. It is a *conte* well told and it is a capital excuse for a spectacle. This, I repeat, is both gorgeous and imaginative, and he will be a poor playgoer who does not go and feast his eyes on this beauty."

To read such things the next morning was ample compensation for a disagreeable moment or two the night before, and I soon began to feel myself at home again in London. Knoblauch's house, in which I stayed as guest during my visit, was in the Regency style and an excellent example of it. Edward Knoblauch was a sensitive, artistic, and highly cultured man, and his friendliness and hospitality to me were heart-warming. He introduced me into houses which contained treasures which would have graced any museum. He showed me the Zoffany paintings in the Garrick Club, and I also went with him to visit a craftsman who made picture-frames and upheld the tradition of his forefathers, who had made frames for Hogarth and other great artists. Later on, when he lived in Brighton, I went with him to see the fantastic interior of the Royal Pavilion.

Before I go on to describe a very important phase of my life, my work for the films with Lubitsch, I should like to mention the "Fashion Theatre" I did, although it really belongs to the pre-war period. It was actually more of an exhibition than a theatre. In a large hall there were examples of the fashions of all ages either behind glass or portrayed by mannequins. The *pièce de résistance* of the exhibition, however, were six stages joined together by a connecting platform. Living pictures— the action was mimed with musical accompaniment—demonstrated the influence of fashion on the attitude of human beings in standing, walking, dancing, etc. The first episode showed a number of elegant Empire ladies seated in a blue salon, who were then joined by the fantastically uniformed officers of the Grand Coalition. Waterloo had been fought and won and a new era had dawned, bringing with it the Reaction.

The beauties of 1813, wearing very little and with bosoms almost bare, were now shocked at themselves and felt undressed at the sight of their successors in much more solid clothing with flounces, and already in corsets. With this the curtain descended and the audience moved on to the second stage, where the curtain rose to reveal a garden salon in which four pairs dressed in the fashion of 1830 were dancing. The corset and tight-lacing now reigned supreme, and the wasp-like waists of the ladies made their rather short skirts of heavy stiff silk appear wider than they actually were. At the same time enormous leg-of-mutton shoulders and the large collars above them made them look almost as broad as they were long.

The third picture, 1840, showed two horsewomen dressed in velvet riding habits before a romantic sham-gothic palace. They rode on real horses and as they dismounted they revealed to the audience that underneath their riding habit they wore long, narrow, lace-trimmed white knickers which reached down to their riding boots. A real coach with real horses waited at the steps of the palace and a large family dressed in the coats, cloaks and hats of the Gavarni period billowed out of the doorway and took their places in the coach, which then drove off complete with baggage and postilion.

For 1850 there was an ice-skating scene with artificial ice. A tenderly attentive gentleman pushed his beloved along in a sledge shaped romantically like a swan. All around were skaters of both sexes, and at the end of the scene there was a general collision with skaters falling in all directions, legs going into the air and causing a wholesale revelation of the most discreet details of the ladies' underwear—an incident which was always heartily applauded.

The 1860 scene was an exact replica of a picture very popular in Berlin entitled "Die Kranzler-Ecke" and depicting the famous corner of Unter den Linden and the Friedrichstrasse, on which the famous Café Kranzler stood, until 1913. The picture showed ladies in crinolines sitting on the terrace drinking chocolate or eating ices and attended by very affected and extremely elegant bewhiskered Prussian officers.

For the sixth and last scene I had taken a fashion salon, in which ladies tried on the exaggerated fashions of 1870, including enormous corsets like suits of mail, and equally enormous bustles—to the great amusement and enjoyment of the audience. The scene ended with a jealous clash between two fops over a particularly beautiful and voluptuous blonde. In the end she fled half-dressed off the stage along the connecting gangway, followed by her rival lovers and all the other types of the previous scenes in chronological order to Offenbach's *cancan* music.

CHAPTER XIII

THE FILMS

AN ACTOR OBTAINED an interview with a film producer and presented him with a number of photographs. Nothing unusual about that; it was happening every day, except perhaps on Sundays. The producer looked casually at the photographs, and then with greater interest. They all showed a man in the Prussian uniform of the eighteenth century. On his head was the highly decorative tricorn of the day, and in his hand he held a stick on which he leaned for support. In another photo he was playing the flute, and a third showed him carefully taking a pinch of snuff.

"By God!" exclaimed the producer, "The spit image of Old Fritz. Is that you? By the way, what did you say your name was?"

"Gebühr. Otto Gebühr," replied the actor.

Gebühr's physical resemblance to Frederick the Great, or "Old Fritz" as he was affectionately called, was really extraordinary. And it was not only a question of physical resemblance. Gebühr was a highly intelligent man, and having taken Frederick the Great as his subject he had studied it in the utmost detail. He held himself like his model; he walked like him; he adopted all his well-known mannerisms; he had even learned to play the flute because it was the favourite relaxation of the greatest of all Prussian monarchs. And, above all, though it was still the day of the silent film, he had even learned to talk in the clipped Franco-German fashion of the King. It was not long before the time spent in that respect was seen not to have been wasted.

The producer made a film with Otto Gebühr as Frederick the Great, and Gebühr immediately became famous. His popularity in Germany was quite astounding, and they were even people who spoke in all seriousness of the possibility of a transmigration of souls, so perfect was the resemblance according to all the graphic representations we had of Frederick the Great and all we knew about his ways, mannerisms and habits.

I knew Gebühr well long before he became famous. He had

acted at the Deutsches Theater for years. He was a cultured man with a high degree of artistic sensitivity. He painted and sketched and he had a real feeling for style. Without that he would never have been able to do what he did. A number of films were made with him during the war, and, of course, they were propaganda for the military spirit of Prussia and as such they were zealously encouraged by the authorities. Gebühr himself became a hero. He was invited here, there and everywhere in officers' clubs and casinos, and the aristocratic Prussian officers, whose forbears had actually served under Frederick the Great and commanded his soldiers in peace and war, stood to attention and felt themselves honoured when the sagacious Otto Gebühr consented to address them.

The upheaval brought about by the lost war, the abolition of the monarchy and the establishment of the Weimar Republic did not cut short Gebühr's Frederician career by any means. On the contrary, he now became the perfect instrument of reactionary propaganda, and the supine, impotent Weimar Republic tolerated it all. To some extent it even encouraged the politically reactionary films which were produced with Gebühr in the leading role as Frederick the Great, and it even permitted shots to be taken in the historical palaces and other buildings, which were now Government property. Not only that, but it even allowed whole companies of the new Reichswehr to be uniformed in the style of Frederick's grenadiers, etc., in order to act as supers in Gebühr's films.

I was asked if I would co-operate in the making of such a film. I am no politician and I was not even German, anyway, and if the German Government had no objection to what was going on why should I bother my head? So I accepted. I was attracted by the task of reproducing a contemporary picture of the colourful and picturesque eighteenth century, and when I look back at the sketches I made for the interiors and for the exteriors with coaches and horsemen they still delight me. A great part of the film was shot in the palace and grounds of Rheinsberg in the Mark Brandenburg, both of which were preserved exactly as they had been in the days of Frederick the Great. My co-operation gave me ample opportunity of observing Gebühr not only on the set, but in his free time off it. He literally lived his role, even when he had every reason to suppose that he was unobserved. During the lonely walks he would make through the park, he was still Frederick the Great in his carriage, his gait and all his movements. An astonishing man.

*   *   *   *   *

After a good deal of sporadic work for the films, I settled down with Lubitsch permanently. Our first film together was "Die Bergkatze", or "The Mountain Cat". It was not a very serious film—and there wasn't a single real villain in it. The old robber chief was a good-natured old soul and though the commander of the fortress swaggered tremendously and played the old swashbuckler, in reality he was more interested in good food and wine than anything else. His soldiers, good-natured and lazy, lived in peace and plenty. The bandits, armed to the teeth and behaving themselves very fiercely, were really chiefly anxious to share some of the good food the soldiers enjoyed, and when they broke into the fortress their prime concern was the kitchen. Other amusing characters were the pompous wife of the commandant and her goose of a daughter, and the handsome, soft-hearted young bandit who was in love with the daughter of the robber chief, the mountain cat, and wept bitterly because she loved the gay lieutenant.

The title role was played by Pola Negri, who was already famous, at least in Europe, even in those days. The lieutenant was played by an amiable young actor who was not afraid to make fun of himself. All the military and all the robbers were definitely comic roles. My job in designing the background and the costumes was determined by the grotesque theme of the film. The officers and soldiers all had magnificent—rather too magnificent—uniforms, with over-splendid gold braiding and flourishes and over-corseted waists. The robbers were fantastically garbed with tall and strangely shaped fur hats and splendid fur-lined boots and so on. The fortress interior was interpreted as a caricature and generously sprinkled with military emblems, and there was even a military motif in the boudoir furnishings of the commander's wife. The exterior scenes were taken in the Bavarian Alps, and this was an error; Nature cannot be caricatured except inside a studio, but I was unable to persuade Lubitsch of this. However, it was a good film, humorous, witty, full of clever camera tricks, and intelligent, amusing entertainment. It was not a very great success. But for me the six weeks I spent in the Bavarian Alps on location were a very pleasant experience.

We arrived in Partenkirchen shortly before Christmas, and the work of erecting my gun-bristling fortress with its crenellated walls and towers began at once. Then we journeyed off on sledges to find suitable landscapes for the exterior takes. The company had not stinted with the expenses and we were all provided with beautifully warm, fur-lined coats, hats and gloves, so that the cold, which was in any case dry and frosty, meant nothing to us. In the New Year the whole company, soldiers, robbers, Pola and her maid as the only women, moved up to a small hotel 3,000 feet above sea-level. The hotel was situated in fantastically beautiful scenery, and all around were frightful chasms and impressive crags. Below us were great

My fortress in the Bavarian Alps for the film, "The Mountain Cat"

expanses of level snow framed by forests of pine trees and in the distance rose a chaotic medley of great Alps jutting into the sky. The view from my bedroom window was breath-taking, a tremendous winter panorama, and I worked eagerly to set it down in all its aspects, including moonlight and snow-storms.

When the weather was too bad to allow us to work out of doors, or after our meals, and particularly after the evening meal when the work of the day was done, I would sketch whole series of actors or peasants, of whom we had about a dozen or so with us for various purposes. They were all robust young men, the typical rugged peasants of the Upper Bavarian Alps.

Confident and bursting with life and energy, they wore their handsome folk costume with its saucy green hat and feather, its leather trousers and wool and leather decorations, with the air of Nature's noblemen. None of them had ever had anything to do with film work before, but they were very willing, particularly as for them it was an easy and pleasant way of earning extra money.

Dressed up as soldiers and handling their rifles easily as to the manner born, Ludl (Ludwig), Sepp (Joseph), Loisl (Aloysius), Ferdl (Ferdinand) and all the rest grinned at each other happily and sprang and danced around like big children out for a lark. They had used rifles before in Flanders or the Carpathians, but here it was a great joke and you even got paid for it. They grinned even more broadly when our Assistant Producer Mathias informed them one morning:

"To-day, gentlemen, you're to be robbers, not soldiers. You'll have different costumes and hunting rifles instead of military rifles. Did you all hear what I said? Hunting rifles."

And when he winked at them and grinned broadly they all grinned back and whispered to each other. They were not mistaken, Herr Mathias knew what he was talking about. Everybody did in Garmisch. On Christmas Day we had been told to go along to the Town Hall, where we should see something of interest. We did so and there in the square before the Rathaus we found a crowd of people around six freshly shot chamois deer. Round the neck of one of them was attached a piece of white cardboard on which the words had been printed: "A Christmas present for the women and children of Garmisch-Partenkirchen." It was inflation and times were hard for poor people. When the deer became venison there were tasty Christmas meals for a good many of the poor people of the town. When we asked who had been so generous, we got old-fashioned looks and shrugging shoulders. "It's a bit of a secret, you see," said one old man. "There are still good people in the world," added an old woman. And we had to be content with that. Except Herr Mathias; he had his own ideas on the subject, and Loisl, Sepp, Ludl and Ferdl owed their engagement with our company to the fact that they were notorious game poachers. Herr Mathias was fond of venison and he thought that if he engaged the poachers the company might occasionally feast on venison—and so it turned out.

Our exterior takes took rather longer than we had reckoned

and when we left Kreuz-Eck, which was the name of our picturesque hotel, and descended into Garmisch again to start the takes in and around my citadel it was the end of February and there was no more snow. That was a catastrophe and we scratched our heads in dismay, but as soon as our ingenious and cheerful poachers heard about it they settled the problem at once by organizing the transport of tons of snow from the higher levels, where it still lay thick, down into Garmisch to decorate our citadel, and they kept up the supply as long as our takes lasted. There was snow in plenty, not only to plaster the walls, but to cover the ground as well, and everyone was happy again, particularly Loisl, Sepp, Ludl, Ferdl and their many friends, who earned a lot of money carting down the snow for us.

In our next venture we went from one extreme to the other, from the snow-covered Alps to the burning Nile, to produce "The Wife of Pharaoh". Nowadays a film company—one of the bigger ones, anyway—would promptly organize an expedition to the Pyramids if it intended to produce a historical film with an Egyptian background, but we weren't so particular in those days, and we were full of confidence in our own ability to produce a convincing Nile, desert, Pyramids and all at home.

"Egypt is, as you know," the author of the story lectured us, "largely sand through which a famous river, the Nile, flows."

"Largely sand"—well, at least, we weren't short of that in the neighbourhood of Berlin. The Mark Brandenburg has not been called "The sand-sprinkler of the Holy Roman Empire" for nothing, or, at least, it was in the days when people still dried their letters with sprinkled sand instead of blotting paper. So Lubitsch and I went off on a search for suitable locations in the Mark Brandenburg. We travelled around for days without finding anything, because although the basic earth of the Mark Brandenburg is, in fact, sandy, it is not easy to find places where it really looks like a desert. We were beginning to feel that we had been too optimistic when our Berlin cockney chauffeur discovered what it was we were looking for. He immediately exclaimed the Berlin equivalent for "Gor' blimey! Why didn't you tell me before!" and drove us to an ideal place at once.

There were mounds and hills of sand of various heights and between them there were expanses of sand without a tree, a bush or a blade of grass. We discovered that this strange

Egyptian landscape was known to the Berliners as Goshen, the very name of that part of the desert referred to in the Bible. This was a real find and we were delighted. Unfortunately, however, there was no way of turning the diminutive Spree which abuts on this modern land of Goshen into the broad and mighty Nile and we had to think of something else. The Elbe, someone suggested. That was broad enough, but unfortunately the Elbe was a proper and orderly German river throughout its entire length; wherever it was broad enough to suit our purpose it was neatly enclosed in solid stone embankments, a well-behaved and civilized modern river without a trace of wild romanticism anywhere. It was once again our Berlin chauffeur, a helpful and cheery fellow named Hoyer who solved the problem of the Nile as he had solved the problem of the desert. He drove us out of Berlin towards the eastern suburbs and there he introduced us to an old sandpit which had been abandoned by the builders because it had been "drowned". It was completely under water and the result was a long narrow lake which we decided would serve us well as our artificial Nile. This sandpit lake was kept narrow by rocky declivities on either side about 20 feet high. Now, as the Nile itself also flows between rocky banks in parts this place too was ideal and our location troubles were over.

Since those days film technique has greatly developed, and models of buildings, landscapes, etc., are often sufficient for distant takes, but in those days we had to build up everything we wanted life-size, and so we set to work on palaces, walls with towers and moats, and, in particular, the treasury of Pharaoh, which was in the form of a gigantic sphinx. We leased a plot of sandy land in the Berlin suburb of Steglitz for our building operations. There were modern buildings visible on its edge, but we built our own palaces, etc., high enough to mask them. There was no difficulty about finance, as we were working for American backers. It was still the inflation period and even a single dollar was quite a lot of money, so we had no time-robbing financial calculations to make and we went to work cheerfully with a "Damn the expense" outlook.

The script was almost preternaturally feeble: the all-powerful Pharaoh loses his head and heart to a Greek slave, and chasing after her he loses his throne and his life to her accepted suitor. But there were some lively scenes in it, including a war between Egypt and Ethiopia. Still, the quality of the script didn't interest me very much as art director. All I had to do was to provide the buildings, the statues of Egyptian gods and goddesses, the war chariots, the costumes of the Egyptian and Ethiopian armies, the costumes of the people and so on—all fascinating subjects for me. It so happened that Egyptology had always been a hobby of mine, and I had even dabbled in hieroglyphics with the assistance of Dr. Erman's famous book on the subject. Thus I was in my element and my drawings were accurate in detail and lettering.

There were mass scenes in the film, and so I had to have 2,000 costumes prepared, and whilst our building activity was proceeding feverishly in Steglitz I was no less busy arranging for the production of the more or less scanty costumes our supers, etc., required. The organization of our costume supply needed a little thought even after the costumes were all ready and delivered. Each type of costume, Egyptian warriors, Ethiopian warriors, priests, slaves, dancers, ladies of the court and so on, was photographed on a picked super and the photo was pasted into an album, each photo being numbered and a note made as to the number of such costumes available. All Lubitsch had to do then was to take this album, go through it and jot down exactly what he wanted for the day's filming: "500 No. 4's, twenty No. 15's, sixteen No. 23's" and so on.

There was a catastrophic amount of unemployment in Germany in the post-war years, but at least it was favourable

Film, "Pharaoh's Wife" (1921). Egyptians at tank with brown make-up

to us, because it meant that we could get as many supers for our mass scenes as we needed. In normal times it is not easy to find large numbers of powerfully built young men for film work, but now there were tens of thousands of demobilized ex-soldiers without jobs. And as for women and girls, they practically mobbed our casting offices, which were at the entrance to the site. It was no easy job to manage thousands of supers in mass scenes and to have them all correctly clothed even in detail and at the same time to remain in style and character and to make them convincing when they moved about before our monumental edifices in the background. I had had no such mass experience before, but when I saw the swarms of Ethiopian soldiers going out to do battle on foot and on horseback and in authentically constructed chariots, I was very well satisfied with myself.

We had leased a number of Spree pleasure steamers to bring 1,200 men along to our "Goshen" sands for the battle scenes. The supers got into their costumes and made up their arms, legs and faces on the journey in order that no time should be lost when they arrived. We had erected fantastic and, as far as we could discover, quite authentic camps decorated with military signs and statues of gods and so on, and there were many horses and pack mules ready corralled. The men arrived and all went well. We took cavalry charges, wildly careering chariots and fierce engagements between the hostile armies. Our supers entered into the spirit of the thing and hammered away at each other's shields with their wooden swords and battle-axes and shrieked with excitement. That was still the days of the silent film so the noise and the Berlin dialect did not matter. Lubitsch watched it all with delight, encouraging the warriors from time to time through his megaphone:

"That's the style, lads. Carry on."

And when he thought a scene was ripe he would shout to the cameramen: "Take!" And then the shout would be taken up by his assistants with their megaphones: "Attention! Attention! Take!" And the warriors would redouble their frenzied efforts.

But on one occasion no sooner had the shout "Attention! Take!" gone up than the hostile warriors flung down their weapons and ceased fighting. The Egyptians and the Fuzzy-wuzzies embraced each other tenderly and all other action apart from this odd scene of fraternization ceased. But the cameras were still whirring. Lubitsch danced with rage.

It was a strike for more pay. Lubitsch didn't like being held up to ransom like that, and a long and heated discussion began, during which the character of the scene changed again. The waiting supers, realizing that their demands were not going through, grew impatient and bedlam broke loose. The hotheads amongst them began to shout threats and before long they were

Film, "Pharaoh's Wife." Egyptian scene

doing their best to smash up the place, knocking over the statues of the gods and generally wreaking destruction. At that moment a new surprise occurred. A large group of mounted Fuzzy-wuzzies had held themselves to one side when the trouble started and now they galloped forward into the riotious mob of supers and began to press them towards the nearby Spree. Shouts and protests were of no avail, the horsemen knew their job and in a very short while the rebellious mass of supers had been pushed over to the Spree and many of them had been pushed into it. The majority then calmed down and there was no further trouble.

Our assistant director, Mathias, the cautious and far-seeing,

had triumphed again. The mounted Fuzzy-wuzzies were
actually mounted policemen. A little anxious at the assembly
of so many unemployed ex-soldiers together, and fearful for the
possible effect on public order, the authorities had provided
Mathias—for cash, of course—with a force of mounted police,
horses and all. And so ended "The Battle of Goshen". In the
evening on their way home on board the pleasure steamers our
supers were quite happy again and singing in harmony, as
Germans tend to do when they get together, particularly when
they have been provided with free beer.

"The Flame" was the next film Lubitsch made. It played in
Paris in the 'sixties and there were boulevards and cafés to
design and construct. Its theme was the tragic love story of a
young musician and a cocotte.

This was still inflation time and anyone being paid in
dollars was very well off. I was one of the lucky ones. I and
others were approached by a businesslike man who advised us
to invest our dollars, or part of them, in real property whilst
the going was good. He had bought land lying on the shores of
a lake about forty-five miles out of Berlin, and he wanted us to

Our country cottage

buy it in lots and have houses built. The whole thing was to
become a sort of film-actors colony. It seemed a very good idea
to me, and after a little thought I bought a couple of acres on
the shore of the lake. A good-sized cottage was built for me and

a garden laid out. The lot cost me 250 dollars: land, house, interior decoration and equipment, the laying out of the garden, including fruit trees, a landing stage and even a boat to go with it. During the course of the next ten years I greatly enlarged the cottage until it became a house. My daughter spent her childhood there and I felt myself so much at home there that I could see myself ending my days peacefully in Pieskow, as the nearby village was called. My wife was not so enthusiastic; the climate of the Mark Brandenburg near the chain of lakes did not suit her. She needn't have worried: our house in Pieskow, literally "built on sand", was not destined to see the peaceful end of me. One day going into town I saw the reflection of a great fire on the horizon. It was the Reichstag burning. The Thousand Year Reich—in which there was no room for us—had dawned. To-day my house and its big garden are in the Russian zone behind the Iron Curtain.

"Revue"

CHAPTER XIV

THE REVUE

IT WAS STILL DURING the First World War when a young
man applied for an engagement as a dancer in our ballet
company. Frau Gydda Christensen put the rule over him and
then recommended his engagement. That young man, still in
German Army uniform, was Erik Charell. In the end he did
not take up his engagement with us, but went off and founded
his own company of dancers and then disappeared on tour in
neutral countries.

When Reinhardt produced "The Miracle" in New York
after the war Charell again came into touch with him and
became his assistant. Whilst he was in the United States he
made a very thorough study of American revues, their organization and their staging. He was an ambitious young man and
he had the advantage of knowing exactly what he wanted.
When he returned to Germany with his plans, the new lessee
of the Grosses Schauspielhaus, considering that revues would
be just the thing for his vast theatre, engaged Charell as

producer. It was very soon seen that Charell had a sure hand for all matters connected with the stage and a very real artistic feeling. In addition, he was full of ideas, energetic, and himself an expert dancer. By the second season he was the independent director of the Grosses Schauspielhaus and had arrived.

My film work with Lubitsch was now at an end and Lubitsch himself had gone to Hollywood for good. I became Charell's Art Director and worked closely with him for over twelve years. After all I have written in this book of memoirs concerning my longing for painted décor rather than three-dimensional plastic scenery, the reader can perhaps understand the enthusiasm with which I now turned to this new work. Reinhardt was wedded to the revolving stage, and that, of course, demanded three-dimensional scenery and the plastic build-up. The revue offered me an opportunity of doing what I wanted. Of course, I did not imagine myself in any way a pioneer; far from it, I was merely giving something back to the theatre: the painted backcloth and painted scenery. Three-dimensional props, such as steps, platforms, etc., were merely auxiliary aids when the exigencies of the piece demanded them. All that was new in what I proposed to do was the kind of scene-painting, the new modern technique. And even then I made no claim to being a pioneer; the Russians had already introduced it, and many others too had worked to give scenic decoration a new birth. As a professional painter, what was more obvious for me than the transfer of the Impressionist method from the easel to the scenery?

However, if I had been forced to rely on the assistance of the old scene-painters with their out-of-date methods and ideas, the translation of my designs to the larger scale of the stage would have proved well nigh impossible. Fortunately, many of the decorating firms had young men on their staffs who were intelligent and unprejudiced enough to grasp what I was aiming at, and capable enough to carry my designs into execution satisfactorily. They realized at once that only a technique of painting which avoided the petty detail could hope to be successful on the large scale; it was the general impression that counted. Impressionist technique of my sketches on paper had to be transferred just as it was, though greatly enlarged, to the scenery. They succeeded, and the result on the big scale was the same as the impression on the small.

"Paint with a broad brush!" we were told as art students. Even the layman will find it easy enough to recognize that the object of this piece of advice was to prevent us from losing ourselves in petty details. A principle of that sort which is necessary for easel painting is still more necessary for painting on the large scale of theatre scenery. There above all, attention must be concentrated on the main forms and never lose itself in fiddling details. My young decorators soon abandoned even their broadest brushes and began to use something like brooms, and in the end they abandoned brushes altogether in favour of the colour spray. In the United States and on the Continent scenery is laid out flat on the floor of the atelier and painted; in England it is usually painted upright. Where the former method is used there is much less risk of the colours running, and the artist can therefore use his brush—or his paint-gun— more generously.

The special nature of the revue form and the endless variety of the scenery used in connection with it, scenery which is often only vaguely linked together, gives the scenic artist endless possibilities for the exercise of his art and his imagination; he can let himself go as he pleases; no limits are set to his fantasy. What more can a scenic artist wish for than—as was the case in one of our revues—a richly decorated baroque hall scene, followed by a prospect of the Venetian Rialto at night, followed by a stylized Delphian oracle scene, followed by a jungle scene with wigwams and redskins?

I am afraid that the mass of Berliners showed a preference for our colourful kaleidoscope of scenes and our variety of programmes rather than Reinhardt's classics. Evening after evening 5,000 people sat happily in Reinhardt's old "Theatre of the Five Thousand". Such audiences were more interested in Negro singers from across the Atlantic, belly dancers from Algiers, and Tiller girls from over the North Sea than in Goethe, Schiller and Shakespeare—particularly when the abolition of the censorship was soon followed by the abolition, or very great reduction, of costume in revue. It may be very sad, but that's the way of the world.

After staging three big and successful revues of this kind, Charell decided to try his hand at the revue-operetta, and so we both set off—not to France—but to the United States to find inspiration for our proposed production of "The Three Musketeers".

The S.S. *Leviathan*, on which we travelled, was the former German liner, *Kaiser Wilhelm der Grosse*, which had been handed over to the United States under the Versailles Treaty. It now operated for an American company and with an American crew but the unspeakably pompous interior decoration scheme of the *Kaiser Wilhelm der Grosse* had been left untouched, and there was even a bust of the Kaiser still in the Music Saloon. However, the tremendous impression of a first Atlantic crossing made me forget Hohenzollern bad taste, and when we arrived in Manhattan it was like landing on another planet.

What interested and impressed me even more than the American show world was New York itself. Nineveh and Babylon must have been very small beer by comparison. Day after day I wandered around with my sketch-book and sought a solution to the problem of representing the skyscraper decoratively. The architectural surroundings were fantastic;

New York

gigantic shapes reared into the sky on every hand. At first I found the thousands of symmetrically bored holes in these vast shapes—the windows—very disturbing, but in the end I managed to dismiss them from my consciousness, but when at last I thought I had found the way to represent them effectively, seizing what I regard as the essential and ignoring the unimportant details, it was time for us to return. Still, when I look at the dozen or so watercolours I did then I think I was on the right road.

The most valuable tip we picked up on Broadway was the

way in which American producers would follow up a lyrical-sentimental scene with a humorous or even low comedy scene. For post-war Germany in which even a loaf of bread cost thousands of marks, laughter was a cure for many things. Charell therefore decided, and very wisely in my view, to make two of his three musketeers comic figures and to have only one the swashbuckling gallant pictured by Dumas, and this latter was, as the revue demanded, an opera singer. When "The Three Musketeers" was produced and I signed for the décor and the costumes, an American correspondent wrote back to his paper:

"American producers who are neglecting to employ Ernest Stern to frame their entertainment are missing the most exceptional dictator of colour and line in the international theatre. Under Eric Charell's enthusiastic encouragement he has recreated the Paris of Dumas in tones of modern Impressionism. For pure unadulterated voluptuousness we will back his scenes in the camp at Rouen and in the courtyard of the Louvre against anything that the other capitals have to offer!"

Well-intentioned and highly complimentary for me, what he says about "Impressionism" was not in the least true of "The Three Musketeers". I had spoken my own language, unconsciously. Although the tasks I was set were all very different and all new, there was something in my work on them all which was related, something in common. It was my own style whatever the task to be performed. The Oxford English Dictionary defines style as "the distinct manner of an artist", and that is precisely what it was in my case. "A real Stern" was a common description of any scenic design to which I put my signature. I am not able myself to define what goes to make up the characteristic peculiarity which unmistakably links up my work on such totally different objects as, say, "Casanova" and "White Horse Inn", or to say what it is exactly they have in common.

The next revue-operetta Charell staged was "'Madame Pompadour" with Fritzi Massary, who had created the role in an earlier piece. She was, incidentally, the wife of that wonderful comic actor, Max Pallenberg, to whom I have already referred, and who was unfortunately killed in an aeroplane accident. The famous portrait of the Pompadour hangs in the Wallace Collection. She is dressed in a wonderful blue dress with a pale pink scarf. In the same collection are many Watteau groups of charming women in shot-silk dresses. It was this colourful and perfumed elegance and discretion I sought to convey in my work on "Pompadour"—but only up to a point. I never had to forget that I was working for the Grosses Schauspielhaus, which seated an audience of 5,000, and delicate, dreamy, smiling rococo was not enough. One of the scenes in the piece was the study of Louis XV, who was represented as a rather foolish and comic old fop. He and his equally absurd courtiers fall over each other in a comic finale, climbing over the throne, jumping over the writing desk and so on; the study is turned into a nursery. Thanks to this, I was given the possibility of exaggeration and caricature in the décor. For the writing desk I had two gilt ladies modelled in life-size in all their nakedness, and for the mahogany walls I had four 15-feet-high naked caryatides made in imitation marble, also plastic and voluptuous.

Whilst we were still engaged on "Madame Pompadour", Erik Charell was already considering Gilbert and Sullivan's "The Mikado" as his next attempt at revue-operetta. As it happened, just at this time I had an offer to go to Oslo, not only to design the décor and costumes for the same light opera, but also to produce it. The idea attracted me, and I had sufficient confidence in myself to believe that I could take on the double task. The proposal was also attractive from another point of view—namely, the financial. If I accepted, I should earn good solid Norwegian crowns, and foreign exchange was vastly high, of course, in a country which was still suffering nightmares of inflation.

The contract with the Casino Theatre in Oslo came about through my friend the Swedish conductor, Einar Nielson, and I received an advance—in Norwegian crowns. I knew "The Mikado" from the days of my youth in Vienna, where it was popular even then. I plunged into my new task with readily understandable enthusiasm—Norwegian crowns! My good spirits were transferred to my interpretation and my Japanese were stylistically rather exaggeratedly Japanese. I had everything made in Berlin, for reasons of economy, quite apart from the fact that it was much more convenient, and I sent on a detailed production script.

I arrived in Oslo in December, which was mid-winter for the Norwegians. I neither understood nor spoke Norwegian, but that didn't matter in the least, because everyone at the Casino

G

Theatre understood, and many of them spoke, German. Thanks to my production script, the preparations had been carried out excellently. My scenery, which was on the folding-screen principle, functioned perfectly. All the leading roles in the piece were in the hands of first-class actors and comedians, so everything promised to go off well and I felt I had every reason to be satisfied.

"It is winter. Oslo is under snow, as you can see for yourself, Herr Stern. At three o'clock in the afternoon it is already dark." The speaker was the Director of the Casino Theatre, and we sat together in his office. "Now, the darkness and the cold explain why my countrymen are accustomed to fortify them-selves with alcoholic drinks, usually hot, rather more than people do in other countries," he continued, and he then raised his steaming glass of punch to me and we drank. "In conse-quence, the Oslo theatre public is accustomed to flock to the theatre bars twice during every evening performance. I need hardly say that this habit has a very favourable effect on my bar profits. I take it, Professor Stern, that you understand what I'm driving at?"

I didn't. I had listened without any very great interest to what he had to say. Bar profits didn't concern me. In fact, bar profits were often in inverse ratio to the quality of a perform-ance. "The bar turn" is an international phenomenon. Seeing that I obviously didn't grasp what it was all about, he went on:

"In order to give my public the usual opportunity of drinking twice during the course of the evening and for the benefit of my own pocket, I need two long intervals. Now, unfortunately 'The Mikado' has only two acts and therefore only one interval, and thus, my dear Professor, what we need is an act in the middle to give us two intervals."

My jaw dropped and I stared at him in consternation to see whether he was really serious. He was. He raised his glass to me jovially again, drank and then continued encouragingly:

"With all your profound experience of the theatre, Herr Professor, you will certainly find it a very simple matter to introduce another act between the existing two. I rely on your inventiveness."

And with that he called in the conductor of the orchestra, who arrived already prepared with a bundle of various items of Sullivan's music, some of which he played to us on the piano in the director's office. No bright ideas came and I proposed

that I should go back to Berlin and see what I could do with
the help of librettists there to fake up some sort of intermezzo—
it couldn't be more than that, but the director set his face
against it. He wanted the première in ten days, for Christmas.
Any further scenery could be prepared in Oslo. In the end
I decided on a pantomimic dance act with no spoken or sung
words. Fortunately, quite a number of the female members of
the Casino Theatre ensemble were also professional dancers.
I quickly designed some fantastic scenery for them and we
knocked together a wretched botch job consisting of a hodge-
podge of Sullivan's music from "The Gondoliers", "H.M.S.
Pinafore" and so on—and the theatre-going public of Oslo was
provided with the usual opportunity for its double noggin.

Then I shook the snow of Oslo from my feet and returned
thankfully to Berlin, to arrive there on Christmas Eve to spend
the traditional festival with my family. In my pocket was my
hard-earned and satisfactorily fat packet of crisp Norwegian
crown notes, a very fine Christmas present to bring home to my
family in inflationary Germany. But Man proposes . . . And
that financial wizard Herr Hjalmar Schacht disposed. When
I set foot on German soil again on the morning of Christmas
Eve I learned that the currency situation had changed overnight. The mark was firm again and my beautiful Norwegian
crowns now meant nothing more than if they had been ordinary
marks. Perhaps that was a punishment for my sacrilegious
interpolation of a middle act into "The Mikado". But I had
treated the piece itself with proper reverence, whereas Erik
Charell just played Old Harry with it—and nothing happened
to him.

He turned it into a revue, and an American revue at that,
as the critics were not slow in pointing out. Even the music
was syncopated and played in new tempos and rhythms. And
as for the plot and the libretto! Nanky-Poo became an American, and Katisha as well. She was a smart and fabulously rich
president of a jam concern who rushed through a very Chinese
sort of Japan in a big American car. Yum-Yum and her ladies
danced and sang in a modern apartment with sliding doors and
a swimming pool. But Koko, played by that prince of comics,
Max Pallenberg, was supreme. On one occasion he appeared
on the stage with forty other Kokos of assorted sizes; and
trying to commit *hara-kiri* and talking "Japanese" to himself
all the time, he was excruciating, whilst his rendering of the

Tit-willow song must have been pretty well an all-time high.

For the appearance of the Mikado in the second act I designed a great palace whose portals, galleries and pagoda-like towers and curved roofs decorated with fabulous Oriental beasts swayed and jerked to the rhythm of the music. One of the critics declared that the scene was so compelling that the audience began to sway in sympathy. In any case, both Charell and I received generous praise for our respective parts in this "Mikado".

When Charell and I went to London to produce "White Horse Inn", we stayed at the Savoy in some style. Now, the owners of the Savoy are the gentlemen who have set themselves the task of preserving the joint heritage of W. S. Gilbert and Sir Arthur Sullivan with love and piety, and they do so with the utmost rigour. Not a word of the original text may be changed and no extemporization of any kind is permitted to the actors. Their feelings at the gross sacrilege committed by Charell can be imagined, and they expressed them, as far as it was possible to do so, by sending us both to Coventry. I must say that I quite appreciated their point of view, and I realized that their motives were exclusively artistic. But in the end they relented, and they did so very graciously. One day on our table in the restaurant appeared a bouquet of flowers with a card attached bearing the inscription: "In spite of the Berlinese Mikado!"

"The White Horse Inn" scenery

CHAPTER XV

"WHITE HORSE INN" AND "CASANOVA"

WHILST WE WERE PLANNING the production of "Casanova", Charell and I had motored from Salzburg to Ischl to visit the composer and librettist. On our way back we passed through Sankt Wolfgang, a village on the lake of that name. Emil Jannings was living there at the time and so we decided to drop in on him. Walking with him along the lake, we came to an inn. It was built in the characteristic style of local peasant architecture and it overlooked the lake. The high roof had large and projecting eaves and the walls were whitewashed. The many wooden balconies and verandas and the window frames were all painted turquoise blue. Over the entrance hung the inn sign, a magnificently prancing white stallion with flowing mane and long tail, bearing the inscription "Zum Weissen Rössl", or "White Horse Inn".

It made altogether a delightful picture and Jannings told us about a comedy which had taken its title from the name of the inn. I knew the piece to which he was referring. I had seen it performed way back in the 'nineties. It had once been very popular and its innocent theme made it suitable even for schoolgirls. The inn, the situation, the lake, the pine forests and the mountains in the background all made a picture which charmed us, and it was one in which the cheerful, healthy, good-looking inhabitants of Sankt Wolfgang fitted admirably.

Jannings had the script of the play. It was by Blumenthal and Kadelburg, and as a sort of explanatory motto for their effusion they had prefaced it with a quotation from their third act, in which one of the characters, Dr. Hinzelmann spouts:

"I feel myself urged out into the mountains, into the whispering woods. And when I stroll through the peaceful morning and my eyes drink in all the beauty around me, the magic of the journey begins to work. And then everything which a little while before appeared so important and so depressing now appears petty when seen from the mountain heights! How far away and forgotten and unimportant is all that left below! And it's the magic of the mountains which does all that. Just try it!"

This gives a very fair idea of what sort of thing the original "White Horse Inn" is: sentimental, commonplace and flat-footedly lyrical. When the theatrical experts, i.e. our jealous rivals, heard that Charell had bought the rights in "White Horse Inn", they wagged their heads incredulously: "What! That worn-out, falsely sentimental botchwork! How do you think you're going to fit all your usual frothy display and your dancing girls into that sloppy rubbish?"

But we had our own ideas on the subject.

A Berlin father and his daughter land in an inn by a lake— "White Horse Inn". A sentimental waiter is in love with the landlady; there is no landlord, so his shy attentions are perfectly legitimate. But the landlady is in love with a smart Berlin lawyer, who is also staying at the inn, whilst the lawyer no sooner sees the young lady from Berlin than he is after her. Our prosy-poetic Dr. Hinzelmann is also a guest at the inn with *his* daughter, and, of course, she has to have a young man too.

As our jealous rivals observed contemptuously: "Any idiot can see the general 'happy end' coming a mile off!" I didn't bother to wait for the result of the re-writing which was going on, and I immediately set to work. How often had I fled into the mountains with my kit in a rucksack as a young art student in 1900! Clambering up endless mountain paths, marching through scented pine forests, tramping across mossy slopes

studded with wild flowers, until finally I came across one of
the many cosy mountain inns tucked away in all that magnificence—just like "White Horse Inn"—with painted balconies
and verandas and gay window shutters reflected perhaps in
some mountain lake. And seated at a table before the house—
perhaps it was called "The Golden Stag" or "The Silver Swan"
or some such traditional name—I would be served with a well-
prepared and simple peasant meal by some buxom pleasant
wench dressed in the delightful costume of the country, with
thick plaits arranged in a crown on her head. And then I would
sketch. I knew exactly what it was that was wanted, and my
old sketch-books of those days provided me with everything
I needed. One book in particular contained splendid material
for my task. In a youthful hand and with many flourishes, I had
written on it "Gamshof, 1897"—"Chamois-Deer Farm". How
well I still remembered the place!

Wastl (Bavarian shortening for Sebastian) was a friend of
mine at the Academy. He was a young peasant by origin, and
he still wore the short leather trousers, the decorated green
jacket and the gay hat with the feather of the Bavarian peasant.
He was a big, fair-headed and good-natured fellow—and
talented too. Apart from the portraits and studies in the nude
which he carried out as a part of his studies, he would sketch
trees and landscapes in particular, and I was much struck with
the natural decorative character he gave them. We became very
good friends and one day he invited me to go home with him
and stay for a while. His father confirmed the invitation in a
friendly letter and I accepted. It was about ninety minutes'
train journey from Munich, and from the station we had to
continue our journey on foot high up into the mountains.

The morning was one of those described by Dr. Hinzelmann,
complete with pine forests and mountain magic. Up and up we
went along a mountain stream, and at last we came out on to
a plateau on which the house and farm buildings were situated.
The vast wooden-tiled roof was weighted with large stones, so
that when the thick snow began to thaw in the spring and slide
off the roof in great slabs it would not carry the wooden tiles
away with it. Carved balconies ran along the whole front. The
window shutters were carved and painted with baroque ornaments and the white walls were decorated with frescoes of
hunting scenes in which chamois deer and stags leapt gracefully
from crag to crag, pursued by eager hunters firing old-fashioned

blunderbusses. In the triangular gable was a large painted representation of St. Florian, the patron saint against fire, in baroque helmet and harness engaged in pouring a bucket of water on to a flaming house. Over the richly carved oak door was an inscription engraved in the lintel:

"Known to all men in our land
As the Gamshof, here I stand.
God's blessing, friend; swing wide the door.
Bring luck within, and roam no more."

The Gamshof, or Chamois-Deer Farm, was a magnificent example of its kind and I paused involuntarily for a moment or

"Chamois Court," Bavarian peasant's house

two in admiration. On the stone flags before the door stood a row of wooden clogs with leather uppers, for even in the richer peasant farmhouses the women never dream of walking over their spotlessly scrubbed wooden floors in anything but bare feet.

Within we found the mistress of the house, Wastl's mother, sitting in front of a monumental and highly ornamental tiled oven, looking as imposing as her house in a dress of mauve silk with leg-of-mutton sleeves and a pleated skirt of heavy satin. A black moiré cap was on her head, and at her ears, around her neck and on her fingers was the kind of peasant jewellery which passes as heirlooms from one generation to the next. She blessed her son and me as we came in, and her two daughters rose and curtsied naturally and gracefully. They were both fine, well-made and healthy peasant girls, and when many years later I came to design the costumes for Josepha, the landlady of the White Horse Inn, and her waitresses, Wastl's sisters, Leni and Bärbl (Barbara), with their long blue- and white-flowered, narrow-waisted dresses and their starched petticoats were my models.

Whilst the girls were laying the table and we were chatting to Wastl's mother, his father and two brothers came in. The peasant-farmer was a broad-shouldered giant with a deep voice and a jovial manner. He wore a coloured velvet waistcoat with two rows of large silver buttons, and across his stomach—where most men of his age carried their paunch—was a heavy ornamental watch-chain. The two younger men, dressed in the style of the country with short chamois-leather trousers and green stockings with embroidered tops (the so-called *Waden-strumpf*, which goes from below the knee and ends above the ankle, which it leaves free), greeted their brother with friendly shoves and hearty slaps on the back. Towards me, the guest, their attitude was amiable and polite. The food was then brought in by an old aunt who lived with the family. She wore a peasant dress of heavy brown silk and the traditional black cap on her hair. Helping her was Nandl, the cow-girl, in a starched print dress. The meal, plain and excellent, was as typical as the peasant dresses around the table: a savoury soup with liver-dumplings floating in it, loin of pork on *Sauerkraut* and fritters. And for each man there was the traditional litre mug with a hinged top filled with home-brewed beer.

Every plate, every dish, every piece of crockery on the solid oak board was the product of a local workshop, Bavarian handicraft art. And everything in the magnificent room was in style and keeping. Not a scrap of it all owed anything to modern industrial production. Compared with its length and depth, the room was rather low, and the master of the Gamshof could easily have touched the massive carved timbers of the ceiling with his upstretched arms. On either side of the main wall of the house were four windows in a row, each about 4 feet high, each with geraniums on its broad window-sill and blue-and-white check curtains to frame it. Along the wall underneath the windows was a comfortable bench. Above it and between the two sets of windows was a wooden crucifix with the carved figure of Christ. An old grandfather clock standing in a corner had the sun, the moon and the planets on its face. Old coloured engravings of Biblical subjects in wooden frames decorated the blue-washed walls. The tiled stove was a splendid example of antique ceramic art with blue-glazed chubby-cheeked cupids, each with its aureole.

The living-room of the Gamshof was a classic example of the traditional Bavarian peasant handicraft work coupled with instinctive and sure artistic feeling. And the same was true of everything else in the house. The banisters of the stairs were a masterpiece of peasant wood-carving. Up above in the broad passage hung primitive but colourful holy pictures and along the walls were carved and painted old chests and wardrobes. The furniture of the room in which I slept was every piece a museum treasure, every piece carved, painted, decorated. The head and foot of the decorated bedstead were of silver.

Recalling all this, I would gladly have made use of it for "White Horse Inn"; unfortunately, all the action takes place outside, "before the Inn", and never inside. But it was not only the house itself which contained such treasures. In the sheds were sledges beautifully carved and decorated and as solid and serviceable as the day they were made, and the well-fed draught horses were kept in a stable which was itself a work of art. There is one scene in "White Horse Inn" which plays "in the cowshed". Here at least I could use my sketches of the stables and sheds of the Gamshof.

On the Sunday morning I was privileged to watch the women of the Gamshof carefully take their Sunday best out of wardrobes and chests and lay them out ready for wear. The inherited traditional garments, the heavy silk, satin and embroidered clothing, the frilled and beribboned aprons, the fur-trimmed coifs were unchanged and still worn by all the women as they had been worn from time immemorial. To see the whole population walking sedately to church dressed in all this finery was a feast for the artistic eye. In the procession which marks the arrival of the old Kaiser Franz-Josef in "White Horse Inn" I used similar costumes.

Feierabend the Bavarians call the evening of a working day when its labour is over and they can gather to enjoy themselves. The girls of the village sit outside with their zithers and guitars and play. Men and girls sing together or dance traditional country dances. Whilst the men engage in their favourite dance known as the *Schuhplättler*, the girls look on and clap their hands in time with the movements. We introduced this virile male dance with its rhythmic slapping of calves, thighs and faces into "White Horse Inn", and everywhere it created a sensation. "Terrific!" said London. "*Formidable!*" cried Paris.

There is a particular village in Bavaria where the local lads are famous for their *Schuhplättler*, and so off we went to Oberdorf to recruit a dozen of the best lads for our Berlin production of "White Horse Inn". We found the Mayor, a bearded and impressive old father of the village, sitting at a table in the local inn with his litre of beer. When we explained to him what it was we wanted he went to the door and blew a series of piercing whistles on his fingers. From the wooded hills around the village echoed similar whistles and within a short while the young men of the village were gathered around the old man, who explained to them in pithy Bavarian dialect what it was all about. There and then they did their *Schuhplättler* for us and we chose the dozen we wanted. Returning to his table in the local inn, the Mayor wrote down the names and particulars of the men we had picked and we transferred them to the contract we had ready. But before the signing started, the Mayor coughed and addressed us:

"You gentlemen from Berlin have picked out twelve lusty fellows," he said, "and when I say lusty I mean lusty. Not only do they eat and drink a lot and sleep soundly, but they . . . they . . . they . . . Well, perhaps you know what I mean. In short, they must have a dozen girls to go with them."

Around the door of the inn stood a crowd of comely, full-bosomed, broad-hipped young peasant girls all gazing in eagerly.

"You've only got to pick them out," he said. "We'll make it cheap."

But firmly we declined. We were quite prepared to see that his young men should eat well, sleep comfortably and—up to a point at least—drink well, but as for the rest we were disinclined to accept responsibility.

"Well, perhaps just six would do," urged the Mayor. "They're good strong girls, and willing."

We remained firm.

"Just three, then," he wheedled.

But we were adamant and in the end the contract was signed for the twelve lads, whilst the Mayor sorrowfully wagged his head and insisted that he was greatly worried at the idea of their going off to "that sink of iniquity, Prussian Berlin" without their own womenfolk to look after them.

After that I went to Munich to obtain real old peasant materials for our costumes through the so-called *Tracht*, or traditional peasant costume associations, which set themselves the task of preserving the old local costumes, encouraging the inhabitants in the rural areas to continue wearing them, and encouraging the production of materials based on traditional styles and qualities. In addition, I needed authentic peasant hats, which I could also obtain only in Bavaria.

"White Horse Inn" was a tremendous success, not only in Germany, but everywhere it was shown. The corny old comedy had been completely re-written and many scenes added to it, including a visit by the old Emperor Franz-Joseph, which gave us an opportunity for our usual lavish display. In March 1949 there was a production in Manchester which won the acclaim of both Press and public, and at the moment of writing at least one "White Horse Inn" troupe is touring the provinces.

The new era at the London Coliseum, when the house changed from musical hall to operetta, was opened with "White Horse Inn". The décor I chose was chiefly my old love the painted background, but I also used three-dimensional props and a revolving stage, because for scenes in the mountains and hills by a lake-side the "box of bricks" on the revolving stage was very useful. It's not the technique itself I object to in its proper place; it's only when it is used exclusively to oust the painted scene. As the dimensions of the revolving stage at the Coliseum were the same as ours in Berlin, I just had our décor copied to the inch. When we began our rehearsals in London everything was ready: the inn with its balconies, the hills, the lake and the forest, the steamer and the famous cowshed with its complement of four life-sized cows with movable heads and tails.

The English stars had all been to see the performance in Berlin and they were quite *au courant*, and our Bavarian *Schuhplättler* had no need to translate their dance into English. Their success was particularly striking, and when a "White Horse Inn Touring Company" was formed they willingly joined it. When the Second World War broke out they one and all refused to let themselves be shot at for Hitler, although, of course, they were all of military age and lusty, upstanding young fellows. They preferred to stay in England.

"*L'Auberge du cheval blanc*" proved a success in Paris, too. It was produced at the Mogador Theatre. At the full-dress rehearsal the French actor who was portraying the old Emperor Franz-Joseph appeared as a perfect replica of the old man, whereupon the manager had misgivings: Franz-Joseph had been an enemy of France in the First World War and his appearance on a French stage might lead to unpleasantness. We thought the whole thing absurd, but we made no attempt to join in the discussion, which ended by the actor's agreeing to alter his whiskers. When he came back we had all we could do to prevent ourselves from bursting out laughing: Old Franz-Joseph had lost his side whiskers and he was now a typical Hohenzollern, and not only a Hohenzollern, but Wilhelm II himself with his up-bristling moustache! However, the manager was satisfied and French audiences raised no objection.

It was 1935 before we produced "White Horse Inn" in New York. Like all American theatres, the Rockefeller Centre had a longer stage than is usual in Europe, but by no means so deep, and so we had to change a good many of the scenes. My work on this production—which lasted much longer than usual —chiefly remarkable for the fact that I gained a new assistant, my fifteen-year-old daughter, Babette, who had obviously inherited the family talents. From her earliest childhood she had played with all the fascinating things she found in my studio—paper, colours, paste and glue, and so on. She saw what I did and she was soon trying to do the same, snipping away, painting and pasting. It was the same with me. My grandfather manufactured military hats, caps, etc., for the Roumanian Army, and that was in the days when military headgear was not the utilitarian thing it is to-day. Cutting out and putting together came naturally to him. And as I found paper, cardboard, pieces of material, scissors and paste on his work-table, I did just what my daughter did after me. In Odessa, from where he originally came, my grandfather had made theatrical costumes. Thus the line of inheritance is plain enough.

"White Horse Inn" was a hearty, rollicking, peasant piece. We followed it up with something for finer palates, something more aristocratic—"Casanova". The historical period in which the great adventurer went from country to country was one of great brilliance; it was the peak point of the rococo era. Louis Quinze was on the throne in France, Maria Theresa in Austria and Catherine the Great in Russia. And the Venice of that time was the Venice of Canaletto and Longhi, the Venice for which Tiepolo painted his pictures. I had read Casanova's memoirs long before there was any question of building up an operetta around him, and I could see him and his times very graphically. In addition, I knew all the places in which the plot unrolled, except Petersburg.

In designing for plays of the same period, such as Lessing's "Minna von Barnhelm" and "Emilia Galotti", and Schiller's "Kabale und Liebe", I had been to some extent limited by the nature of the plays to everyday rococo in clothing and environment. In "Casanova" at last I was fortunate enough to have an opportunity of letting myself go in all the pomp and glory of the

"Casanova" in Venice

period. An adventurer must have an adventurous environment, rich, brilliant and scintillating. And, of course, our "Casanova" was to be a sort of revue-operetta with singing and dancing, but this time for a change, the action was to be logical and even serious: Casanova, the gallant who could win the heart and person of any woman, fails to win the only one he really loves, and finally leads her into the arms of another. In other words, we presented Casanova in a new and unexpected role; we showed him renouncing his desires in favour of another. Whoever went to see "Casanova" in the hope of enjoying prurient situations, lustfulness and bed business was disappointed.

The title role was played by an operatic baritone both in

Berlin and London, and the music was by Johann Strauss the elder; that is to say, we took motifs from his lesser known works and used them to make a new score for "Casanova", and with great success. And as for the scenery . . .

Silver-blue ghostly moonlight and deep shadows. A canal spanned by a high and graceful bridge. A beautiful Venetian sings on a balcony; Casanova stands on the bridge and listens. Another beautiful woman descends from the gates of a palace to enter a gondola. That was Venice in our opening scene. The next scene was a gaming-room, also in Venice. A large crystal chandelier and numerous wall lights. A great ornamental ceiling painted in the style of Tiepolo. The ladies wore enormous crinoline-type dresses of deep red with silver embroidery. In contrast, all the male characters were dressed in black. The next episode took place in Potsdam in the period of Frederick the Great and the famous dancer, Barberina. In another scene the great hall of Maria Theresa's palace in Vienna was done in gold and white with mirror walls. A 15-foot-high statue of the Madonna decorated the façade of a Spanish convent and from the great doorway emerged a procession of eighty nuns in pink dresses trimmed with lace. In the Palace of Dux in Bohemia the curtain rose to reveal Casanova deep in thought in an enormous library. The finale of the piece was the traditional "Carnival in Venice". Throngs in black, white and gold clustered on balconies, rode in gondolas. Palaces and campaniles turned in the moonlight.

"If a show plays twice nightly to crowded houses, what more do you want?" That and similar questions were asked again and again when the Coliseum management proposed to take off "White Horse Inn" to make room for "Casanova". It was true "White Horse Inn" had been running for fourteen months and it seemed to be getting more popular rather than less as time went on. The pretty waitresses in their saucy green hats and the lads in their leather shorts and their calf socks thought Sir Oswald had gone off his head. The fact was that originally Erik Charell had not been too optimistic about the success of "White Horse Inn" in London and contractual obligations now compelled Sir Oswald to take off "White Horse Inn" and stage "Casanova".

The English production of "Casanova" was to be even more dazzling than the German, and for London the Potsdam scene had been changed to one in Petersburg. The monumental bed of Catherine the Great was the chief prop in a splendidly decorated room with blue pilasters. After a magnificent levée scene into which a ballet was introduced, there was a rapier duel with Casanova, in whom the light-hearted Catherine was more than a little interested, as one of the swordsmen. On both sides of the proscenium palace-like buildings in the Venetian style were erected, connected above the stage by a bridge, which incidentally is still there.

The grand finale in London, the "Carnival in Venice" scene, outdid its predecessor in Berlin both technically and in the magnificence of its costumes. In Berlin the palaces, campaniles, the bridges and the gondolas had turned on the moving stage, but in London they did so threefold because the Coliseum stage had three moving platforms, each of which could revolve independently. Casanova's last words to the audience are:

"Sing! Dance! Love! Laugh! That is life."

As far as I was concerned, I could afford to laugh. My work was once again at an end and all my troubles and worries had been overcome.

CHAPTER XVI

STAGE PEOPLE

THE JOB OF PRODUCING the same play or piece in various countries offers an interesting opportunity for comparative psychological studies. For instance, although the stage-hand system is much the same in Germany, France and England, racial differences show themselves clearly in character and temperament. The German, used to military discipline, does exactly what he is told to do, often blindly. He never makes any personal contribution. He always builds up his props in the same way, using the same technical aids and following the exact instructions he has been given. In other words, he is somewhat of a robot, but a very reliable robot.

The French stage-hand—let us suppose that it is a question of a quick-change scene—wants you to explain to him first exactly what it is you're after. He also wants you to tell him exactly how much time he is to be allowed for the job. How it's to be done he doesn't want you to tell him; that's his job. Once he knows exactly what it is you want, he withdraws with his colleagues to the nearest café and discusses the matter at length. After that he usually comes back and tells you that, say, a minute and a half is not enough; it can't be done in the time; it needs two minutes. Whereupon you point out that the London stage-hands did it in exactly one minute. This gravels him for a moment, but he's got his comeback: the English are better paid. However, what they can do the French can do, but . . . More pay or it won't be done at all. The Frenchman is a born individualist.

His English colleague does the same quick change of scene efficiently in precisely the time he has been asked to do it in. If you praise him, you put him on his mettle and he says, "Oh, that's nothing. We'll do it even quicker next time." He then insists that you take a stop-watch and time him. And when the job is done you find that he has improved on his time by a few seconds. At which he grins proudly. The Englishman is a sportsman and he would rather have liked to bet you on it.

Experienced and capable foremen in England bear the modest title of "Head Carpenters", and they put their backs into it with the others. In Germany the same man would bear the more resounding title of "Stage Inspector", and that would effectively prevent his lending a hand himself.

I have met some astonishingly ingenious and superb craftsmen amongst stage workers, men who were literally capable of turning their hands to anything. The more out-of-the-way things you required, the more you put them on their mettle. Such men were jacks-of-all-trades—and masters, too. Carpentry, joinery, carving, modelling—anything. Nothing came amiss and any material could be worked in and put to good use: felt, canvas, wire, cardboard, paper. They would make you convincing exotic flowers out of coloured shavings and use goose feathers for the leaves. An old yellow parchment document with impressive seal hanging from it? An old ikon or holy picture? An Indian fan? You had only to say the word and in a very short space of time you had what you wanted. I remember on one occasion asking for a royal sceptre and getting an astonishingly impressive one made out of the back of a carved chair.

It is not surprising that such wizards are themselves often oddities and eccentrics. Whether their fantastic occupation made them odd, or whether they adopted it because they were odd to start with, I don't know, but oddness and eccentricity belong to the theatre. Despite all modernistic innovations, despite the introduction of the latest word in technical aids, the old German theatre still retained much of its romantic character. And every time you wandered through the labyrinthine passages and stumbled up worn stone steps and through neglected rooms, whose original purpose had long been forgotten, to emerge at last on to the stage during a rehearsal, you found that the romantic and mysterious was still alive. No one connected with the theatre is immune to it.

In the dim light of perhaps a single lamp shadowy groups stand around whispering. The star turns up his coat collar and murmurs with Hamlet: "The air bites shrewdly; it is very cold." And even the ghost appears. Suddenly coming out of the shadows—even more uncanny than at Elsinore—a bundled-up something slops forward. Only when it reaches the unlighted footlights and a yellow electric bulb lights up over a small desk do you realize that the strange being is a bent old woman with thick glasses. Squatting at the desk, she licks her finger and turns the pages of a dog-eared script, muttering to herself, shivering and pulling her shawl closer around her shoulders. It is the prompter. On the Continent there's no "prompt side"; she sits just under the front of the stage with her head on a level with the actors' feet and concealed from the view of the audience by a sort of shell-like hood permanently fixed at the footlights.

In the meantime, more shapes have come on to the gloomy stage. Towards the front is a table and someone takes his place at it; that's the producer. A number of chairs are put here and there for various other observers. "Lines" begin to be spoken, half loud and in a monotone. Now and again the voice of the prompter sounds loud and sharp. The producer sits at his table, his head resting on his hand, seeming to show little or no interest in the proceedings. Suddenly, abrupt and urgent like lightning in the darkness, the words rattle out:

> *"Art thou a devil*
> *Escaped here from Hades?*
> *Then look on this sign,*
> *To which all must bow,*
> *The black hosts of hell!"*

Faust speaks! Once again Goethe's masterpiece is being revived. The words are stirring. They are no longer murmured like the mutterings of a crowd. The prompter speaks louder. The light gleams in her glasses.

I have often found that lines seemed more effective on the gloomy stage with the empty auditorium stretching away into the darkness than afterwards during a performance to a packed house. But after a while everything falls back into the old jog-trot of the rehearsal. The actors mutter their lines, go over them rapidly and half inaudibly. Walk up and down mechanically, making a half-hearted gesture now and again or striking a pose. The producer stares down at the floor; then suddenly he rises, leaves his desk and walks over to the spot he has been gazing at, stoops and picks up a pin, which he then carefully sticks into his lapel. He is superstitious like all theatre people, no matter how enlightened he may be outside. To pick up a pin is a compulsive act; to leave it lying would bring bad luck. Even the ultra-modern theatre man Reinhardt had a collection of pins, rusty iron nails and bits of horseshoes picked up in this fashion. I have known actors who religiously kissed their scripts before going on. There were others who had to spit three times before each performance. And I remember once a well-known actor who simply refused to go on at all at a full-dress rehearsal because he had spotted a peacock's feather in a hat.

Amongst my old sketches are many which were made at such rehearsals, more or less rapidly sketched groups or individual figures. Many of them were subsequently useful in my painting, and I made some of them into lithographs for a series entitled "Behind the Scenes". I was particularly impressed by the old girl who acted as prompter. With her thick glasses and wrapped in her heavy shawls, she always struck me as the secret, invisible source of strength; it was she who first had to speak the words before the actors could utter them. One evening I decided to watch her at work without her knowledge. It was a performance of "Faust", and before she appeared I went down into the gloomy depths below stage. By the light of one small and much-used yellow bulb, I made my way between the heavy props which supported the stage timbers above my head. All sorts of apparatus for raising and lowering platforms now no longer in use encumbered the space. Everything was covered with thick, greasy dust. When the first bell rang up above and informed all and sundry that there was just ten minutes to go, I withdrew into the darkness. After a while I heard the old woman coming. She made her way through the labyrinth even more wrapped up than usual, carrying a large bag and mumbling to herself. No more convincing witch ever trod the boards above us. She felt her way along the wall and then she switched on another miserable yellow bulb, which revealed a narrow flight of steps leading upwards to the prompt box. She sat down on the lowest step, took a pair of carpet slippers out of her bag and put them on instead of her shoes, which she put down at the bottom of the steps. Then she took out her script and a rug from the bag and climbed the steps with much grunting and groaning. At the top she turned round and sat down. All I could see now was the lower part of her; her head was already in the prompt box on a level with the stage. Then she tucked the rug around her and made herself comfortable. The rug was very necessary; it was draughty below stage. The second and then the third bell sounded and a moment or two later I heard her whisper sibilantly:

> "*As of old the sun begins its song,*
> *Still rivalling its brother spheres.*"

And then the same lines were repeated loudly on the stage above. Raphael had spoken the opening words of the "Prologue in Heaven". The play had begun. The stage above was bathed in light; below the stage in semi-darkness was the old woman wrapped into a shapeless bundle. And there she sat cooped up throughout the whole performance, hidden from the audience by the prompt shell. Before her on a level with her chin was the floor of the stage, and just below it, faintly illuminated by a carefully screened lamp, was the script of "Faust". Below, her rheumaticky old legs were protected from the draughts by the rug, and above the dust of the stage blew into her face. And the whole time she had to pay close attention to the piece, whispering the words with the players. To know that she was there following every word lent confidence even to those who knew their roles by heart and never made a slip. Those who knew their roles indifferently relied on her almost entirely. Others occasionally needed to hear the first word or two of their lines. Still others declared that the prompter hissing away below them put them off their stride and insisted that she should be silent for them, and then if they tripped up they blamed her for letting them down. The life of a prompter is a hard one. It must have been bitter, in particular, for our old girl—she had once played leading roles herself, including Juliet and Margerita.

When I was designing for a musical in an old Viennese theatre just after the First World War I made the acquaintance of another of these prompters, Fräulein H. She was long and angular and had once been an actress, but she had been prompting then for almost a quarter of a century. She invited me to visit her, saying that she had an interesting collection of curiosities connected with the theatre which I would probably like to see. She lived on the fourth floor of an old house in Vienna, and when I climbed the stairs she opened her door dressed in a loose lilac gown with a train and invited me to enter. On her head was a blonde wig with a diadem on top. Theatrical bracelets decorated her bony arms, and her bronze coloured sandals were ornamented with coloured glass beads. The odd thing was that the ageing woman did not look ridiculous in this get-up of former days. There were still very definite traces of her former beauty in her cadaverous face, and her fine eyes sparkled.

With a queenly gesture, she indicated the odds and ends of theatrical memories with which her room was filled. There was an artificial palm with dusty leaves on a rickety gilt table, a memory of some long-past piece. In a plaster vase was an enormous bouquet of coloured grasses—a "Markart bouquet" they call it in Vienna. Curtains draped the door and window, painted to imitate brocade. The walls were covered with the photos of actors, most of them dead and gone; theatre programmes and reviews in frames; and long-dead laurel wreaths, still with their faded ribbons and gold lettered inscriptions. On

I visit the former prompter

an easel was a large painting of my hostess in the role of "Iphigenia" dressed in a light blue tunic and with a golden band around a lovely head of blonde curls. And all over the place were books—on the window-sill, on shelves, on the floor, even on the iron stove. Apart from the couple of rather wobbly gilt chairs on which we sat to drink coffee, there was nothing else on which to sit. It made me wonder what she did when she wanted to rest, to make herself comfortable, to read one of the many books piled up everywhere. She picked up Goethe's "Iphigenia in Aulis". Would I like to hear her in her greatest role as "Iphigenia"? Naturally I declared that I would love it.

Whereupon she pushed aside a high screen painted with roses and butterflies to reveal a strange piece of furniture. It was a high seat and a number of steps led up to it; instead of ordinary arms, the narrow seat had high sides and back which enclosed her, whilst on the top, crowning the whole strange edifice, was a sort of shell. Fräulein H. clambered up the steps, sat down, lowered a desk top, placed the Goethe on it, found her place and began to declaim her old role with passion and emphasis. Suddenly I realized the significance of that strange piece of furniture; it was a replica of a prompter's box. Accustomed for nearly a quarter of a century to declaim the world's masterpieces in the narrow limits of her prompter's box, she had had a replica made for use at home.

"You see," she explained when she was finished, "seated up here I can control the work of my pupils with particular authority—I teach, you know. The narrow seat doesn't disturb me in the least; in fact, I need it now in order to be able to live the part, to let myself be carried away with the ecstasy of the role. As a theatre man, you know that we artists have our whims and eccentricities. Why, my colleague Sarah Bernhardt slept in a coffin for years."

CHAPTER XVII

"FAUST"

From time to time in this book I have spoken of Goethe's "Faust" and quoted from it, but I have not yet mentioned how intensely the scenic problems raised by both parts have interested and occupied me. I mentioned the illustrated edition of Shakespeare's works which was in our modest library at home and how it awakened my enthusiasm as a lad. We also had an illustrated edition of Goethe's works. I don't think anyone mentioned either Shakespeare or Goethe to me as a boy, and my attention was drawn to both of them by the pictures rather than the text. I had no idea what Goethe's "Faust" was all about, because poetry was a closed book to me, and it was only when I saw "Faust" played at the Vienna Burg Theater that I found out. At the same time, I was strongly critical of the way in which it was staged, because—which was not surprising—the scenes on the stage were nothing like the pictures in my book. The illustrator had kept faithfully to Goethe's descriptive text. Faust's study he had portrayed as a tall, narrow gothic type of room, and he had taken over this gothic narrowness in all the other illustrations, whether in the street, in the cathedral or in the castle. The witches' kitchen, Auerbach's cellar, the rooms of Gretchen and Martha and the little garden were all "narrow", and the scene of the action was circumscribed. In my view, this was a correct interpretation, because the plot unfolds in a small gothic town surrounded and pressed in by its walls.

Consider Scene 2, "Before the City Gate", when Faust says to Wagner:

> *"Out of the hollow gloomy gate,*
> *The motley throng come forth elate:*
> *Each will the joy of the sunshine hoard,*
> *To honour the day of the risen Lord!*
> *They feel, themselves, their resurrection:*
> *From the low, dark rooms, scarce habitable;*
> *From the bonds of work, from trade's restriction;*
> *From the pressing weight of roof and gable;*

> *From the narrow, crushing streets and alleys;*
> *From the churches' solemn and reverend night,*
> *All come forth to the cheerful light."*

The productions of "Faust" that I saw all failed to convey this sense of restriction. All the scenes I have mentioned took place on the full stage. This was not only formally against the directions, but it even contradicted the tendency of the play, Faust's longing to break out of the narrowness into the light:

> *"Ah me! this dungeon still I see,*
> *This drear, accursed masonry,*
> *Where even the welcome daylight strains,*
> *But darkly through the painted panes."*

And in this falsely interpreted scenery actors strutted around in silks and velvets decked out in Renaissance costumes instead of in gothic garb. I always thought of Faust, Mephistopheles, Gretchen, Martha, Valentine and so on as though Dürer had drawn them. They would then have looked very much more like Goethe's idea of his characters, I thought. But in this I was to prove wrong. In the Vienna Music and Theatre Exhibition there was a costume for Mephistopheles which Goethe himself had designed. I went to see it and came away disappointed. The doublet and the baggy hose were made of some common red woollen material, cheap and banal and not at all in gothic style.

In the end I realized that in Goethe's day people just did not bother about such things as historical style for stage performances, and costume anachronisms did not trouble them in the least. Many years later, when I was faced with the task of costuming Goethe's characters, I had won through to a greater freedom and I invented my own style to suit the piece. The more I regarded "Faust" and the harder I thought about the problem, the more taken up I was with the piece itself. Much of it I knew by heart, and I knew the exact sequence of all the many scenes without having to consult the script. If anything was left out it struck me as sacrilege. Serious German theatres (including the Austrian) usually began the piece with the "Prelude on the Stage" in which the Manager, the Dramatic Poet and the Merry Andrew discuss everything connected with the piece. And only then came the "Prologue in Heaven" in which, after the three Archangels praise the Creation (I can only describe their words as tremendous), the voice of the Lord speaks to Mephistopheles and grants him Faust, so to speak, for experimental purposes.

> *"Enough! What thou hast asked is granted.*
> *Turn off this spirit from his fountain-head;*
> *To trap him, let thy snares be planted,*
> *And him, with thee, be downward led;*
> *Then stand abashed, when thou art forced to say*
> *A good man, through obscurest aspiration,*
> *Has still an instinct of the one true way."*

Apart from Faust's pact with the devil, which first appears in a book by Johann Spiess entitled "Historia von D. Johann Fausten", published in Frankfort-on-Main in 1587, the whole of the first part of the tragedy, i.e. the Gretchen tragedy, etc., is completely Goethe's work. The Helena scenes, which appear in the old German puppet play of Dr. Faust, were used by Goethe in Part Two.

I once saw this puppet play, "Dr Faust", in Munich. It begins with a prelude in Hell, a grotesque and fantastic scene with the evil spirits of Lust, Drunkenness and Avarice. Faust sells his hope of eternal salvation to the tempter for "Wine, Women and Lust," and he never uses his new power for higher ends. The scope of this puppet play is restricted to the ideas and desires of the groundlings and never rises above them.

Quite by chance, whilst I was engaged in writing this part of my book, I was given a ticket for a production of Marlowe's "Tragical History of Doctor Faustus". At that time Marlowe was a poet of whom I knew little more than the name, and I had never seen or read this particular play. I went to see it and I was astonished to think that such a work had been written before Shakespeare, at least before Shakespeare had written his masterpieces. In particular, I found the idea of presenting Mephistopheles as a monk a touch of genius, and also the constantly present, changing personifications of Good and Evil (the Good and Evil Angels). The fantastic scene of the seven deadly sins I found tremendous. I was deeply impressed by Marlowe's treatment of the theme. And how I envied the stage-designer, the painter Morris Kestelman, who had done his work excellently!

The two operas on the theme, "Mephistopheles" by the

Italian Boito, and Gounod's "Faust", left me with very mixed feelings.

A production of Goethe's "Faust"—if it could still be called Goethe's when the producer had finished with it—was staged in Paris at the Odeon Theatre by the French producer, Antoine, who had something of a reputation in his own country. It was practically a parody. The two parts were run into one and contained both the Gretchen tragedy and the Helena scenes. Antoine obviously saw his Faust as a typical German professor—or what is popularly considered to be a typical German professor by people outside Germany. Antoine turned poor Gretchen into a voluptuous, full-bosomed person with thick golden plaits. The light-blue dress with puff sleeves in which she was presented made her look even fatter. And in the final scene when she is dressed in a penitent's shirt in her cell she looked like an elephant. It was quite clear that for Antoine Gretchen was what popular belief in France holds to be a typical German woman.

"Faust," Witches' Sabbath

The programme was drawn up as a sort of guide without tears to the plot. "*Faust endormi dans une prairie pres de Magdebourg*" it said in one place—to my enormous astonishment. Magdeburg of all places! Magdeburg, almost a symbol of the sober North-German plain! After much cogitation it occurred to me that this must be Act I, Scene 1, of Part Two. Goethe says nothing about Magdeburg, of course, and is content to entitle it "*Anmutige Gegend*" or "A pleasant Landscape", and he goes on to say, not that Faust is asleep, but that he is lying on a flowery sward "tired, restless and seeking sleep. Ariel and his sprites, graceful little figures, hover around him." In Goethe's version the sprites seek to comfort Faust and Ariel sings:

> "*Who round this head in airy circles hover,*
> *Yourselves in guise of noble elves discover!*
> *The fierce convulsions of his heart compose;*
> *Remove the burning barbs of his remorse . . .*"

In Antoine's version the elves were the pupils of Isadora Duncan's dancing school, and they pranced around the unfortunate Faust "in the neighbourhood of Magdeburg". It was deplorable. The only compensation in the whole production was the performance of Mephistopheles, and I hope I shall not be thought to be taking my revenge on Monsieur Antoine if I say that the nature of the role, brilliant, mocking, devilish, was one a Frenchman could play superlatively well.

It would take us too far if I now described all the various stagings of "Faust" we produced. Let it suffice to say that we did our honest best to give Goethe's masterpiece a worthy setting. But at the risk of appearing vain, I propose to quote an appreciative critic, Schultze-Naumburg, on my work in connection with the staging of "Faust", Part Two. After all, what the critics write about us theatre folk is, unfortunately, all that remains tangible of our work.

"I recall a performance of 'Faust', Part Two", writes this critic, himself an artist, which is a change. "At the conclusion the skies were filled with the heavenly hosts. In view of what we have all experienced in the way of living pictures set up for the purpose, the idea is one to fill the soul with anguish. But we needn't worry where Ernest Stern is concerned. As though painted by Fra Angelico on a gold background, a mosaic of angelic lines fills the space, faint, without shadows, like disembodied spirits, whilst only a slightly heightened glow of light surrounds the Blessed Virgin in a dreamlike aureole."

Goethe took the traditional figure of the old necromancer and lifted it to higher spiritual regions. He turned it into the tragedy of man's spirit striving towards the light, into the fate of mankind as a whole. In view of the eternal values in "Faust", and the impressive and thrilling fashion in which Part One lends itself to staging, and considering in particular the excellent translations available, I find it astonishing that English theatre circles show so little interest in it. I have often tried to persuade leading producers and actors in this country to stage the tragedy—unfortunately, without success.

In 1932 Luise Dumont, the highly talented and artistic director of the Schauspielhaus in Dusseldorf, asked me to do the stage and costume designs for a production of Parts One and Two at her theatre. I accepted gladly. A melancholy significance attaches to that work—it was the last I was fated to do in Germany.

The Three Magi, Cochran revue, "Follow the Sun"

CHAPTER XVIII

GRAND OPERA

BEFORE I BEGIN to deal with a completely new phase in my life—my permanent settlement in England—I must go back to one or two interesting things which took place in the post-war period: post-First World War, that is.

Bruno Walter, now internationally famous as a conductor, was at that time Musical Director of the Charlottenburg Opera House in Berlin, and he asked me to design the scenery and costumes for his production of Wagner's "Tannhäuser". I was delighted. At last the chance of doing grand opera; something I had always wished for. To translate music into form, line and colour—an ideal job for me. I knew the opera very well, having heard it on a number of occasions in Vienna and Munich, and I had always taken strong objection to the visual settings chosen.

I pointed this out in talks with Walter, and he declared that it was due to the bygone taste of the year 1845, when the opera was first produced, and to the excessive reverence with which the staging traditions of "Tannhäuser" had since been treated.

"But we have chosen you to do it for us," he went on, "and we have every confidence that you will carry out a difficult and important task in a thoroughly worthy and artistic fashion."

Deeply gratified by his words, I could only assure him that if I didn't it wouldn't be for want of trying. He than played me the whole opera magnificently, and it was a great musical experience for me. In the subsequent weeks I sat at my drawing board and sang or hummed the melodies from "Tannhäuser" as I worked—out of tune perhaps, but enthusiastically.

Tannhäuser was a wandering troubadour, what the Germans call a *Minnesänger*. According to the legend he remained, devoted to pleasure and unmindful of his Christian duties, in the pagan Venusberg. But at last the prick of conscience made itself felt and he went on a pilgrimage to the Holy Father in Rome to obtain forgiveness for his sins. The Pope refused him absolution and he returned in despair to the halls of Venus. Wagner linked up this legend with the singing competition in the Wartburg. In the opera the competitors are Walther von der Vogelweide, Wolfram von Eschenbach, both famous German *Minnesänger* and poets, Tannhäuser and others. Whilst all the other singers praise knightly and human virtues in their songs, Tannhäuser sings a song in praise of passionate love. Exhorted by Elizabeth, the daughter of the Landgrave and master of the Wartburg, to do penance, Tannhäuser makes the pilgrimage to Rome.

The Wartburg, which still existed up to the Second World War, is also the scene of a popular Luther legend. It is, or was, built in the romance style of architecture, which was considered in the nineteenth century to be the only fitting background for poetic and romantic happenings. This would perhaps not have been so bad, and not so far out, if the background had been left as it was: original, primitive and untitivated, but thanks to Wagner's artistic advisers or perhaps, feeling as I do, it would be better to say Wagner's art advisers and leave the question of their artistic qualities out of it—the background and the environment were given a false and saccharine-like sweetness, *Verkitscht* as the Germans say. At the same time the valuable and unique documentary evidence which is readily available concerning the *Minnesänger* was deliberately ignored to suit the book of the revisors. The result was that Wagner's characters, not only in "Tannhäuser" but also in "Lohengrin" and "Parsifal", were turned into figures out of an amateurish masquerade, and decked out in silks, satins and velvets of jarring colours.

In every production of "Tannhäuser" I saw, the unfortunate hero had to wear a sort of long nightshirt whilst his partner in the lists of love, Frau Venus, always looked like a school-teacher swathed in white cashmere. Elizabeth always wore a long dress with a train that would not have been altogether out of place at a modern dinner party. And as for the ballet on the Venusberg, the less said the better. When I told Walther that I proposed to make a complete break with this musty old tradition and take flamboyant gothic as the style for my decorations and costumes, he was obviously a trifle shocked. He pointed out that the title of the opera was "Tannhäuser or the Battle of Song on the Wartburg" and he advised me to go to the Wartburg and see the background for myself.

Off I went to the little town of Eisenach in Thuringia. The Wartburg stands, or stood, on a tree-covered hill near the town. Seen from a distance, the conglomeration of buildings of all epochs certainly made an impressive and most picturesque whole. But when I came to examine it closer I found that the so-called Landgrave's House, the Elizabeth Gallery and the Hall of Song, the real Romanesque buildings, outdid my most pessimistic fears. It appeared that Wilhelm II had had it all "thoroughly"—read "ruthlessly"—restored. Everything which had once been authentic Romanesque architecture had disappeared and had been replaced by Wilhelm's architects, who had taken precisely the traditional Wagnerian décor as their model. It was profoundly depressing. There were even new frescoes depicting, not the original saga, but the saga as Wagner had re-cast it for his own purposes. I fled for comfort to the old part of the Wartburg, which had been left untouched, and recovered my spirits in the small room in which Luther had lived for a year in hiding. It was there that he is supposed to have thrown his inkpot at the devil who came to tempt him—and if you don't believe it, there's still the mark where it hit the wall.

So the style was to be Romanesque? Very well, let it be—but I took my inspiration for the architecture of the Hall of Song from anywhere but the Wartburg, and yet when it was finished everyone exclaimed: "How just right!" And as it had to be

Cave of Venus, "Tannhäuser"

Romanesque, I went in for it thoroughly, and the usual "cave" in which Venus sings had to put up with the style too. It became the ante-room to a romance hell; great caryatids writhed painfully up the stone walls; arches curved up to the ceiling vainly trying to find some support and ended in great stone grotesques in the shape of devils' heads desperately biting into involved Romanesque ornaments. Fortunately the opera singer who was to take the role of Venus was a beautiful woman with a lovely figure, and fortunately too she was no prude and consented without a murmur to wear the sinfully tempting costume I designed for her. Instead of the traditional ballet, I surrounded her with a horde of green furies and shaggy satanic demons.

The majestic entry of the guests into the Hall of Song is the visual peak of the opera. I had my own ideas on the subject, and they were much opposed to the usual trooping of a few hundred singers and supers over the stage. I found the producer very understanding, and together we worked out a procession which bore some relation to the various musical motifs and sought to create a harmony between décor and music; that is to say, we illustrated the music psychologically and decoratively. Lyrical and melodic music we marked by the entrance of girls, pages or young couples. The less impressive music was for the married couples. The *fortissimo* passages saw the entrance of the warriors, and the triumphant fanfares accompanied the knights. It was our intention to reinforce the music with action, and we found that our audiences actually grasped what we were driving at.

All the costumes were inspired by the famous Maness manuscript, which is a collection of coloured miniatures done in the thirteenth century, showing Walther von der Vogelweide, Wolfram von Eschenbach and many other famous *Minnesänger* in knightly garb with their coats of arms. The result of all my efforts was highly gratifying, and although I had deliberately avoided the traditional, even the authorities who usually clung obstinately to tradition even in small things had to admit that it was a success.

One episode in connection with the designing is worthy of mention because it shows how wrong even the experts in stage matters can be. Wolfram von Eschenbach sings the famous song to the evening star in an autumn landscape. For this scene I gave him a full cloak with broad stripes of light and dark brown. This cloak was the only garment amongst the hundreds I designed to which the costume experts of the Charlottenburg Opera House took any serious objection. They didn't like the stripes and they found the cloak jarred with the

H

lyrical nature of the song. However, I was quite certain of myself in the matter and I refused to budge, so Wolfram von Eschenbach appeared to sing his famous solo in my striped cloak—and almost all the critics mentioned that cloak in particular as a touch of genius in costume design!

Another opera for which I did the designing was Hugo Wolf's *"Der Corregidor"*. It was originally to have been entitled "The Three-cornered Hat" after the story by the Spanish writer Alarcon, *"El sombrero de tres picos"*, but the Spanish musician Falla had already based a ballet on the story and used

"Der Corregidor," Opera by Hugo Wolf

the title, so Wolf's title had to be changed. Incidentally, another Spaniard designed the scenery and costumes for this ballet when it was produced by Diaghilev, Picasso. I don't know where Picasso took his inspiration from, but I carefully studied the Gobelin designs of Goya and Bayeux, two more Spaniards, for mine, and I did my best to make my Spanish characters, both male and female, as like them as possible.

Hugo Wolf's reputation was based, of course, on his *Lieder*, and his music was regarded as undramatic. His opera consisted largely of a string of songs. Bruno Walter worked hard to make a success of the famous lyric composer's only operatic venture, but the general public was not enthusiastic. As far as I was concerned, *"Der Corregidor"* gave me a welcome opportunity to try my hand at a Spanish background, and when I look again at my sketches I am still grateful to Hugo Wolf.

It was in this post-war period that I returned to Vienna. Laughter through tears is not an exaggerated way to describe it. Neglected, shabby and poverty-stricken, Vienna still retained her old charm. I had gone there to design the scenery and costumes for a production of "The Duchess of Chicago", an operetta which calls for no comment. But the theatre in which it was produced was the one in which I had first heard *"Die Fledermaus"* of Johann Strauss when I was a youngster with curly hair and a small and anxiously cultivated moustache. I was now clean-shaven—and baldish. Saxophones and susaphones grunted and whined in the orchestra, and on the stage, where once the Viennese waltz had held graceful sway, exotic stampings and gyrations went on. But over the entrance to the theatre the figure of Pappageno decorated with his feathers and carrying a bird-cage was still enthroned against the yellow wall, for it was in this house that Mozart's "Magic Flute" was first performed in public. Before the building still flowed the little river of Vienna and on the other side still stood the old building with the attic in which Susanna had lived and in which she had encouraged me to abandon the pen of the clerk for the brush of the painter. When I walked along the narrow river I saw the building of the Commercial Academy, grey, squat and graceless, with the winged baton of Mercury still on its roof.

The rich baroque façade of the Belvedere still faced the world in all its old splendour. When I was young the proud buildings of Vienna seemed to have something almost arrogant and unapproachable about them. They seemed secure in their everlasting grandeur. Now they seemed to be warning me: "Now that you're here again, set us down before it's too late." Even the tremendous black gothic dome of St. Stephen's, whose stern Catholicism once seemed so intimidating, now invited my admiration purely as a masterpiece of architecture.

The lively movement of the Vienna streets was much the same as ever. You could still meet the peasants dressed in their local costumes. There were Czech and Hungarian peasant girls, and old women in their wide frocks and their embroidered bodices selling fruit and vegetables, but their countries were no

longer part and parcel of the old Austro-Hungarian Empire.
The Peace Treaty of St. Germain had hacked the old complex
to pieces, and now its separate parts vegetated independently,
able neither to live nor die.

But Vienna still exercised all her old attraction and her
citizens paid little attention to the new frontiers, though in
one striking respect the Vienna street scene had changed: the
colourful and smartly dressed soldiers and their elegant
officers had gone. They had been a sight worth seeing, a fact
which was forcibly recalled to my mind in April 1949 when
I was asked to design the uniforms of a dozen Austrian officers
of the 'eighties for a revival of Noel Coward's "Bitter-Sweet".
"The Imperial and Royal Austro-Hungarian Army" was the
book which once again inspired me—what a wonderfully
artistic sense of colour those old uniforms revealed!

"Pag' and Cav'"' were being given in the momumental
Opera House on the Ringstrasse. I had witnessed the première
of Cavalleria Rusticana" in the 'nineties and Mascagni himself
had conducted the orchestra. Music and song in post-war
Vienna were still on the very high level of the days of the
Empire, but the glory of the Opera House itself had faded. The
worn and patched seats were now occupied by an audience in
the drab every-day clothing of the street and the joyful spirit
of former days had gone.

"Faust" was being given in the Burg Theater. How could I,
as a former "Regular", fail to see it again? "Again ye come, ye
wavering figures!" cries Goethe in his Dedication. But the men
and women on the stage were all unknown to me, and even
Apollo and the Nine Muses in their sacred grove painted on the
curtain had grown worn and colourless. The attendants who
showed us to our seats were wounded ex-soldiers. Thin and
bent, they thanked us profusely for a small tip. And in the foyer
during the interval the buffet which once served iced champagne and everything which went with it now served hot dogs
and beer. *O tempore, O mores!*

But the most moving experience in post-war Vienna was
meeting people I had known in other days. One night a man
approached me at the stage-door, greeted me politely and
mentioned his name. He was grey and his moustache hung
down in a melancholy fashion. His suit no longer fitted his thin
body and it was worn and shiny. On his head was an old-
fashioned panama. At first the name stirred only a faint recol-

lection, and then suddenly I realized who he was: a former
captain on the Imperial General Staff, a highly cultured and
much-travelled man. I had spent many pleasant hours in his
apartments, where he kept his fine collection of Chinese and
Japanese *objets d'art*. He invited me to visit him again and I
readily agreed. On the way he suggested that we should go
into a cafe and have a drink to celebrate the renewal of our
acquaintance. He ordered a bottle of Tokay and a plate of
sandwiches. He ate the sandwiches ravenously and we finished
the bottle between us. When the waiter came with the bill he
fumbled clumsily in his pockets and then confessed shame-
facedly that he had forgotten his purse. I paid.

He still lived in the same apartments, rents at least were
cheap, but the impression I received was very different now. It
looked poverty-stricken and neglected. I could see at a glance
that his collection was much reduced, and the reason was easy
enough to guess, but there were still a number of interesting
things left and when he spoke about them he recaptured something of his former fascination as a host. He made no mention
of his present deplorable situation, and when I left he literally
forced a small Chinese bronze ornament on to me "for my wife".
The next day I received a bill—three Austrian crowns!

Owing to the fact that the newspapers had published inter-
views with me, particularly about my memories of the Burg
Theater in the days of its glory, my presence in Vienna was well
known. One day a lady came to see me in my hotel. Once again
the name was vaguely familiar, but the hotel vestibule was not
very well lighted and I could not see her too clearly. I invited
her to dinner and we sat in the restaurant and discussed the Burg
Theater. And then suddenly I remembered the handsome and
elegant young student actress who had been one of our fellow
regulars in the Burg Theater queue. She was now in the late
forties and still well dressed, and she was wearing a big brooch,
a miniature studded with small stones, which was obviously
valuable.

During a pause in our conversation I asked her how she had
got on during the war. For answer she undid the brooch and
handed it to me, and then I could see that the subject of the
miniature was the late Emperor Franz-Joseph.

"His Majesty gave it to me in person," she said, and she
pronounced the words with reverence.

She had been fortunate in her career; she had gone straight

from the stage school to the Court Theatre, and there she had been a success. She had been noticed by the old Emperor himself and one evening she had been summoned to the salon behind the court box and there received by His Majesty, who had complimented her highly on her acting. For some years she had been honoured with such summonses from time to time, and on one occasion the old Kaiser had presented her with the brooch, and with it had gone a life pension.

"It was paid regularly even after his death," she said, "but when the catastrophic collapse came with the lost war our money was worthless, as you know, and so was my pension. To-day I have nothing. I could sell the brooch, of course. It is valuable. But I can't bring myself to part with it, and I think you will understand that."

Her voice was low and trembling, as she spoke of her misfortunes. Such scenes, and there were so many of them, were terrible. These people were not professional beggars with the carefully invented hard-luck story. They were cultured and talented people who had been crushed by misfortune and reduced to beggary. And what could a man do beyond give them a little to tide them over? It was no solution of their problems. Their position was hopeless.

She was not the last of my old acquaintances who came to me for help; not by any means. One morning when the first rehearsals of "The Duchess of Chicago" were taking place and everything was still in a more or less chaotic state I was handed a letter. "The gentleman will call at eleven o'clock," I was told. I tore open the envelope and inside it was a letter dated January 1898 from Munich and written by me to my "Dear friend", T. T. was also one of my old acquaintances of the Burg Theater queue and gallery. Promptly at eleven o'clock he arrived. A sort of spectre with feverish sunken eyes dressed in a frayed suit came limping out from the wings towards me. T. was the theatrical type, but there was no play-acting about his condition. "If you can't help me," he declared, "all that remains is this," and he drew out a revolver. I did manage to settle his problem; I found him a job as a call-boy.

The end of my last visit to Vienna was, however, not without its kinder sentiment. Erik Charell was planning a production of "*Das Drei-Mäderln-Haus*" (subsequently produced in this country as "Lilac Time") for the Grosses Schauspielhaus in Berlin. The composer plays the male lead in this musical and

the score is made up exclusively of his music. The story deals
with his love for three Viennese sisters, and there is still, or was,
a charming old gabled house which is popularly supposed to
have been the house in which the three sisters lived. It was
know as the "*Drei-Mäderln-Haus*" to the Viennese. I don't know
whether it actually was the house in which the three pretty
girls in their flowered crinolines lived, but, in any case, it was
a lovingly preserved bit of Old Vienna. It stood together with
a group of other such houses on the last remaining part of the
old Vienna Bastion. I made sketches of it and of Schubert's
house in the suburbs and of his grave, next to that of Beethoven's. And with that the melancholy visit to my much-loved
Vienna came to an end.

Paris

CHAPTER XIX

END OF AN EPOCH

IT WAS ONE AUTUMN in Paris that I finally realized that I was taking Hitler and his Thousand-Year Reich too lightly. It was my intention to return to Germany, and the evening before I dined with some friends and made the acquaintance of a tall, good-looking man, a German, Count Yorck. He learned that I was going away the next day, and, no doubt to make conversation, he asked me where I was going. When I said, "Berlin," at first he laughed and thought I was joking, but when he realized that I was serious he, too, grew serious,

"You're lucky enough to be here amongst human beings," he exclaimed, "and yet you're thinking of going back to Nazis!"

Like many other people, I had not taken Hitler and his plans and, above all, his racial theories, seriously. And now, thanks to Count Yorck, my incorrigible optimism received a jolt and

I realized that it was time I did something about it. Two hours later I put through a telephone call to our house in Pieskow where my wife and daughter were living.

"I'm leaving for Holland to-morrow and I hope to meet you both there," I said laconically.

It was impossible to go into any details or offer any explanations. I just hoped that she had understood me. We had good friends who lived in Bussum near Amsterdam.

Windmills in white, green and brown. Yellow-painted swing-bridges over slow-flowing, silver-shining canals. Red and blue houses with tiled roofs and white-painted window frames. Red, yellow and purple rectangular patches of ground where millions of tulips stood upright. Heavy-beamed, rounded golden-yellow barges against a long row of cobalt blue houses. Men in long, baggy trousers, wooden clogs and flat, round hats carrying neatly arranged rows and rows of red Edam cheese on a sort of stretcher. Girls in pointed stiff lace caps and check aprons polishing brass utensils until they shone. And everywhere quaint children, plump and happy, clattering around in their clogs. And suitably fat white clouds rolling over a blue sky—how could the clouds be other than white, round and fat here?

So much for the outward appearance of Holland to the stage designer. That's the way I saw it and that's the sort of Holland I sought to create on the stage when Reinhardt produced Maeterlinck's "Blue Bird".

My wife arrived safely in Holland with my daughter, and it was time. Already, I learned, the other children and the authorities had begun to find her non-Aryan father objectionable. After carefully weighing up the pros and cons, it was decided that my wife should return to liquidate our household. In the meantime, I stayed in Holland—and painted. And there was plenty of inspiration for the artist amongst the old Dutchmen. It was then that I got the idea of a fantastic ballet based on Breughel's type of hell, but I have never been able to find a producer to do it or a backer to put up the money for it. Backers for anything but a cast-iron, guaranteed success—or what looks like it—are rarer than rubies nowadays, and for their revues and Christmas pantomimes producers use the old scenery and costumes theatre designers have made for them for quite different productions. And they pay us no more for this re-use of our work. They don't even mention our names. No one bothers to consider that our ideas are our intellectual property and ought to be protected as such. Anybody can exploit them.

Incidentally, my designs for the production of "White Horse Inn" in the United States in 1935 are at least protected. Like all other stage designers, I had to join a trade union, together with my colleagues, the paper-hangers, though how we got together I don't know. I had no objection to joining, but I refused to pay the 500-dollar entrance fee; our American backers had to pay that. Off I went to the union headquarters, which were in Forty-Second Street, to "sit" for my entrance examination. For about two hours my examiner asked me all sorts of questions, such as: Who was the composer of "Madame Butterfly"? Who was the composer of "Carmen"? What happens in "Hamlet" (and one or two other Shakespearean plays)? How do you reckon out the dimensions of a stage set? And so on. I also had to make various extempore sketches both on paper and on a blackboard. In the end the examiner came to the conclusion that "obviously" I knew my job. Having passed my entrance examination, I was then allowed into a room in which my future American colleagues were assembled; perhaps the paperhangers were there as well, I don't know. Three men sat at a table under the Stars and Stripes, and I had to raise my hand and repeat a form of words after them. Unfortunately, I have forgotten what it was, but I expect it was a solemn promise to uphold the dignity and honour of our profession, which, in any case, I have always striven to do. After that I was earnestly congratulated on having been accepted as a member and handed a certificate of membership and a small rubber stamp with which henceforth I had to stamp all my designs so that the stage hands, stage printers and so on should know that I was organized and not "black". I was also informed that in the event of my death my wife would receive a burial grant of 250 dollars from the union. If anyone dares to plagiarize my work or steal it, at least in America I can have the union on them.

My wife returned safely to Holland, after having met and overcome countless difficulties raised by the Nazi authorities. Even to-day, almost twenty years later, she still recalls that experience with discomfort. From Holland I went to Paris, where I signed a contract with the Fox Film Company to go to Hollywood. As I was due to take up my duties under the

contract only in the following February I occupied the time in
between by carrying out a project I had first formed in 1900.
I painted a series of sixty watercolours of Paris which I entitled "Dramatic Architecture". At the same time I enjoyed
my stay in Paris to the full. I lived in the old artists' quarter in
Montparnasse and took part in the local *bohème*. The hotel in
which I stayed was opposite the famous Café du Dome, and
on its terrace, completely surrounded by glass and heated by
charcoal braziers, an international crowd of artists of all sorts
congregated. It was there that I got to know Madame Zack,
a very lively little lady who ran a modern art-dealer's and
played quite a role in Paris art circles in those days. She exhibited a couple of dozen of my watercolours under the title
"*Paris vu par Stern*".

There was one thing which made me regret that I had left
the carrying out of my project so long, and that was the fact
that the human background had grown so much less picturesque with the passing of the years. The students no longer wore
beards and top-hats, artists no longer wore their hair long or
dressed so fantastically, the girls of the art quarter no longer
wore knickerbockers, and, above all, I missed the colourful
soldiers, their blue greatcoats buttoned back to reveal their
striking baggy red trousers, their shakos with the red pompoms
on top, always worn at a gay angle, and their white gloves. And
their counterpart, the *nounous*, or nursemaids, in their colourful
costumes, had disappeared from the Luxembourg and the
gardens of the Tuileries—or, at least, they no longer wore their
old costumes. With regret I recalled the old French song:

> "*Trois petits soldats en gants blancs,*
> *Se promenaient les bras ballants,*
> *Ils traverserent la Seine pour*
> *Voir le jardin du Luxembourg*
> *Ou les bonnes et les nounous*
> *Ont un faible pour les Piou-Pious!*"

When the job was finished off we went to New York. This
time my wife and daughter went with me. The Nazi nightmare
was over as far as we were concerned. All our possessions were
in Hamburg ready packed, waiting to be shipped to the United
States. With us we had three big trunks and a number of
small cases, a gramophone and two cases of my theatrical
designs. As my wife had not been allowed to take any money

out of Germany, she had bought herself practically everything the heart of a woman desires—why not? Money was no object; rather spend it on luxuries than leave it behind for the Nazis.

For five days all we had seen was water and occasionally a school of dolphins, and now the first thing that greeted us when we arrived in the New World was a vast advertisement in gigantic letters which called upon us to chew Wrigley's gum. It was my third visit to the States and I was therefore not disappointed. In any case, the disappointment does not last for long and then it is replaced by one of the grandest sights of the modern world. Gigantic buildings loom up almost as though materialized out of the clouds, and as the Babylonian pomp of Manhattan appears it is almost as though one can hear the majestic accords of Dvorak's "New World Symphony".

On the train we had our own little compartment, which was our home for three days and nights as we rolled across a continent, and every evening the Negro attendant turned it into a three-bedded sleeping-room. At the end of the train was an observation car, from which we could get magnificent views over the countryside. From time to time the train stopped at stations, or perhaps at mere places for taking in water. Soon the names I saw began to recall half-forgotten boyhood memories. One day I actually read "Arkansas" on a name board and soon afterwards I was able to assure myself that the rolling prairie really does exist and is not merely an invention of the Wild-West story writers. At dawn one morning I was looking out of the train window when I saw two mysteriously wrapped-up figures before a primitive hut from which a woman emerged with a clumsy water-container. They were "Redskins"! Redskins in person! More and more frequently now primitive settlements were visible by the side of the track, with houses made out of boards and painted in bright colours. On both sides the track was enclosed with barbed wire. Were there still really herds of buffalo, and was this the way they kept them off the line? We looked out over the endless, steppe-like landscape eagerly. Yes, there was certainly something or the other moving in the greyish yellow scrub which covered the prairie. At first we could not make out what it was, and then we could see that whatever it was it was not galloping, but rolling, and as it rolled it grew larger. It was being blown along by the wind, picked up from the ground and rolled into fluffy lumps which soon festooned the barbed wire at the side of the track. Alas, no buffaloes!

And then came the day when our train puffed steadily higher and higher up into a region of pine forests and snow. In the plain on the other side we saw our first orange groves, clumps of palm trees, cactus and other sub-tropical flora. We were in California.

The same sub-tropical growths were in the garden of our apartment house at Santa Monica, and on the other side of a boulevard lined with palms was the Pacific. For the next six months we were settled. Apart from a double bedroom and a living-room which also became a bedroom at night, our very nice little flat had two bathrooms and a kitchenette which contained just everything. I bought a second-hand Willys-Knight car for 150 dollars and engaged a young Swiss named Keller as chauffeur—he was the son of a pastor and he had run away from home to make his fortune in the New World.

The film script I was to work on was still in the formative stage, so for the moment I had nothing to do. The best motor roads in the world stretch out temptingly through what we were assured was God's own country, and therefore, of course, the best in the world, a sort of earthly paradise. We set forth in our second-hand car to make its acquaintance. The inhabitants of Los Angeles and Hollywood are not prepared to admit that there is ever bad weather in their part of the world, and if it does rain they say: "It's just mist from the Pacific." The climate of California is indefinite, a sort of midway thing between the climate of the Riviera and the northern line of the tropics, the tropic of Cancer. Palms are not indigenous growths in California, but they do quite well there. Geraniums grow into small bushes, and oranges and avocado pears hang round the doors. The indeterminate nature of California's climate is best illustrated by the behaviour of the imported Australian eucalyptus trees. They can never make up their minds exactly what season it is and they put out new green leaves when the old ones are still on the branches.

During the long motor-car trips we made almost every day, I did a great deal of sketching, and I was astonished again and again at the chaotic nature of the landscape. In parts the countryside looked as though Nature had not yet decided what it was to be, as though it were still unfinished and she was still experimenting with it.

The character of the landscape seemed to have determined to some extent the character of the architecture, and a great number of the houses were of a provisional and temporary kind, or, at least, that was the impression they made. Very often, particularly those on the coast, were just knocked together, usually made of wood—to say timber would give a too solid impression. Most of them were gaily painted and seemed to have been constructed according to no particular principle and without an over-all plan. When we commented on the flimsy character of the buildings, we were told that it was

Santa Monica

because of the possibility of earthquakes. One of these settlements, which bore some quite grandiloquent name, was a positively classic example on the part of the jerry-builder run wild. High above it towered an imposing castle—that is to say, it was imposing enough at a distance, but when you got closer it was seen to be a hollow mockery, a sort of film structure, all façade. We were told that the owner of the building land had had it erected to attract people to purchase his lots. It would have driven me out of sight.

Hollywood then was not the town it is now. For one thing, it, too, appeared provisional and unfinished. Built-up areas were followed by vacant and often hilly terrain. Only the broad, well-lighted main streets were completed. The various film stars of the day lived in houses around the town, houses of all sorts, all periods and all styles of architecture. There was timbered "Tudorbethan" or stockbroker style, crenellated mediæval castles, Moorish *alcazars*, Spanish *haciendas* and so on in an astonishing jumble. And the speed with which this type of building was carried out was equally astonishing. One day you would come across a not more than half-finished building which looked as though it would take months to complete, and a few days later you would pass by the same place and find that the building had been provided with imitation columns and decorative statues and so on and was now ready for occupation. In short, the film technique was applied to building the homes of film stars and others. Bare plots of land were turned into flowering gardens in the same short space of time, and the trees and bushes would be reflected in a newly laid out swimming pool. I witnessed such a quick-change scene at first hand.

Lubitsch had had himself a *hacienda* in the Mexican style built on a hill. All around the luxuriously appointed and picturesque building the land was bare, without even a blade of grass. Lubitsch was entertaining his guests, of whom I was one, on the terrace when, quite literally as we sat there, "Great Birnam Wood to high Dunsinane hill" came. Trees hurried along the road towards the house on lorries. The roots of each tree were still encased in enormous clumps of earth, and as we watched they were dropped into already prepared holes. Before long there were leafy trees of all sorts around, looking as though they had grown there. The rest was left to the fantastically fruitful soil of California. The *hacienda* was now in the shade of a grove of trees, whilst in the garden bushes and flowers bloomed as though they had always been there.

The Fox Film lot was in the centre of the town, situated on a group of hills and surrounded by a high wall. It was a small town on its own, even a small world. There were buildings of all kinds, offices, workshops, studios, storerooms and so on, and between them were excellent streets, squares with plots of grass and so on. A number of picturesque bungalows set in exotic gardens were at the disposal of the stars whilst they were working on a film. In addition to these more solidly built parts of the Fox Film lot there were also the fantastic and ephemeral edifices set up temporarily for the particular films which were in process of shooting. Real trees and bushes and ordinary landscape formed the background for these artificial and frequently changing constructions.

There was a certain fascination about this mixture of the real and the fake. A typical Wild West street would suddenly change into a bit of New York with half-a-dozen fake sky-scrapers. Clustered round a bridge over a dry depression, which could be filled with water at need, was a picturesque village, complete with village church. As there was no particular epoch or style in the construction we soon succeeded in transforming it into a Hungarian village for our film. On the edge of a steep declivity at the bottom of which was a great pool of water stood Chinese houses erected on piles. A formal garden with steps, balustrades and statuary belonged to an Italian *palazzo*, or rather to the façade of an Italian *palazzo*, and on the other side of it was a typical American colonial-style residence with tall narrow columns. A jungle which had been made for a film by sticking plants provisionally into the earth was now bloom-ing away on its own. When I first saw the lot a number of fine New England houses had just been completed and provided with shade from real holm trees. About a week later I saw a party of men with ladders carefully picking the leaves off these trees. The producer was now about to shoot a late-autumn scene with leafless trees and bare branches. Later on he decided to do the summer scenes and then the same men with their ladders were busily engaged in fastening foliage to the same trees. Why he didn't shoot the scenes the other way round was just one of those many small mysteries of Hollywood.

Trees, bushes and nature in general had a lot to put up with in Hollywood. I remember one take in the open with a clump of real trees in the background. On examination, the producer decided that the trees were too dark and therefore looked too close, whereupon the unfortunate trees were sprayed blue, because blue looks light in the take, and the scene was then taken again. Once again the producer was dissatisfied; this time the trees were too light, so they were sprayed again, this time with a deeper tint of blue. That was satisfactory, but it left the clump of trees blue, and as the colour could not be washed off the trees were sprayed green again.

Through one of the valleys between the hills ran a railway line complete with engines, carriages, trucks and so on. This was not for transport, but for film purposes. Over-topping the whole lot were the masts and funnels of an ocean-going liner.

Only half the ship was there, but that half was complete in every detail, with decks, portholes, derricks, lifeboats and so on. The ship was rooted solidly in concrete, but by an ingenious trick it could be made to appear in the film as though it were

Fox filmtown, Hollywood

sailing away. This ship was the one used in Noel Coward's "Cavalcade" film, which was made by Fox. The illusion of movement was obtained by moving the landing stage at the side of the ship.

"Land of unlimited possibilities"—the worn-out phrase certainly applied to the film world. For a picture with a Hungarian background, Erik Charell and I left the real Hungary thousands of miles behind us to fake up the land of *paprika* and Tokay on the coasts of the Pacific Ocean. The film was "Caravan", and the hero, played by Charles Boyer, was a gipsy fiddler who travelled around in his caravan. His gipsy companions were brown-skinned, dark-haired Mexicans. The gipsy wagons were the typical American "covered wagons" camouflaged. The only thing which really was Hungarian in the whole film was the gipsy orchestra, and that happened to be on tour in the States, and we brought it to Hollywood for the film. An important role was played in the film by the vineyards and the picking of the berries, so for these scenes we faked a vineyard on the side of the hill with the tall vine-poles in use in Hungary, and on the vines hung real bunches of grapes which came to us in masses from the southern states.

When I came to have the costumes for the Hungarian characters made up according to my designs, I found to my great satisfaction that there were plenty of authentic materials available—the businesslike Hollywood costume firms had taken advantage of the collapse of the Austro-Hungarian monarchy and the subsequent inflation to buy up masses of material and costumes. There were magnificent examples amongst the selection and innumerable real peasant garments and real uniforms. I was able to equip a whole troop of Hungarian hussars correctly down to the last detail.

An upright old gentleman in whom you could see the ex-officer a long way off came to us to offer his services. He had been a cavalry staff officer in the Austro-Hungarian Army, and he was anxious to make our hussars drill correctly. However, I had to reject the services of Captain von So-and-So as unnecessary in "Caravan", as also the services of a specialist in medals and orders who presented himself, another von, a big fat man with a monocle and a German naval officer's peaked cap. They were typical examples of the human wreckage flung up on the shores of the Pacific in Hollywood by the war, revolution, and the collapse of a social world. This was particularly true of the Bolshevist Revolution, which had emptied masses of Russians into Hollywood. There was one group which hung together and claimed to be of the Petersburg *haute volée*. Others went around in magnificent Russian beards and were only too anxious to point out that real beards were much better than false ones, which was perfectly true. And, of course, there were the women who claimed to have been ladies-in-waiting to the Tsarina. Perhaps some of them were, but if they all were then the Tsarina must have been liberally supplied. Many of them certainly came from the highest circles of the Russian aristocracy. They all spoke French perfectly and they proved of great assistance to us in the French version of "Caravan", which was also made by Fox in Hollywood.

The film itself was the usual romantic tripe: the rich young and beautiful heiress to land, palace and a fortune falls in love with the handsome and attractive young gipsy—Charles Boyer—whose charms are reinforced by his playing of the fiddle. His romantic way of life almost persuades the heiress to run away with him, but she is saved in the end by the re-appearance of the young hussar officer, whom, she discovers, she loves after all. And with one wet and one dry eye, as the Germans say, she lets the gipsy go on his way. The film was lively and well made, with much humour and some fine music, but it wasn't very successful.

By the time we left California six months later, our daughter spoke excellent English and was in a position to hold long and obviously interesting conversations with the other children on the deck—thirteen is a good age to learn a language. The ship on which we left was the S.S. *President Pierce* and put out from San Diego. We motored there, using our faithful old Willys-Knight car for the last time, after which we gave it to our Swiss chauffeur Keller together with our Scotty "Kockleburr", known for short as "Cocky".

Like most things in California and filmland, our departure was not normal. The first thing we noticed was that the dock-side was alive with armed guards keeping a very close eye on the dockers doing the loading, which seemed to be proceeding at an unusual speed. It consisted of crates of tomatoes, and the loading was so hurried that many of the crates fell into the hold and burst. No one seemed to be much disturbed by that, and all they seemed to want was to get those tomatoes on board as quickly as possible without bothering too much about the condition in which they arrived. There was a general air of nervousness, and the presence of so many armed men greatly heightened it. At last all the tomatoes were in the hold, and then came some smaller cases, very solid and obviously very heavy. The loading of these cases was supervised with particular care. Up they went in the nets, swung round and rapidly followed the tomatoes into the hold. Passengers and crew stood along the side of the ship and watched the proceedings silently. At last all the cases were on board too and then the armed men pressed the dockers away from the ship and off the quayside altogether.

The *President Pierce* was the last ship the dockers loaded before joining the general strike which closed all the Pacific ports. The contents of the heavy boxes which had followed the tomatoes consisted of silver ingots—hence the general nervous-ness.

We steamed south along the Mexican coast. Blue-black clouds hung threateningly over the chain of rugged, many-toothed red and violet mountains on the horizon. Swarms of flying fish leapt up around the ship. It had become oppressively hot. The following morning the sea was covered with yellow and green snakes curled round and round and floating along. Then we passed a number of islands with emerald green tropical vegetation. We were in the equatorial zone. Along a channel cut through solid rock, past half-swamped forests, and with low-lying clouds which seemed only just above our heads, we steamed through the Panama Canal lock by lock until we were finally lowered to Atlantic level on the other side. I am afraid I broke all sorts of regulations on the way, for I sketched furiously and took many photos.

In Cristobal we were able to go ashore for a few hours and stroll under coconut palms and through arcades of Indian and Chinese shops. And everywhere there were Negroes in all shades from black to coffee-brown, a vast number of whom were joyfully chattering as they loaded still more goods on board the *President Pierce*. The voyage to Havana was terribly hot, but at least I was rewarded when we got there by finding that a part of the town was still old Spanish in style. At last, after fourteen days' voyage, we landed once again in New York.

CHAPTER XX

LONDON

DURING THE WINTER, which we spent in Paris, I did the designs for a musical entitled "Mandrin", which dealt with the adventures of a gay and amatory robber chief in the days of Louis Quinze. In the spring the long-awaited telegram arrived from London—and a new life opened up for me.

I sat in Hyde Park, watched the sheep grazing and admired the magnificent trees with their thick foliage—and the Continent seemed much farther away than just those few miles across the Channel. I had a studio at my disposal in the old Alhambra —what a pity it no longer exists!—and there I worked busily on the designs for "The Flying Trapeze", a circus show complete with arena, auditorium and orchestra. In my old sketch-books I find circus motifs again and again; it is a world which has always interested me. I remember in particular a clown who was the darling of us youngsters in Bucharest. He was an Englishman named Harrison, and he spoke Roumanian with a comic accent which we all tried to imitate. He always wore a white costume covered with hearts, diamonds, spades and clubs. He died in this costume, sacrificing his life trying to save the circus horses from a fire which had broken out. I had sketches of him, but I couldn't bring myself to use his pathetic costume for one of our Alhambra clowns. And there were acrobatic riders of both sexes, clowns of all kinds, high-trapeze men and women in inimitably affected poses—and magnificent horses galloping around with their tossing plumes!

I remember one summer night at the Lido near Venice. Suddenly over the black silhouettes of the trees as I walked appeared a sort of glowing pink pyramid against the deep blue of the night sky. As I came closer I realized that it was "the big top" illuminated from within. That was now down in my sketch-book too. And then there were memories of my good friend Susanne. I have already mentioned that to eke out her existence as an artist she sometimes went off with touring circus companies. Whilst I was still a student in Munich, I got a letter from her from the Bavarian town of Landsberg where she was appearing in "Rio Muni's Circus." I went to Landsberg to see her and I found her, together with a number of other women, doing the cooking in the open.

It was a colourful gipsy encampment with washing and tights hung up to dry all around and horses grazing here and there and wandering about at will. The background was a line of primitively painted and over-decorated caravans in blue, green, gold and heaven knows what other colours. Circus folk have a knack all their own of making a decorative whole of gilt mermaid figures, fantastically formed vases with flowers, garlands and all sorts of strange and wonderful birds and animals and all the colours of the rainbow. The outside of the circus tent was decorated with highly-coloured and daring figures, and there were so many figures painted over the ornate red plush curtains which flanked the entrance that the spirit wilted at the idea of counting them. There was a Sultan on horseback surrounded by a horde of Janissaries; at his feet knelt another horde of highly decorative ladies with voluptuous proportions and very little clothing, but to make up for it a mass of chains, jewels, hangings and ornaments of all sorts. They no doubt represented the female booty of his latest expedition. This, according to the inscription, was "Kara Mustapha the Invincible". And underneath in gigantic letters was "Rio Muni's World Famous Oriental Wonder Show!" Susanne danced in the show in a turban and baggy trousers loaded with "jewels". I sketched it all at the time and there it was in my sketch-books and very, very useful to me now in my work on "The Flying Trapeze". The horses' heads in gold medallions, the mermaids with balloon-like bosoms, long yellow hair and golden tails, and all the rest of the primitive-naïve decorations were ideal for our circus on the stage and heart-warmingly authentic.

In front, adjoining the arena, I erected the box of the Empress Eugénie, the wife of Napoleon III—the piece concerned the adventure of a trapeze artist (Jack Buchanan) with one of Eugénie's ladies in waiting. The "plot" was helped out by the usual circus clowning, dancing, Chinese jugglers, Neapolitan brigands, feathered blackamoors and—in memory of Susanne—a beauty in a turban and baggy trousers hung with jewels.

I have always been fond of circuses and fairs, and when I am in London I never miss a Bank Holiday at Happy Hampstead. Unfortunately, the quaint and lovable atmosphere of the old circus and fair has almost disappeared. The old-time decorated wagons are now utilitarian motor caravans, and I usually have to be content with sketching the still gaily-painted wooden horses of the roundabouts or the façade of some wandering menagerie. Times change and the old gives place to the new. I suppose that is inevitable, but it's a pity the new is so depressingly sordid and banal.

"The Flying Trapeze" was also to be produced in France, but the French demanded a thorough overhauling of the whole thing. "*Tout cela est bien lourd*", they objected. It is the usual French criticism of everything not originally produced in the City of Light—including the works of Shakespeare. I went off to Paris ahead of my family to find somewhere for us to stay whilst we were preparing the production of "*Le trapeze volant*", and my daughter began to study French industriously. But the French were beginning to be upset about the political situation: Hitler and Mussolini were getting on their nerves. They were unwilling to commit themselves, and in the end the project came to nothing and I returned to London, where the whole atmosphere was much more calm and peaceful. How wonderfully safe you felt on the right side of the Channel! I shed no tears over "*Le trapeze volant*" and continued to sit in Hyde Park and watch the sheep peacefully grazing. I always had my sketch-book with me, and I sketched the sylvan scene, the swans on the Serpentine and one or two of the older houses in Park Lane with their bay-windowed fronts. Spouters' Corner also attracted me, and in my sketch-book is many a gesticulating orator engaged on his endless task of putting the world to rights.

I had no very definite plans, but I was anxious to settle in England, because my profession demanded that I should have a permanent domicile. Thanks to my good London theatrical friends, we obtained an indefinite extension of our permission to stay. Although we had arrived with German passports, we were not refugees in the ordinary sense. Incidentally, since 1925 I was no longer a Roumanian subject; I had taken out naturalization papers under the Weimar Republic. Whilst we were in London, however, our passports became invalid, because the Nazis revoked all naturalization orders made before their accession to power.

Once settled in London, the contracts began to come in. In 1929, at the instance of C. B. Cochran, I designed the Vienna Café with all its types from the 'eighties for Noel Coward's "Bitter-Sweet". When I came to do the same thing again for a revival in 1949, with the old-type Austrian officers and the ladies of the period with their saucy bustles, I discovered that the delightful musical had not aged. I had been in London again in 1930 to do the designing for "The Song of the Drum" at Drury Lane. The scene was India, but I was informed that "for political reasons" it was to be called Huzbaria and that

"The Song of the Drum"

I could invent my own Orient. I did, and it was a mixture of Persian and Arabian and "The Thousand and One Nights". I built up my models in a spacious dressing-room next to the stage: "Blue Bazaar", "The House with the Red Door" and the palace of "The Ilkhani of Kahlek" with its cupolas.

The atmosphere of the old theatre still exercised all its fascination. Even the façade had remained more or less unchanged. The old antique niches are still on either side of the entrance, the columns supporting the portico still bear traces of the same blue oil paint, and as often as I pass I still observe with satisfaction that the old lamps are there, supported on their ironwork arms decorated with wrought flourishes. There were many things I wanted to sketch, and in particular the church by Inigo Jones in Covent Garden, but I had very little

time then, and, in particular, it was November and there was
a good deal of fog, which made it difficult to see.

My friend and fellow scenic-designer, the late Aubrey
Hammond, used to meet me every evening in Drury Lane,
and then we would go off to dinner together, popping in on the
way to various pubs, for Aubrey was a great one for a drink.
He knew me to be an admirer of Dickens and invariably it
would be: "Now, this is a little place Dickens used to go
to. . . ." Dickens may well have dined at Rules in Maiden
Lane, but I doubt if he visited all the pubs I went into with
Aubrey.

My work on "The Song of the Drum" came to an end; the
first night took place; the reviews were published.

"As for the sheer gorgeousness of the Ilkhani's palace and all
its incidental pageantry, these are things quite beyond my
powers of description." So wrote one enthusiastic reviewer. In
the best case with a friendly observation of that sort, our work
is consigned into limbo. After the full-dress rehearsal the work
of the scenic artist is done and he can go back to his private
life. I always think of Schiller's lines in "Fiesko": "The Moor
has done his duty; the Moor can go."

I believe there are many people who love "first nights", but
for me they are always disagreeable. The thing that only a rela-
tively few people in a small circle have seen is now exposed to
the critical gaze of many. And I am sitting there amongst the
audience on the first night discovering with dismay all sorts of
sins of omission. Or I sit there grinding my teeth as some false
lighting or the other ruins my most carefully planned effects.
It has happened on more than one occasion that I could stand
it no longer and have fled from the auditorium, convinced that
I have just witnessed that tragedy of theatre tragedies, the
flop. But when I succeed in holding out to the end there is the
victory celebration, the champagne dinner in a more or less
extended society consisting largely of people I have never seen
in my life before. And then I sit and hear their comments.
"Quite nice", says someone, and he is referring to something
I have almost sweated blood over. Or maybe the comment is:
"Very clever, I must say." Why must you say? I think. It's
a pity. Or the lady at my side asks disdainfully: "Did you really
like Miss X's green dress?" and turns up her pretty nose. And
that green dress was probably one of my best ideas. "Pretty,"
admits another one, "but odd; distinctly odd," and then she

holds you spellbound with the description of her daughter's talent. The girl it appears, designs masterpieces of the scenic art for her school theatrical performances. Or the influential critic demonstrates clearly by what he is saying that he really hasn't a clue as to the respective shares of the producer and the scenic artist in the show.

A letter arrived one morning from Basil Dean inviting me to come to the Ealing Film Studios to discuss a proposed Mozart film to be entitled "Whom the Gods Love . . ." Prague, Vienna and Salzburg in the rococo period. Scenes from "The Marriage of Figaro" and "The Magic Flute"—theatre in film! It was at about this time, I think, that my diary contains an entry: "If one could only get out of this world without dying first!" Here was my opportunity. Here was an opportunity to forget persecution, hatred and poison in a dream world of the past, a world which I could create myself. The scenic artist doesn't have to sell his soul to the devil like Faust in order—shall we say?—to see Helena in the flesh before his eyes. All he has to do is to take a piece of the best cartridge paper, sketch the lady as he imagines her, colour the result, and soon the lady will live, breathe and move in the flesh before him, speak, sing, laugh, cry, dance and play the spinet.

I was used to that, of course, but in the film the artist experiences the Pygmalion miracle rather differently. On the stage he sees her, so to speak, two-dimensionally, in relief against a background. In the film she is not merely against a background, but in space, in a new world, and she appears more plastic and three dimensional.

"Whom the Gods Love . . ." dealt with the life of Mozart in short episodes from his childhood until his early death. In one scene he was depicted as a child together with Marie Antionette, who was the same age, in the presence of the Empress Maria Theresa. Another scene showed him at the clavichord leading an orchestra. For the operas I build up not only the stage with the proscenium arch and the curtain, but also the theatre auditorium with its boxes. My inspiration was the wonderfully preserved auditorium of the Munich Residence Theatre—since destroyed, thanks to the Führer. It was a splendid example of a court theatre and I heard Mozart's operas in it for the first time in my life. Italian decorators of the eighteenth century did its walls and ceilings beautifully with *scherzi e divertimenti*. The auditorium was decorated with scrolls and flourishes and a great variety of delightful fauna. Garlands of roses with flying ribbons wound round slim and gilded pillars and balustrades. Over the boxes tumbled droll and charming cupids. And the sprites who hovered on the ceiling in flying garments looked to the audience below like a graceful acrobatic ballet in the air. The whole was music translated into the plastic arts. Unfortunately I had to go carefully with such precious—and costly—decorations in my film theatre. I had to be content with the *scherzi e divertimenti* principle for "The Magic Flute" alone.

The plot of "The Magic Flute" is naïve. The two lovers, Pamino (with the flute) and Tamina, are subjected to all sorts of trials and tribulations, but in the end, of course, they are united. The Queen of the Night, the coloratura singer, represents the principle of Evil. The High Priest Sarastro, the bass, represents the principle of Good. But the most popular figure in the opera is easily Papageno, the bird-catcher, in his feather-bedecked costume. In the end, to the satisfaction of all, he is provided with a Papagena.

Obviously, the subject-matter calls for anachronistic and fantastic caprioles. The style of Louis Quinze has to be Egyptianized and the Egyptian style has to be given a baroque air. I went to the British Museum in search of inspiration. There were Egyptian art exhibits in plenty and the most delicate and graceful *objets d'art* of the Louis Quinze period.

It was at this time that our furniture, pictures and books arrived and were kept in storage for the time being by Whiteley's. On one occasion when I was having some of the cases opened an English book came into my hands. "Facetiæ, being a general collection of the *jeu d'esprits* which have been illustrated by Robert Cruikshank", London, 1831. I picked it up on a bookstall in the harbour of Naples on account of the Cruikshank illustrations, of which I already possessed a goodly collection. As a former caricaturist, I regarded him as a colleague and I eagerly collected new examples of his work as they came my way. The same was true of the often-shameless Gillray, and the fact that he had spent some part of his early life wandering around with a troop of strolling players increased my interest in him. And, of course, and above all there was Hogarth. Better judges than I have dealt with the work of this great English master, and I will confine myself here to his work from my own standpoint as a stage-designer. Both from the point of view of scenery and costumes he has given us invaluable descriptions of eighteenth-century England.

It so happened that in Cochran's production, "Follow the Sun", for which I had been engaged, there was a scene entitled "Sleigh Bells" which was supposed to be in 1830, i.e. in the time of Cruikshank. And another scene was called after Hogarth's engraving, "Strolling Actresses dressing in a Barn", a work of real genius. I found it a fascinating task to translate this two-dimensional picture as Hogarth has left it to us into plastic perspective, to make it live. There is a sort of balcony filled with theatrical odds and ends. In one's interest to make out just what they are one is almost tempted to apostrophize Hogarth's ladies: "Do please step aside a moment, my dear, and let me see those things behind you." Hogarth's inventive genius was great, I know, but at the same time I am sure he actually saw that scene with all its variety of odds and ends.

As "Actresses dressing in a Barn" is an engraving and therefore in light and shade only, the scene had to be coloured. I had the costumes made of white linen and then sprayed in various shades of brown. The fully-dressed persons of the original engraving and the various props had to be carefully fitted into the scene. A number of supports invisible to the audience assisted them to maintain their characteristic poses. And when they were all assembled in the picture and properly clothed, I took brown colour and a brush and with a few strokes here and there I heightened the effect by stressing the shadows. Hogarth himself in a fur cap and a long coat appeared in person, carrying palette and brushes, to look at his gold-framed picture.

"Sleigh Bells" was the winter finale of the revue. There was snow not only on the Achilles statue at Hyde Park Corner and over old Regent Street with the quadrant, but Cruikshank's ladies and gentlemen were also snowy; white layers of snow lay on their hats and on their shoulders like collars of ermine.

"Follow the Sun" was to appear at Christmas, and Cochran accepted a suggestion of mine for a suitable Christmas scene. There is a charming, childlike and almost naïve poem of Heine about the three Kings. Everyone they meet they ask the way to Bethlehem, and no one can tell them until at last a golden star appears in the sky and guides them, stopping finally over the house of Joseph:

"The star did stop over Joseph's house,
And the three Kings went within.
The ox did low and the babe did cry,
And the three Kings raised their heads to sing."

That was the end of the poem. I remembered it well from my Munich days. I had heard it sung one Christmas in a cabaret by a male trio to a delightful tune. Fortunately, I was able to get hold of the original music for the song, which was then sung in a scene which I had designed like an old illuminated missal against a gold background.

When I returned from the first performance of the revue— it was in Manchester Opera House—it was Christmas Eve. In the train on the way back to London it was snowing and the landscape was white. Looking through my Cruikshank again, I found the inscription in my handwriting, "Christmas 1913, Naples".

CHAPTER XXI

THE THEATRE UP TO THE WAR

MY FIRST ACQUAINTANCE with "The Boy David" was when Sir James Barrie read it to Cochran and me, sitting beside the great fireplace, in which a huge log was burning, in his study on the top floor of one of the old Adams houses in Adelphi Terrace. From the corner windows there was a magnificent view over the Thames from the Houses of Parliament to London Bridge.

"The Boy David" has been described by the critics as Barrie's Biblical "Peter Pan". I am not a dramatic critic, and I can only say that the poetry of the play impressed me deeply and that I found the Biblical period as Barrie presented it enthralling. I was doing the costumes for the play and not the décor, which was in the hands of Augustus John. Previously I had always refused such a division of labour; not from sheer vanity or ambition, but because I was convinced—and still am—that in such cases the proverb, "Too many cooks spoil the broth", usually holds good. In this case the personality of Augustus John made things rather different. I found him a true artist and moved only by his devotion to his profession.

In his studio in Chelsea he showed me a whole series of Biblical landscapes. He was keenly interested in his new task, but, of course, technically he was a complete tiro where the theatre was concerned, and he was intelligent enough to recognize it frankly and to welcome the assistance and advice of an old hand. Given such an attitude, co-operation becomes an easy matter. John occupied himself with the scenic landscape and left the interiors, Saul's tent, the visions, the props and so on to me.

After long preparations and much hard work, everything was ready for the first night of "The Boy David" in Edinburgh, when Elizabeth Bergner, who was to play the title role, fell ill, and the first performance had to be postponed for several months. Such a postponement, shortly before the first night, when all the actors have lived themselves into their roles and are ready to begin, is much feared by all theatrical people. Everyone is keyed up to concert pitch and then the expected relief is snatched away. It is an anti-climax which can have seriour results. When the performance is finally fixed all the work

has to be done over again. One might think that at least the
scenic artist and costume-designer have no such troubles, but
that is not so. The one or the other, or both, suddenly discovers
that what was thought to be an appropriate solution of this or
that problem a month or two before now appears to require
revision, alteration or even replacement altogether.

When the Edinburgh first night at last took place and the
play was then transferred to His Majesty's the chopping and
changing began in earnest. Some scenes were cut out, new
scenes were introduced. In particular, the role of Goliath was
cut out altogether, because, despite all our arts and tricks, it
proved impossible to make the giant convincing on the stage.
However, nothing could save the play, and "The Boy David"
was withdrawn after a very short run.

There was one minor frustration for me in the staging. The
blowing of the ancient horn summoning the Hebrews to battle
seemed a matter of importance to me, and I proposed to represent it in the traditional fashion with the ancient ram's horn,
known to the Jews as the *Shofar*, an instrument which has a

"The Shofar"

short conical bore of very large calibre and a very limited
scale of notes. Such *Shofars* are still blown to-day in the synagogues on the anniversary of the day Joshua brought down
the walls of Jericho, and as a boy I had often witnessed this
ceremonial blowing of the *Shofar*. A ministrant would appear
dressed in a white prayer mantle with black stripes. He was
completely covered, even to his hands, and where his face

would have been was a black space. This ghostly figure would then produce long, wailing notes interspersed with short, almost grunting noises from his strange instrument. The sounds are nothing like ordinary trumpet signals; they are eerie, primitive hootings, and that was exactly what I wanted for "The Boy David". After trying in vain to borrow a *Shofar* from the synagogues, I finally succeeded, to my great delight, in buying a real one for the modest sum of 15*s*. in Petticoat Lane. But my delight was short-lived—I was unable to find anyone able to blow it, and so, to my deep regret, the project had to be abandoned.

At last, after long delays, "White Horse Inn" was to be produced in New York. My wife and daughter looked forward to the visit, and I welcomed the opportunity of tackling the artistic problems of skyscrapers once more. Europe began to fade into the background a little for us, though, of course, we were not entirely ignorant of the fact that trouble was brewing between Italy and Abyssinia at the time; something about a disputed watercourse. It all seemed unimportant. But war came, and then one day I read in the "Telegraph" that Mussolini had proclaimed the King of Italy Emperor of Abyssinia.

Shortly after that the telephone rang. I found it difficult to understand what was wanted, but I caught the word "Abyssinia". "Yes, yes," I said. "I know all about it; I've just read it in the newspapers," and with that I hung up. I was busy. But a few minutes later the telephone rang again and the same voice began to talk about Abyssinia, or so it seemed to me—until I realized that I was being asked to design an Abyssinian scene to be inserted in "Black Birds", the all-Negro revue which was playing so successfully in London at the time.

There was also another commission I undertook in the few weeks before the S.S. *Paris* left to take us to New York. Gordon Selfridge asked me to call on him to discuss the decoration of the façade of his famous department stores for the coronation of King Edward VIII. He was anxious to have the building completely covered with rich and colourful décor, and pictures in relief of important historical events were to stand between the pilasters. Above the main entrance was to be a group showing Britannia with all her Colonial and Dominion children gathered around her. The whole was to be crowned by a gigantic representation of St. George slaying the dragon, which was to stand on top of the building. In other words, it was theatrical décor on the grand scale. Gordon Selfridge and I came to an agreement, the contract was signed and I set to work on the designs at once. I was to be away three months, and in the meantime my project was to be carried out in detail by the draughtsmen.

Whilst I was in New York I received an intimation that Edward VIII approved of my designs, but that instead of St. George and the dragon on the roof he wanted to have a symbolic figure of "Peace". Returning to London, I got on with the work at once. I had three draughtsmen to carry out my decorative ideas, and my compositions for the historical scenes were handed over for execution to various sculptors. I would have liked to present the "Britannia" group as Britannia holding the door open for refugees from oppression, but it had to be the old symbolism of Britannia and her Colonies and Dominions.

In December 1936, when we were already far enough advanced to try out the velvet and gold hangings, came the bombshell of the Abdication. One of our artists observed regretfully that if Edward had realized all the trouble we had put ourselves to he would have thought twice about it, but we all brightened up at the thought that there would have to be a coronation after all. And so it proved; the same designs served equally well, with minor alterations, for the Coronation of George VI. A new medallion showing the ruling pair, and rather more use of the Scottish thistle as a motif, and everything was in order.

We lived in Stratford Court in Oxford Street, and from our windows I could observe the work which went on to hoist the great figure of "Peace" on to the roof of Selfridges in sections and set her up there. On May 10th, 1937, two days before the Coronation, "Peace" was in her proper place illuminated by floodlighting. I am not being wise after the event, but I didn't like the lady; something seemed to warn me that she was a fraud.

From all I have written about my work as a scenic artist and costume-designer for the theatre the reader might think that I had been entirely devoted to it. It certainly took up most of my time, but I find a note in my diary, written after a visit to August John's studio, which indicates my real feelings:

"How I envy him as he stands there in front of his easel with palate and brushes. It is painful to be regarded as a sort of outsider when one is really heart and soul in it."

No, my heart was not exclusively in the theatre and I did not

I

regard my scenery and costume designing as the be-all and end-all of my existence. I envied my colleagues of the palette and the easel. They practised the art for which I had been trained. Many of my old Academy friends are now amongst the recognized few who play an important role in the world of art and whose pictures, hanging in galleries and famous collections, are regarded as of significance for the technique of art. I may be wrong, but when I used to meet them after I had taken up my theatrical work I could not avoid the feeling that they regarded me in some way as a deserter. To some extent I even regarded myself in that light.

In my last years at the Academy I had good reason to look forward to my future career as an artist with some confidence. I had won the prize for a Christmas competition with the theme "Struggle". The artists who entered for it had to submit some picture or composition which expressed the idea of struggle. I put my name down for the competition and I gave a great deal of thought to the thing, but something in me revolted at the ordinary banalities: wrestlers, warriors and so on. For all my cogitation, I came to no satisfactory result and I was on the point of withdrawing my name when chance came to my aid—as it has done so often in my life.

A colleague was paying me a visit in my studio when the bell rang. A young girl was at the door. Nervously, shyly and obviously in some embarrassment, she asked me if I wanted a model. I did and I engaged her to pose for me there and then. After a while she emerged from behind the screen towards the light, anxiously holding on to her last vestige of clothing, her shift, and obviously inwardly struggling before she could abandon the last stitch and expose herself in all her nakedness. Seeing the poor girl's struggle, I had my subject for the competition in a flash and the composition as well. All I had to do was to paint the scene just as it presented itself before me. There sat my friend on a divan carelessly smoking a cigarette and quite indifferent to the girl who stood before him, grasping her chemise around her and fearing to take the plunge. The empty canvas for my entry was already standing on the easel, and had been for some days, warning me to start work. I began at once and worked swiftly, because there were only two days left.

The next afternoon my friend and I carried the finished picture to the selection committee. In my haste to get it finished, I had ignored details and done the work with broad, rapid brush strokes: there was the beginner, her fear of the altogether clearly depicted, and there was the artist, my friend, sitting casually on the divan smoking a cigarette and waiting for the upshot of her inner struggle. I think it was the rapid technical

"Struggle," for which I got the prize

performance which helped me to the prize quite as much as the psychological strength of the subject itself.

My picture "Struggle" brought me in more than the prize. The Munich "Sezession", the association of modern painters, invited me to exhibit my picture in their gallery and to become a member of the group. It is easy enough to imagine the feelings of a young beginner who is invited to join the acknowledged masters of his profession and see his picture exhibited together with theirs. I continued my painting with tremendous enthusiasm. Commissions began to come in from art dealers and others, and I even had the satisfaction of seeing my picture, "the girl in the chemise", widely copied. And the art critics were benevolent and prophesied a favourable future. "The unfermented juice is excellent", wrote one of them; "let us look forward to the wine." But although I was beginning to sell, cartooning brought in more, and then came the offer to go to

Berlin, and the income attached to it was too tempting because it enabled me to get married. And after that came Reinhardt and the theatre.

For long periods my conscience lay quiescent, and in the moments when it troubled me I began to sketch—my consolation. And when, years later, I made the acquaintance of the English countryside a passion for watercolours arose. On a coach journey from Bournemouth to Swanage I fell so much in love with the delightful scenery of Dorset that I left the coach at a small hotel which was beautifully situated, and there I took rooms for us. There were in a cottage, which was not part of the hotel proper, but a sort of annexe at a distance from the hotel, to which we went—up a hill and through a copse of fir trees—to take our meals. From the hill one could see the Channel, with the Isle of Wight like a golden cloud in the distance. To the north the lonely heath landscape extended to the bay of Poole, and to the south, by the old village of Studland, steep and fantastic rocky cliffs reared out of the sea.

My motifs began right at the door of our cottage. Behind high hedges was a picturesque and somewhat dilapidated farmhouse and at the end of a deep, overgrown cutting were the colourful ruins of a brick kiln. Beyond that the hills rose higher and higher and on them cropped a few peaceful old horses and sheep. Rather farther away began the brown, grey and green of the treeless heath. The chief feature of the landscape was the Agle Stone, an enormous deep-red stone in the form of a mushroom, which looked as though it were of Druid origin. Under the small clouds which constantly crossed the sky some parts of the heath, almost as lonely and mysterious as though it were on another planet, were in shadow whilst others gleamed colourfully.

The rolling dunes along the shore with their pale green grass and their yellow sands were in strong contrast to this landscape, and they ended in a sudden steep drop down to the broad sands proper, on which the frothy breakers fell ceaselessly. Beyond the dunes and the shallow arc of sands, a high ridge of rocks thrust itself forward into the sea, and then came higher country with great cliffs and a sheer drop to the sea.

It was an exceptionally lovely summer and in the rich soil of this much-blessed isle everything grew luxuriantly. I could stand and watch the exquisite perfection of a single bush or a single branch, each leaf as though carefully and perfectly carved. And then the magnificent trees! English people are used to them, but to visitors from the Continent their glory is a never-ending source of wonder. Artists above all immediately notice the difference between England and continental Europe, because it is their business to represent what they see—just how they do it is their business. They immediately notice the intense green of the grazing land, for example, and of the grass in general, and for them the enclosing hedges gives the landscape something finished, something definitive. These hedges with their numerous gates and stiles are something typically English, and so is the architecture of the cottages and farm-houses.

Their ground plan is obviously determined by the position of their hearths. In continental Europe the chimney is almost invariably in the centre of the roof; in the English countryside the chimneys usually rise at one end of the roof, at the narrower end of the building, and they are often exceptionally tall. The innumerable thatched roofs which still exist in the English countryside, with eaves rising in a graceful curve over the upper windows, fill the stranger with particular delight. And so it is with innumerable other things, many of them of quite a minor character, which are typically English. For instance, the construction of the very fences is different, and the tools of the men who build. The English hayricks pleased me in particular. There are hayricks on the Continent, too, of course, but not in this typical form, and it is not customary to cut lumps out of them as though out of a piece of cake, as it is here.

One of the cliffs I have mentioned is called "Old Harry", and it is rumoured to have been struck out of the Devil's hand just when he was going to hurl it to destroy Salisbury Cathedral —those were in the happy days when the villain always got the worst of it. One morning I was seated in full sunshine 40 feet over the sea and painting a marvellous scene, and yet somehow I was uncomfortable and couldn't tell why. The feeling that someone was behind me was so strong that involuntarily I turned my head from time to time. I couldn't make it out, and I wasn't sorry when the time came to pack up my things and tramp back to the hotel. I happened to mention the strange feeling I had experienced, and I described where I had been sitting. The reply came pat:

"That's not surprising; you were sitting at Suicide's Corner."

For two and a half months we stayed at Studland Bay and I sketched and painted everything that attracted me: the old

Norman church and thatched cottages of Studland, grave-
yards, the manor house, gorges, caves, mist rolling up over the
downs from the sea, the waste of hilly bramble country in the
west, grazing cattle, sheep and pigs and even pigsties—and the
ruins of Corfe Castle. A year after the war I returned there.
There was no war damage, but the lovely beach was cut off
by long lines of rusty barbed wire and the W.O. was still
engaged in exploding the mines which had been laid there.
Where gaily-coloured bathing huts had been were now grey-
green gun emplacements—I sketched them too.

After the welcome Dorset pause came a period of intense
theatrical activity in London. The late George Black often
called me in to assist him in the carrying out of his many ideas.
He was a real theatre man, and he knew that the audiences of
the Palladium and the Hippodrome did not merely want to
laugh and that they gladly welcomed really artistic presentations.

Cochran proposed to stage Franz Lehar's "Paganini" at the
Lyceum and he called me in for the costumes and décor. The
main roles of this musical are those of Napoleon's sister,
Elizabeth Bachiocci, Duchess of Lucca and Piombina, and the
reputedly diabolical violinist, Paganini. The scenes are an inn
in an Italian landscape, a smugglers' cave and various rooms
and halls in the ducal palace. In order to enhance the picturesque effect of the opening scene, already romantically
decorative, I imagined the inn built into the ruins of an old
Roman building with ivy-clad columns, such as I had often
seen in Italy. The smugglers scene was played in a large room
with a vaulted roof, a sort of huge cellar with secret passages
and concealed openings, spiral staircases, and so on. Elizabeth,
the Duchess, lived, received her guests and sang in a palace
done throughout in the most ornate Empire style, a period in
which it was fashionable to flirt with the heroic motifs of Greek
and Roman antiquity. Slim white columns gave support to
richly coffered ceilings and from light blue walls winged genii
stood out in relief. The light-coloured hangings and curtains
were decorated with gold and silver embroidery in the pattern
of stars, flourishes and running scrollwork. The stiff gold and
white furniture demanded statuesque attitudes from those who
used it and the Récamier couches called for classic poses.

The Empire style offers the scenic artist and designer rich
possibilities precisely because it is a style which is in itself all
theatre. To believe the drawings and representation of the day,

all men and women were slim and elegant. The women in particular clothed themselves in semi-transparent draperies and consciously struck antique poses. The fashion journals of the day, "*Le bon Genre*" in Paris and "The Repository" in London, show us slim and graceful creatures revealing almost more of their charms than their draperies conceal. How the poor ladies without such obvious physical charms got on in those days it is difficult to guess. But I hadn't to bother about that, because a careful choice of our actresses allowed me to realize the characteristic features of the costumes of the day with all their exaggerations, and Evelyn Laye as the Duchess was a delight to the eye. Incidentally, it was not the first time I had used the Empire style of costume, for I had been responsible for the costumes of the well-known film, "The Congress Dances". It was quite certain that Lyceum audiences had something beautiful to look at and to hear, but despite the brilliance of the producer, Tyrone Guthrie, "Paganini" was not very good box-office.

I think the reason lay in the story itself. Paganini, as contemporary drawings depict him, was a grotesque even fantastic figure, long-legged and painfully thin, a real caricature piece. He was supposed to have sold his soul to the Devil in return for his magic playing of the violin. Thus Paganini was a violinist and not a singer. Tauber played the title role. He sang, of course, wonderfully as usual, but there was nothing remotely diabolical about his plump figure, and Paganini's magic was supposed to reside in his violin, not in his voice. The basic idea of the piece was impossible, and there was little to be done about it.

I already knew Tauber from Berlin. He had sung the leading role in Lehar's other and much more successful musical, "The Land of Smiles", originally called "Spring in Manchuria", for which I had designed the costumes and the Chinese décor. The last time I saw him before he died was in connection with the production of the old Austrian operetta, "The Bird-Seller", at the Palace Theatre.

I never met Lehar, but I could certainly claim to know his "Merry Widow" inside out, for I did the décor and the costumes for three different productions of it. The first time it was for a fashionable theatre whose management proposed to stage the operetta just as Lehar wrote it. The second time all that was left of Lehar's "Merry Widow" was the music; the rest had been sacrificed to a revue on the usual "stupendous" scale, and this time "the widow" came not from the Balkans, but from

Honduras, which allowed the use of exotic motifs. When this production was given in Paris, the producer made a slight concession to Lehar by bringing in "Maxime's" again, though I turned it for the purposes of the revue into a highly coloured merry-go-round. My "Merry Widow" No. 3 was produced in His Majesty's, and although the Second World War had already

Costumes, "The Merry Widow"

begun and our rehearsals were interrupted by air-raid sirens, both Jack Hylton, whose show it was, and I had every reason to be satisfied.

In the year of Munich, whilst the lunatic over the North Sea was promising gullible Germans world domination, I was still thinking only of my art, and I held an exhibition of my most important scenic designs and also of my Paris watercolours in a Bond Street gallery. It was in connection with this exhibition that I received a charming letter from an unknown admirer who sighed herself "Andrée":

"C'est en donnant le bonheur qu'on le trouve, et vôtre art donne du bonheur à des milliers d'admirateurs du beau."

Whilst a million armed men were engaged in manœuvres in Germany, I designed a "Meissner Porcelain Finale" for the Palladium, and whilst "Le Fureur", as the French pronounced "Führer", was raving away at Nuremberg I was helping Michael Redgrave with the décor and the costumes for "The Duke in Darkness". I also worked for the Hippodrome in "The Fleet Lights Up!" and the subject was after my own heart. The old tea clipper, *Cutty Sark*, came into it and also Javanese palaces in the jungle and a sea battle. But in Kiel the Nazis were building for the real thing, and in the Sudete areas Henlein and his rabid Sudetes were becoming more and more aggressive. But in April 1939 I was still designing such peaceable things as exhibits for the Ideal Home Exhibition at Earl's Court, made of paint, metal, glass, stone, concrete, electricity, coal, fabrics, timberwork, and so on; 7 foot high figures which symbolized the benevolent forces which built men shelters and turned their shelters into homes. But Hitler was building warplanes.

A script was sent to me about this time dealing with the life of the famous and notorious Irish adventuress, Lola Montez, who turned the head of King Ludwig I of Bavaria as a Spanish dancer. It was quite a promising theme, but, unfortunately, the background was Munich and there was little chance of altering that. "Munich!" At that time it had an ominous sound, and the idea had to be abandoned.

And whilst Hitler, Mussolini, Daladier and Chamberlain were sitting hopelessly together in Godesberg I was asked to sketch humorous scenes for the Palladium, in which the famous umbrella was to appear. But we realized that the political situation was too serious and too critical for cheap humour, and it was decided instead to appeal to the patriotic feelings of the public, so off I went one evening to the Tattoo at Aldershot to obtain inspiration. Theatre people have an understandable weakness for military pomp, and with my old master, Reinhardt, I had witnessed the Tournament at Olympia, the changing of the guard and the trooping of the colour. The night tattoo that I now witnessed by floodlighting, contrasting the old thin red line with the modern Army, was a masterpiece of staging. We then tried something of the sort "with drums and trumpets" on the stage of the Palladium with successful results —even the balloon barrage was not forgotten.

Conscription had been introduced in Great Britain in peacetime—a unique innovation. However, we were still amongst the optimists who refused to believe that it would come to war. We lived happily in our Hampstead flat and planted scarlet runners on the balcony. In our spare time we wandered over the Heath, constantly discovering new beauties, and from Ken Wood we admired the dome of St Paul's glistening in the misty sunshine. But for all our optimism, my wife and daughter bought black-out material and began to paste up our windows with criss-cross strips of paper.

Whilst I went on with my painting: dressing-room scenes, rehearsal impressions and other theatrical motifs, Ribbentrop announced the conclusion of the Russo-German Pact to a startled world. And there was no "escape clause"! It meant war. But we still went on living as usual—what else was there to do? We went by steamer to Richmond, or down the river to Greenwich, and we decided that to get the right impression of London's power and glory you should arrive by ship and steam under Tower Bridge.

The optimists were confounded. At the beginning of September Hitler attacked Poland, assuring the world that it was really only a minor police expedition; it would be all over in a few weeks, and then the thousand years of Peace Hitler had promised the world could start off in earnest. But Great Britain had been deceived enough. On that Sunday morning we listened to Mr. Chamberlain announcing the outbreak of war on the wireless—and a few minutes later the first siren sounded. Sober judges put the duration of the war at three years. They were optimists too.

It was an exceptionally mild and sunny autumn. Phlox, asters and dahlias bloomed in all the gardens, but enthusiastic diggers were hard at work excavating trench shelters. At nights there was an impressive spectacle of criss-crossing searchlights and during the day the silver balloons glistened in the sun and covered the blue sky with a fantastic network as far as eye could see. At nights we tested the black-out and found it satisfactory and during the day we carried cardboard boxes containing gas-masks over our shoulders.

In November the rainy weather set in and the hoardings and the wet sand-bags in front of the shops looked more miserable than ever, an eye-sore. And then someone got the bright idea that artists should decorate the hoardings. It sounded marvellous, and we could already see Piccadilly, Oxford Street and Bond Street as endless art galleries. Sir Kenneth Clark opened the exhibition of our designs and we felt confident that soon commissions would pour in from shopkeepers anxious to present an æsthetic façade to the world in war time. But they had other worries; most of them contented themselves with having the signpainter paint "Business as Usual" on their hoardings and left it at that. Art in wartime was a luxury.

December was by no means a wintry month and there were still a good many roses blooming. Regent's Park looked lovely under a golden brown carpet of leaves, and on the lake clouds of screaming gulls had joined the flocks of ducks. In old Hampstead Cemetery we found a quiet romantic corner from which the usual deadly white marble angels were not visible. It was difficult to believe that it was not more than five miles away from the town, but our consciences were clear—we knew it wasn't. I mention the "five miles" because we were now "enemy aliens" and were not allowed to go beyond five miles from the town without special police permission. In reality, we were not even "enemy aliens" any longer, because the Nazis had cancelled our German naturalization papers. I had managed to get hold of the official German decree and I showed it to the British authorities to demonstrate that we were not enemy aliens, but stateless persons. But the police had no time for such fine distinctions, and they consoled us with the "Tribunal" which would sooner or later investigate our case; until then we should have to remain formally "enemies", and so I had to surrender my camera and our wireless set.

I had already made an application for British naturalization, and I showed the police at Bow Street the public declaration of my intention in the Press, in accordance with the provisions, and also an article in the "Star" entitled "Famous Stage Designer wants to be British". Once again they were amiability itself—but the "Tribunal" . . .

On November 27th, 1939, my wife, my nineteen-year-old daughter and myself appeared at last before this Tribunal. The Chairman, a big white-haired old gentleman of imposing appearance, listened attentively and sympathetically to our case. I had never been employed by any German Government and I had never done military service in Germany. I described my professional activities in Germany. "Reinhardt", nodded the Chairman; "a great man". The fact that I had designed the Coronation decorations for Selfridges seemed to be a point in my favour. And then, of course, there were the flattering recommendations of C. B. Cochran and his praise of my work as a scenic artist and designer. The upshot was that I and my family were granted "exemption" until further notice and given permission to live in Great Britain without restriction. I received a document which read:

"The holder of this certificate is to be exempted until further order from internment and from the special restrictions applicable to enemy aliens under the Aliens Order No. 1920 as amended. Refugee from Nazi oppression."

After this official confirmation of my political harmlessness I was enabled to continue my life "as usual". I was offered a commission to design for a revue with the topical title of "Black-out". Another theatrical man told me at great length about a piece he was to produce entitled "The Arms of Venus" and in which he invited me to co-operate. Neither the one proposal nor the other came to anything, but the title of the latter piece reminded me of a comic episode of my Munich art days at the beginning of the century.

I had advertised—as was the custom in Munich—for a model. I wanted a red-haired girl. One morning a mother arrived with her daughter, who was wearing a voluminous large-check cape, such as was popular at the time. The girl certainly had beautiful red hair.

"Are you the *Herr* painter who advertised for the model with red hair?" the mother asked me.

I confirmed that that was so, and asked them to come in. Whilst the girl disrobed behind a screen, her mother unwrapped what proved to be a low stool draped with light-blue velvet decorated with silver stars and put it down in the centre of the floor. I watched this strange performance with some interest; it was the sort of thing a performing dog would sit on before an audience. Then the woman suddenly clapped her hands and shouted "Hoppla!" like a ringmaster, whereupon the red-haired girl leapt out from behind the screen unclothed, sat down on the stool, clapped and also shouted, "Hoppla!"

Except that she didn't clap her hands, but the soles of her feet!

"There you are," cried the mother. "The ideal of red-haired beauty. What do you think of that?"

I was flabbergasted and hardly knew what to say.

"Yes, yes, of course, her hair is certainly beautiful," I stuttered finally, "and she's very pretty too, very pretty. But you see, I want a model with . . . I'm afraid . . . Well, the fact is I really wanted a normal model with arms."

"Arms!" spat the mother fiercely, glaring at me with arms akimbo. "You wanted a red-headed Venus, didn't you? You're supposed to be an artist, and you don't even know that Venus hasn't got any arms!"

CHAPTER XXII

THE SECOND WORLD WAR

ALTHOUGH MANY PROJECTS fell through under the stress of war, there was still a certain amount for me to do: one or two reviews and some work at Blackpool. But what was happening in the world was depressing and on June 24th I wrote in my diary:

"France! I am literally afraid to read the newspapers. I can't stand the news. Is that the France we all knew? The France which marched at the head of humanity for so long!"

And on June 26th: "France is still the great query. What *is* happening there? Has old Pétain taken leave of his senses? For anyone who knows the history of France and the character of the French people it is all simply inexplicable."

And soon after that my diary notes the first air raid and the few hours we spent in our shelter. How indignant we were that such a wonderful moonlit night should be so desecrated! When anything monstrous happens and we are beside ourselves, we always naïvely find it astonishing that Nature herself, heaven and earth, seem to take no account of it. I can still clearly remember walking in the country in Germany on the day the First World War broke out. I passed a mill and there on the green pond ducks were swimming around and quacking cheerfully, as though the world had not just fallen in. The indifference of the ducks struck me as astonishing. They ought to have been affected, too. They ought to have been gathered in silent groups along the edge of the pond, their feathers fluffed out miserably.

The first air raids on London caused many people to lose their heads, and a sudden fear of all foreigners, refugees, of whom there were very many, particularly in Hampstead, arose. "There may be dangerous spies amongst them. Play safe. Intern them all. No notice can be taken of individual hardship." Some of the more sensational newspapers joined in the cry. I made what inquiries I could and the answers were soothing, but the disagreeable rumours continued and so I packed a case with necessities and had a sketch-book and pencils ready.

Early in the morning on July 4th, 1940, a gentleman whose

profession was obvious appeared in my flat and informed me politely that he would be calling for me in an hour and would I kindly prepare a few things for the journey. Oh no, he assured me, I was not going to be interned because they thought I was dangerous, but in order to protect me from the possibility of molestation by excited people who were beginning to see spies everywhere. Ah, well!

Ten o'clock saw me sitting with a group of fellow unfortunates in need of protection in West Hampstead Police Station and watching the constables while away the time playing billiards. At three o'clock in the afternoon a bus arrived to take us and our luggage to a barracks which served as a collecting centre. From there we were all taken in Green Line coaches to Kempton Park Racecourse, where it became quite obvious that real care was being taken to protect us from boisterous elements. The place was surrounded with barbed wire and at every entrance stood big fellows in battle-dress with steel helmets, rifles and bayonets. I began to feel quite sorry for anyone who might try to molest us. My case was searched and a packet of razor blades was confiscated and all the money I had with me—about £20. For this I was given a formal receipt and at the same time a number, "80582—Group 14".

The fifty or so men who shared the room in which I was put turned out to be quite agreeable companions on the whole. We were given mattresses and blankets to make ourselves comfortable on the floor. Two big double doors opened up on to the racecourse, which looked lovely in the afternoon sun. For tea and supper combined we were each given a large mug of hot tea and two thick sandwiches with plenty of butter and cheese. When it grew dark we made up our beds in neat rows along the walls, undressed and put on our pyjamas as though we were in a hotel, and turned in. The lights went out and a certain amount of snoring began to make itself heard. I lay there listening to it and to the regular steps of the sentries outside and wondering whether after the excitements of the day I should be able to sleep.

It was only on the following day when I had time to think things over quietly that I realized that I and all the other 600 refugees with me were prisoners behind barbed wire. The stupidity of it all depressed me. I and my fellow unfortunates had more reason than anyone to hate Hitler and all his works, yet here we were, shut up as though we were his friends. On the other side of the barbed wire, which was already rusty, we could see life proceeding normally: cars, carts and buses rolled by, people went about their business, went to work in the morning and returned in the evening. Housewives did their shopping in the parade of shops we could see, and there was a pleasant-looking little pub. But we, who wanted nothing better than to enjoy the hospitality of this country and help her as far as we could in her troubles, had been turned into pariahs overnight.

During the day the Green Line coaches disgorged further groups of internees. One of them asked me whether I was Ernest Stern, the stage-designer, and when I replied that I was, he informed me that some newspapers were attacking the Government for its policy of wholesale internment and that an article entitled "For Shame!" had been devoted to my special case. All my natural optimism bubbled up again immediately and I felt like Beethoven's Fidelio when in prison he hears the distant fanfare which presages his release. I felt convinced that in a few days, when the authorities had had time to sort things out a bit, I should be released, and that the Isle of Man, or even Canada or Australia—so went the rumours —would never see me. In a much better mood, I got out my sketch-book and began to use my companions as they walked around and talked, sat and played chess and so on as models. Closer acquaintance with our barbed-wire oasis revealed gardens with blue hortensias, and in a clump of trees there was a quiet bench by a small stream where one could read undisturbed. I sketched our guards, too. Small wonder that they were all such big strapping fellows! Nothing but the best was good enough for us, apparently, and only His Majesty's Grenadier Guards had been thought worthy of the job of protecting us.

We were given a stew of meat rice and potatoes in our dixies. It was good and there was plenty of it, and that helped to keep my spirits up. We all began to shake down in our new surroundings. Friendships and acquaintanceships formed. After our dinner, which was at midday, we were allowed to take a siesta. From being depressed, most of us now became cheerful. We thought we could see the silver lining in the clouds already. As an artist, I began to appreciate the humour of our situation and the element of caricature in it. Amongst the internees were some who were nerve-ridden and jumpy; they ran round asking everybody questions and never waiting for an answer. Others put up a ponderous show of dignity and philosophy to impress the rest. Still others argued at the tops of their voices, waving their arms wildly, and overwhelming anyone whose opinion happened to differ in the slightest from their own. Almost all the benches on the racecourse were occupied by zealous card-players, and amongst them wandered a strange, prophet-like apparition, preaching to the empty air and raising his bony hands aloft in warning. Obviously, we called him Jeremiah.

There was one group of young men, most of whom had grown up in and around Whitechapel, and their only language was authentic Cockney. They had their own huts and they

"Jeremiah." Sutton Coldfield internees camp, 1940

seemed to be enjoying themselves, playing football and capering around like cheerful puppies. For them the place was like a holiday camp and many of them obviously found the idea of being fed regularly and for nothing very agreeable. "Business" also started up, and there were groups of *entrepreneurs* who were prepared to do the washing of the other internees for a consideration. Placards began to appear advertising their services. One of them read: "Socks darned—one penny per sock. Clean socks only accepted. Work taken in at 10 a.m."

Soldiers drilled and exercised on the racecourse, and in their free time they played football. A match had already been arranged between them and the interned young Jews. Occasionally officers were visible, but it was not difficult to see that they didn't much care for the job of guarding refugees. But there was one sergeant-major type with a red, beefy face and a white moustache, very smart and upright in a brand new uniform with a row of medal ribbons, who marched around with a swagger cane tucked under his arm looking for cigarette ends or scraps of paper. Whenever he found one he would bawl at the nearest internee: "Pick that up!" Perhaps the man had been a lawyer, a judge or a university professor in Germany or Austria, but now "Mr. Pick-it-up", as he came to be called, could turn him into a scavenger.

Twice a day we had to parade for a roll-call, which was carried out by N.C.Os. I don't know why it was, but they could never get the numbers to tally, and then they would go into a red-faced huddle with our "Group Leaders", refugees like us, but usually not very agreeable types, who arrogated authority to themselves. In the end this sort of "trusties" corps was abolished at our protest.

We were three weeks in Kempton Park before being transferred to Sutton Coldfield, and it soon became clear to us that our guards had a bad conscience towards us. For one thing, after a few days all the confiscated razor blades appeared on a table and anyone who wanted a blade could take one. We were allowed to write post-cards home and newspapers were promised. At the same time, once we had got over the depressing effect of feeling ourselves prisoners instead of free men, we began to grow more exigent. Somehow we managed to send off protest telegrams to various Members of the House of Commons. We also demanded that the primitive fashion of serving our food up in tins should cease and that we should be provided with cutlery and crockery like civilized human beings. A sort of canteen service was actually organized and the restaurant of the racecourse was brought into use. The custom of eating out of tins was, incidentally, becoming very disagreeable, because, owing to the lack of hot water, we were unable to clean them out properly and they began to smell sour.

My neighbour G., a likeable Austrian from Vienna, had discovered camomile growing in the camp and we filled the tins with this. It made everything we ate taste rather over-aromatic, but at least it disposed of the unpleasant musty smell. Letters began to arrive for us. In the restaurant we ate at long tables and were provided with plates and even knives and forks. However, knives in the hands of dangerous customers like us must have struck the camp authorities as unwise, so they posted sentries with fixed bayonets to watch us at meal-times. We organized a protest demonstration against this piece of stupidity, and one day at a prearranged signal we all got up from the table as soon as the meal was served and marched out. After that the armed guards were withdrawn and we were allowed to eat our food—and use our desperate weapons—without supervision.

For some time there had been rumours that we were to be moved to a specially prepared camp with much more comfort than the provisional arrangements of our present camp could offer. To hear our group leaders talk about it, you would have thought that a paradise on earth had been prepared for us. Then one day we were officially informed that we should tell our families that as from August 4th our new address would be: "Aliens Internment Camp, Sutton Coldfield, near Birmingham." And on August 4th we moved. "The exodus from Egypt into the Promised Land", our wits termed it.

First we went by train and then by buses. But our Land of Canaan turned out to be a tent colony surrounded by barbed wire. The camp terrain itself was treeless, but quite close was a pretty lake and a shady wood. A broad dusty path led between a number of large tents through the chaotically incomplete camp. It was immediately dubbed "Fifth-Column Avenue". The cooking facilities and the washing arrangements were all in the open. The tents themselves proved to be quite empty. We were furious at this change for the worse in our circumstances and we staged a noisy demonstration, demanding to speak to someone in authority. The N.C.Os. in charge of us were at their wits' end—which wasn't very far away—and they turned out the guard, which consisted of elderly Territorials, who appeared with rifles and fixed bayonets. However, we put them to flight by waving our raincoats at them and shouting, "Shame!"

Then we discovered that mattresses and blankets were piled

up in a huge marquee. At that there was a wild stampede and everyone loaded himself up with as much as he could carry and rushed off to find himself a place in one of the tents. They were new army tents, and around the centre poles were hooks to hang up our clothes. The canvas could be raised all round the tent to a height of about 3 feet, and this was invariably done during the day.

The Camp Commandant, who finally appeared, did his best to soothe us by pointing out that it was not lack of goodwill on his part. At the first roll-call he addressed us as "Gentlemen" and read us the latest war reports. When he told us that 142 Nazi planes had been shot down in a single day during the "Battle of Britain" the frantic cheering with which this announcement was received should have been enough to tell him, what he knew already, that it was senseless stupidity to intern us—we all hated the Nazis far more than he did and had far more reason to.

He allowed us to send telegrams of protest to the House of Commons, leaving the formulation of the text entirely to us, insisting only that we should mention that the camp authorities were doing their best to improve matters as far as lay in their power.

Each of us was allowed four thick new blankets, and the dixies and cutlery which were distributed were also new. In the meantime, work went ahead to complete the h. and c. showers which were being installed. Reporters were allowed into the camp to interview us, and an article published in a Birmingham paper under the title "Intelligentzia behind Barbed Wire" caused a scene in the House of Commons.

We took our meals in a large marquee, which, for some reason or the other, had a board at the entrance which announced "White Horse Inn". There we sat six at a table, whilst volunteers served out the food.

Each of us received a military ground-sheet which we spread on the heather-grown floor of our new homes and made ourselves a bed for the night. In addition, I had a rubber mattress which could be inflated, lent to me by my friend G., the Austrian. The scent of the heather was in our nostrils, the moon shone, the sentries marched up and down to see that no harm came to us—and we actually slept.

After a while we settled down in our new camp as we had settled down in the old. In my tent, which I shared with five others, who had all been lawyers either in Germany or Austria, we used to regale each other with our experiences and adventures before going to sleep. G., speaking in a Viennese accent, told us about his life as an officer in the former Austro-Hungarian Army. M. came from Frankfurt. S., from Leipzig, spoke with a Saxon accent and so on. My reminiscences as a painter and a theatre man were found particularly interesting, and we even had visitors from neighbouring tents at our sessions.

A canteen was set up in the camp and, amongst other things, we were able to buy bottled beer. Our letters were no longer censored and we began to receive parcels. All parcels had to be opened in the presence of the Camp Commandant. On one occasion I received a parcel of books.

"I oughtn't really to let you have those," said the Commandant.

"But they're only ordinary detective novels," I pointed out. "What harm can they do?"

"When I was a prisoner of war in Germany during the first spot of bother we used to get messages in books from home," he replied. "You just make almost unnoticeable marks under whatever letters you need, and there you are."

"That's a good idea!" I exclaimed.

"Yes, wasn't it?" he replied, and handed over the books.

The summer was a pleasant one and our camp between the woods in the east and the sea in the west was quite a pleasant place. Group life in the open air appealed to me as an artist, and I did a good deal of sketching. This not only aroused interest, but also brought me in advantage. I was invited to picnics at which there were cakes, sardines, paté de foie gras, Nescafé and other little luxuries. The hairdresser, a fellow refugee, used to cut my hair for nothing—what there was left of it. When I say for nothing—"Well, just a little sketch as a memento. . . ."

There were two Alerts whilst we were in Sutton Coalfield, but although the wailing of the siren over the countryside was eerie it conveyed no sense of urgency. The younger men began to dig slit trenches—just in case, but it was really more for exercise than anything else.

"Why don't you join the Pioneers, boys", our guards called out from the other side of the barbed wire. It was advice that quite a number of the younger men took when the opportunity was offered them later.

Our Jeremiah was still with us, but no one took any notice of him. He was obviously quite mad, but he appeared harmless enough. He would take up his stand on a heather-covered mound and deliver his tirades to the empty air, flailing his arms and raising his bony hands to heaven to call down I don't know what judgement on us all.

And then the time came for us to leave Sutton Coalfield. We assumed, correctly as it turned out, that as the summer was approaching its end, we were no longer to be left under canvas. One morning we were all marched off to waiting coaches which took us to the railway station, and we then travelled by train across the country from west to east. This time our destination was "York Racecourse, Internment Camp B", where there were solid huts ready to accommodate us, which we now decorated with bunches of heather we had brought with us from Sutton Coalfield. Apart from our cases, we had half-filled jars of jam and marmalade, and cardboard boxes. Packets tied on with string dangled from our persons and our pockets were bulging with various possessions.

We now lived in big high-ceilinged, raftered huts with real beds. On the window side were tables and chairs, and from morning to night they were occupied by impassioned card-players. Our tent community kept together, and we now began to feel ourselves like civilized human beings once again.

In York we were asked to elect someone from amongst our number to represent us in negotiations with the camp author-ities, and this we did: a former businessman, middle-aged, shrewd, intelligent and good-humoured, who proved worthy of the confidence we reposed in him. From his negotiations on our behalf with the authorities, it became clear that York was the final stage of our wanderings. The camp authority was no longer the War Office, but the Home Office.

We now had a canteen which was very much like an ordinary café, with a piano and a platform for lectures, etc. There were plenty of professional and good amateur musicians in our ranks and a very good orchestra was formed. It also turned out that we had two first-class chefs amongst us and a number of waiters, and at our request the indifferent English cooking was replaced by very good continental and Jewish cooking.

During the day we no longer saw any guards, but at nights we could still hear their heavy, regular footsteps as they marched up and down on sentry-go. We were encouraged to play games and to hold concerts and there was even a small lending library for our use. Our packets were still opened in the presence of the Commandant, but the atmosphere was cheerful and the sight of particularly good things would always produce amiable congratulations and words of encouragement: "Keep your pecker up. It won't be long now."

And most of us succeeded, but there were the unfortunates who were still depressed and miserable. They sat around anxiously and hopelessly. When they talked it was almost in whispers, and when they moved it was with dull resignation. They seemed to hang together on the principle of like attracting like. You would meet groups of them, coat collars turned up, hats or caps pulled down over their eyes and hands in their pockets, looking like dying flies in winter instead of human beings in the pleasant sunshine. For these wretched Jews the warmth seemed to have gone out of the world, and with it all hope. They were pathologically depressed and there was little one could do for them. It reminded me of many of the scenes we had staged where a spot-light would suddenly rest on a group, raising it out of the general mass: a group of drawn and anxious faces, contorted and miserable, grotesque almost in its ugliness and therefore doubly touching. The ceaseless drama of the oppressed and persecuted, the homeless and the hopeless. And in the background I could almost hear the tragic chorus which underlined their woes.

One of them knew of my work in the theatre and he talked to me about a project developing in his mind to write a "De Profundis" of the modern Jews, the tragedy of a people. I listened to him with sympathy, and encouraged him. With his woebegone eyes and his melancholy face, he was a figure of tragedy himself. He could talk compellingly and perhaps he was a poet in feeling, but I doubted his powers of dramatic expression, and, in fact, as far as I know, nothing ever came of his plan.

In the meantime, there were more and more indications that the responsible authorities were ashamed of their first panic and were now anxious to bring the internment scandal to an end if they could find some face-saving way of doing it. The first step was to sort out those who could be released on health grounds, and the doctors in the camp—internees like the rest of us—were set to examining their fellow prisoners. After some hesitation, they thought they might diagnose arterio-sclerosis in its preliminary stages with me. It was perfectly clear that they didn't believe it themselves and, in fact, at the age of sixty-four I had the blood pressure of a man half my age. As a result of these examinations, a number of internees were released, but I was not one of them. Our doctor comrades were taking their job too seriously; they hadn't grasped what the authorities wanted, so English doctors were brought in, and after that things began to move. I came up before one of them. He looked at me, made no detailed examination and then dictated to his secretary:

"Mr Ernest Stern, sixty-four years old, pale and emaciated. If his condition is not to worsen he should have constant attention in his own home under the control of his family doctor."

I think he was helped by my old sports coat. I had bought it too large in the first place, in error, and as I had lost a certain amount of weight in camp it now hung on me and made me look quite pitifully thin. I don't wear it now, but it still hangs in my wardrobe and every time I see it I give it a friendly wink. It did me a good turn and I don't like giving it to the old rag-and-bone man.

Just before this farce of a medical examination, I had given a lecture to my fellow internees on the theatre, and I had everything prepared for a second lecture, but on September 11th, the evening fixed for the lecture, my name was called out by one of the younger refugees who served as messengers, and I was instructed to pack my things and get ready to leave the camp within twenty minutes. I was like the legendary prisoner who was unwilling to leave his prison. I hurried to the office to see if I could go the next day instead; I wanted to deliver my lecture. It was no use; my name was on the list and my place was reserved. I had to pack hurriedly, take messages from fellow internees whose turn had not yet come, and rush helter-skelter to the bus.

"When you get to London you'll miss the peace and safety of the camp," said the Commandant when he paid out what was left of my £20. "London's front line to-day. You'll think of us when you spend the nights in the air-raid shelter."

For the moment the prospect held no fears for me. I thanked the Captain for his kindness and off I went.

The first thing I noticed in York was the seemingly very large number of young, pretty and well-dressed women. Small wonder I got that impression: we hadn't seen a woman for two and a half months. There we stood in York Station, the fifty of us, like a flock of sheep which had lost its shepherd. Suddenly I realized that I was an independent human being again. I was free. Free to come, free to stay, free to go. Immediately I left the forlorn group and mixed with the ordinary public. "I needn't take the train at all," I thought, "or at least not yet. Whilst I'm in York I can have a look round. It must be an interesting town; old Roman foundation and so on."

From the bus I had already caught a glimpse of an old gateway with gothic architecture and coats of arms. That would be worth sketching. And there was still York ham to be bought in the shops. But at that moment the train for London pulled in and the attraction was too strong. York could wait. I wanted to go home. I waited until the others had got into the train and then I found a carriage as far away from them as possible. It wasn't that I didn't like them, or that I wanted to cut myself off from them as human beings; it was just that I wanted to feel myself a free individual again. When the steward came round I took a place for dinner and went into the dining-car. I sat down at a table covered with a white cloth on which wine-glasses chinked together as the train rolled on, making a merry little tune. Stretching my legs out comfortably, I ordered a glass of sherry. At another table two of my former companions had done the same. They caught my eye and we raised our glasses to each other—and the future.

The train was some hours late, as was usual in those days. Several times we waited for no obvious reason in the open countryside, and it was one o'clock in the morning before we finally slid slowly into King's Cross. An air-raid had been on for some time and there was already the glow of fires over the roofs. I went down into a tunnel which was being used as an air-raid shelter and spent the night there. The next morning I made a civilized breakfast of eggs and coffee, bread and butter and marmalade in the station restaurant. Then I got a taxi and was driven off to the northern heights. To stand in front of my own flat door and ring the bell was an enormously satisfying experience. The door was opened by my daughter, who probably expected the milkman. I was home again.

My internment was over, and in my sketch-books its experiences were recorded. "This is Tent No. 38 in Sutton Coldfield. . . ." There were our clothes and our gas-masks hanging on the centre pole; there were the blankets neatly folded; on the guy ropes hung our washing to dry. "And that's where we washed and shaved in the open air. . . ." "This is the canteen queue. . . . There are the fellows sun-bathing. . . ." There they all were: lying around, playing cards, peeling potatoes, standing in front of the barbed wire. Altogether barbed wire, rusted to a dirty orange brown, played a big role in our lives; it was everywhere; it coiled viciously around stakes, rolled endlessly over fields, twisted and writhed over every possible means of escape. How ugly it was with its grim barbs! What a sign of the wretched times!

One of my first visits in London was to my old friend,

York internees camp, 1940

C. B. Cochran, to thank him for all his efforts on my behalf—he had even got into touch with Churchill himself. I was glad to be back in London again, air-raids and all, but it was not a pleasant spot, and in particular my wife's health was breaking down under the strain of constant pilgrimages to the cold, damp shelter, so we decided to go to Oxford.

I already knew the town because on one occasion I had been invited to deliver a lecture on the art of the theatre at New College. "Dinner in Hall" had impressed me particularly. The gothic interior with its paintings, the beautiful old silver, the peaceful, traditional atmosphere, the dons around me and the undergraduates in the body of the hall. And afterwards we had taken port in a beautiful Queen Anne room, seated in a half-circle round a tremendous open fireplace in which a fire of logs blazed cheerfully. The passing of the port with its traditional ritual was new to me, and I enjoyed it hugely, particularly as the port itself was excellent.

It was the uninterrupted tradition of life in Oxford which impressed me most. The very stones of the old buildings seemed less to have been placed there than to have grown up out of the ground naturally, and the result was a perfect whole, a delight to the eye and a consolation to the restless soul.

This time I was in Oxford on my own and we stayed at a friendly little boarding house. It was autumn, and the old town was a fairy picture of red, brown and golden leafed trees. At night, with the moonlight turning the old façades to silver, I had the impression of wandering through a tremendous theatrical décor painted on gauze. There was one spot between the Sheldonian Theatre and the old Ashmolean Museum where I positively expected to see picturesque figures draped in voluminous cloaks turn the corner at any moment and burst into a conspiratorial chorus. And before the Camera with its Roman façade I should not have been surprised to meet the ghostly Grand Commander from "Don Juan" in person.

At first I wandered around lost in admiration and unable to make up my mind where to start, but when I did the work forged ahead and the result was a series of watercolours, "Oxford in Autumn", with a sub-series, "Oxford in the Rain". I did not confine myself to the usual: Jesus, New, Magdalen, Trinity, Christ Church, and I took in various lesser-known buildings, ancient pubs and so on—and, of course, the churches, and St. Peter's in the East, with its squat tower and gnarled tress, in particular. The Thames, now become the Isis, and the Cherwell with their college barges were particularly romantic with the coloured leaves of autumn drifting and turning on their swollen waters.

When the weather was too inclement for outdoor painting, and the wind blew cold gusts of rain through the groaning branches I would take shelter in the quiet, arched interiors of churches and chapels, where the daylight was stained by ancient windows, or in college libraries and other buildings where the stones of the old corridors and the steps were worn away by countless generations. It was on one such occasion that I discovered the ethnological collection with its "masks". The mask belongs to the theatre, but unfortunately I have seldom been able to introduce it even where in my opinion it organically belongs: in many classic pieces. Even Reinhardt, with all his urge to experiment, could not be persuaded: he attached too much importance to the expression of the human face. But what is the make-up of an actor if not a kind of mask? Chinese and Japanese actors have brought the art of the mask to a high degree of perfection. In their art certain colours and certain ornaments are used invariably to represent certain characters. In China and Japan every member of the audience, no matter

Oxford

how far away from the stage he may be, can recognize at once from the blue, green, red, white or black make-up what role the actor is playing. Chinese actors appearing before the Emperor or Empress even wore a mask at the back of their heads in order that no matter where they stood they should never seem to have turned their backs on the Son of Heaven or his consort. Before the Second World War I witnessed a performance of Indian dancers. They all wore fantastic masks, and the effect was very striking. In my opinion dancers should always be masked on the stage. Dancing is the most primitive of arts and there is still much to be learned from the primitive.

One of the things which struck me as most delightful in the old university town was the presence of youth and bubbling good spirits against the ancient background. The undergraduates, with their various college scarves and their highly coloured pullovers showing under their open black gowns, hurried or cycled through the streets, in picturesque contrast to the age-old façades. Against such a background, their youth and high spirits seemed doubly joyful. On almost every lamppost the old rung for the lamplighter's ladder had been bent down by the weight of generations of acrobatic undergraduates; and the grimmer the "climb" the more enthusiastically it was conquered, and more than one day dawned to find Martyrs' Memorial or the ancient spire of some worthy building decorated with a fast-disappearing article of domestic furniture now put to a new use. And the girl undergraduates were hardly behind their male colleagues in high spirits. If they were seldom seen in "The Lamb" and the other well-known pubs, they were very evident in Christ Church Meadows and along the Cherwell, usually in slacks and as gaily coloured as the men.

Oxford was a happy refuge for us in the bitter days of war. Age-old values were being destroyed elsewhere, but in Oxford everything remained the same, an oasis of peace in an insane world. The deer still grazed in Magdalen Park. In the Bodleian the codices and Froissart's miniatures were still on view. Before the Sheldonian the philosophers still sat serenely on their pedestals and looked out over the same old world. But, somewhat regretfully, we decided to return to London. So just before Christmas we packed our cases and returned to our Hampstead flat.

We found a general air of confidence and hope. The preliminary successes in North Africa were encouraging. The theatres were still open, despite air-raids, and we found that even our radiators were hot in the flat. But the cemented air-raid shelter in the garden was as cold and dismal as ever. Out of the question to use it in winter. Friends who had a ground-floor flat had gone away, so we took down mattresses and blankets and slept there at nights and pretended we were safe.

It was still possible to buy Christmas trees, and so we had one

that year and my daughter piously unpacked all the old
decorations we had kept religiously since her childhood and
decorated our tree. The coloured glass globes, the candle-
holders, the naïve Christmas angel, a characteristic product of
Bavarian peasant art, which always topped our tree—they all
awakened pleasant though rather sad memories of other and
happier days. And under the tree we built up the crib again

My little daughter, 1922

with Mary and Joseph and the Babe in the manger, the
Shepherds, the three Kings, the sheep and the oxen. As a child,
my daughter had always found that wonderful. Now I watched
her as she built it up again, a young woman in slacks and jacket,
ready to scoot out with tin hat, bucket and stirrup pump to
tackle incendiaries.

And there was roast goose in accordance with immemorial
custom, done to a crisp brown turn and stuffed with apples and
chestnuts. Even Hitler, Goering and company seemed to have
a heart at Christmas and the traditional season of goodwill
passed without a single air-raid warning. But there was still
that odious mocking voice on the wireless to tell his stiff-necked
countrymen that even more horrible and effective measures
were coming to break the resistance of the obstinate island race.

I had lived for forty years amongst the Germans, and I was
still at a loss to explain how a handful of lunatic brutes had
managed to obtain such control over an industrious and

capable people. And my German-born wife understood it no more than I did. If her Hanseatic forbears had ever dreamt of conquests it was overseas and by peaceable means, and it was in 1906, when we first came to Berlin, that she made the acquaintance of Prussianism. Neither she nor I ever felt really at home there.

At the age of seventeen she had lived in London with an English family *au pair*, an admirable institution which broadens the horizon of young people, opens their eyes to new things and new ways and gives them another language. Returning to Germany in 1902, she went to Munich, where we met. The "arts and crafts" movement was just beginning then. One of its branches was the production of furniture with specially woven and designed materials. The designer of the furniture also determined the kind and colour of the materials used, and the so-called Sherebecker hand-weaving system, which was still traditionally practised in Denmark, was taken over. Not only furniture coverings, but also curtains and hangings in modern designs were produced in this way. My wife learned the craft and soon became a teacher herself, as well as carrying out orders in this modernized old craft.

I have already mentioned that as a fifteen-year-old my daughter had helped me with my model building. When we were finally settled in London she attended an art school, and her studies from the living model showed excellent results; so much so that she soon began to do murals on her own and even to design ballet scenery. At the same time she assisted in the practical execution of my costume designs, showing considerable manual dexterity and inventiveness. To-day, after many years experience with a firm of theatrical costumiers, she and a friend have made themselves independent. The painting and spraying of materials of all kinds, the creation of original headdresses and the modelling of masks has become a speciality for which they are already well known in the theatre world.

Whilst still at Oxford, I had been approached by a number of young people to give lectures on the scenic art, and I had very gladly complied. One of my projects has long been to found a school for scenic art, because it strikes me as an excellent thing that forty years of practical stage experience should, in some form or the other, be placed at the disposal of the next generation. Unfortunately, I have not yet been able to put my project into operation, though I have made various suggestions and offers to the most likely quarters. When I returned to London I began to work on a series of lectures dealing with school theatrical performances. My main aim was to persuade the youngsters to paint their own décor and to design and execute their own costumes. As my object lessons, I took "Hamlet" and "Julius Cæsar" and one of the old Chester Nativity plays.

My first lecture was given in a high school for girls, and I was gratified to discover that I had chosen a manner of presentation which kept my young listeners interested. For the Nativity Play I made them model décor about 18 inches high. They were really double-sided screens. All that was necessary to change the scene was just to turn them round. Mary, Joseph and Elizabeth, the three Kings and the Shepherds, the Tax-collector, the villain of the piece, Herod, and his brutal warriors, the angels, and, of course, the devils with their horns, tails and cloven hoofs, were drawn on paper, coloured, cut out and fixed to boards so that they stood upright, about 11 inches high. I had done my best to give each figure its characteristic attitude as demanded by the scene, even exaggerating it a little. My idea with regard to Nativity Plays was that the actors should mime only. Mary, Joseph, the Kings and all the other normal speaking roles would mime their parts, whilst a special "voice" would speak their lines, the speaker standing before the stage. In addition I had provided for a chorus to support the speaker and underline certain passages, a sort of human orchestra.

It was my view that if the Nativity Plays were given in mime only, so to speak, as a series of living pictures, it would make it easier for young amateurs than if, in addition, they had to speak verse or lines. To act and at the same time to speak is a difficult double task even for an experienced actor. If there were no lines to learn and deliver, and if they heard someone else speaking them instead it would be something like a melody whose rhythm they then had to illustrate in mime. I was happy to find that my young listeners readily grasped what it was I was aiming at. They agreed with me that if they were relieved of the necessity of learning and declaiming lines they would be better able to concentrate their attention on effective mime, plastic attitude and impressive movement.

There was another important point I had in mind when I proposed the mime, and that was the various masks the char-

acters had to wear. The three Kings, the Tax-collector, Herod
and his savage warriors, not forgetting the devils, all wore the
masks indicated. Many were bearded and with characteristic
make-up; some of them—Herod and the devils, for example—
were conceived definitely as caricatures. Such masks make it
awkward for experienced actors; to expect young amateurs to
acquit themselves well in them if they also have to speak is too
much. My ideas were developed from the puppet theatre: the
marionettes move and tell the story in mime, and the "voice"
speaks their lines.

For "Hamlet" and "Julius Cæsar" I had chosen décor of
the simplest possible kind, and I had also prepared little figures
already costumed. I also sought to give my pupils hints and
advice on the designing and execution of their own costumes.
Owing to the shortage of materials in wartime, I assumed that
my listeners would have to find their own, and I proposed the
use of old bed-sheets for tunics and togas, and perhaps black-out
material for Hamlet. They showed the keenest interest in what
I had to say, and from their questions I could see that they had
understood.

"But you've shown the 'Hamlet' figures with black and
brown legs," one objected. "You can't get coloured tights these
days, you know "

"Quite," I agreed. "So if we can't get coloured tights we'll
do without them. I've painted the legs of my figures, as you
point out, and you can paint yours."

"Paint our legs! Of course! What fun!"

Incidentally, whilst I am on this question of theatrical
costumes, I should like to pay a tribute to an agreeable feature
of stage life in this country, and that is the care with which
English actors and actresses treat their costumes, and the
general willingness with which they accept what has been
designed for their roles. I remember one old comic actor here
who always treated his costume with what amounted almost to
veneration. He would allow no one to help him on with it, and
when the performance was over he would carefully take it off
fold it up and lock it away himself. And if ever any repairs had
to be made to it, he would produce needle and cotton and
carry them out himself.

In my experience in this country, I can't recall a single
instance of carelessness or abuse in this respect. It was very
different in Paris, where everyone did just what he pleased

once the first night was safely over. And even in the land of exemplary discipline, Germany, it was not a great deal better. I have always held English actors up to their German colleagues as an example of how to treat stage costumes and I have always stressed that, after all, proper dressing is an important part of their profession. Usually I have been listened to with a lacklustre eye; some have agreed with me, but most have shrugged their shoulders and thought that genius—which they, of course, all possessed—was more important than the handful of coloured scraps they were expected to wear. There were certainly some—and not as a rule those who lacked genius—who seemed to live themselves into their roles only with their costumes. But there were others—of both sexes—who made all sorts of difficulties: some wanted silk when their roles demanded simple materials; others wept when they had to appear in rags. And then there were the indifferent and careless ones who treated their costumes as a necessary evil. I remember one actress who used to dash into her dressing room at the last moment, strip off her street clothes—and underneath she was wearing the Greek tunic she had to wear as Jocasta in "Œdipus Rex".

An episode occurs to me in connection with that genius, Rudolf Schildkraut. He was playing the role of Shylock in our production of "The Merchant of Venice". When the play had been running for about a fortnight I saw it again and it struck me that there was something odd about him. He seemed to have got fatter. In addition, his *caftan* looked longer. I could have sworn that previously his sandalled feet had been visible. When I went round to Schildkraut's dresser the man admitted that he had lengthened the *caftan* by putting in a broad piece of stuff.

"Why did you do that?" I asked. "The *caftan* was made specially for Herr Schildkraut and it fitted excellently."

The man mumbled awkwardly, and I could see that there was something at the back of it he didn't want to tell me, so I took the matter up with Schildkraut himself, who was also a little embarrassed, like a naughty child who has been caught out. It seemed that he was always in a hurry to get away after the performance because his card-playing cronies were waiting for him at the club to make up a table, so he played his role in his ordinary clothes under the *caftan* and all he had to do was to strip it off, remove the grease paint and hurry away. But, as I say, Schildkraut really *was* a genius.

K

Costumes for Russian scene in revue "Fine and Dandy"

CHAPTER XXIII

THE CLOUDS LIFT

THE ALLIED FORCES HAD crossed the Mediterranean. Sicily was safely in their hands. The conquest of Italy had begun. The Palladium then wanted something or the other reflecting these hopeful events and I was commissioned to design a scene in which the troops were singing their songs amidst Italian ruins. When Scottish songs began, the scene changed to the Highlands with marching pipers. And finally a Guards band in peacetime uniforms, red coats and bearskins, played before a décor representing St. James's Palace. The situation on the Russian front had also greatly improved, so that we were now in a position to risk a little humour about the Russians without giving offence. Muscovite scenes were nothing new to me, because I had worked for the famous Russian cabaret, "The Blue Bird". I therefore designed a Russian scene for the finale of the revue "Fine and Dandy" at the Saville Theatre: a snow-covered landscape with a colourful Russian hut in the foreground. In the interior a grotesque tea scene took place around the samovar. When the hut revolved a second interior became visible with gold and silver ikons which turned out to be a bride and bridegroom with their bridesmaids, who

then indulged in a wild and whirling dance with their guests
à la Diaghilev.

"When we Russians are happy we dance!" shouted Leslie
Henson from his sledge, drawn by dappled horses to the accompaniment of a merry jingling of bells.

The American allies were not to be left out of it, and the
Palladium planned a revue entitled "The Discovery of
America" in a series of fantastic scenes. Unfortunately, this
came to nothing, which I much regretted, because all my
sketches were wasted. However, there was "Wild Rose" at the
Prince's, which was redesigned, and for this I was able to utilize
many of my personal impressions of the New World. One of
the high-lights in this show was a cigar ballet, which developed
out of a typical Havana box. I also did "The Duchess of
Danzig" and "The Lilac Domino" in this period.

By chance I came into contact with Donald Wolfit at about
this time, and we naturally discussed his Shakespearean
productions. He complained of the constant difficulties which
were caused by the transport of cumbrous scenery on his tours.
I showed him the "Hamlet" and "Julius Cæsar" models I had
made for my lectures and suggested that he should try some
such simple form of scenery which would fold up into a small
space and be easy to transport. He at once recognized the
advantages of my scheme, and the first commission I undertook
for him was to design readily transportable scenery for "Twelfth
Night". I made the scenery 9 feet high in tryptic form to
fold up, with scenery painted on both sides. By merely turning
the screens round, he could have either interiors or Olivia's
garden. In addition, the scene-shifting pause was cut out; the
change of scenery was carried out in full view of the audience
by four pages to the accompaniment of music. I used the same
screen system for Wolfit's "As You Like It". In both pieces a
coloured curtain gave a semicircular background to the scenery.
Where the scene required furniture, it was just carried on by
the pages or by the actors themselves. Despite the simplicity
of this method, it was very effective and never destroyed the
illusion. When this was written we were discussing the possibility of designing scenery of the same sort to serve for "The
Merchant of Venice", "The Taming of the Shrew" and
"Measure for Measure".

The newspapers brought news of the heavy bombing of
German towns. The day of reckoning had come: Berlin,

Frankfort-on-Main, Hamburg, Nuremberg and Munich. The Germans now had to taste the bitterness of seeing irreplaceable cultural values, the work of generations, destroyed in a night. The fate of Munich saddened me in particular, of course, because the town, with its old streets, squares and buildings, had meant so much to me in my youth, and was bound up with so many of my pleasantest memories. Fifty years had passed, and they all flooded in on me again as I read of the destruction.

By a strange coincidence, I received a letter just at that time which made all those memories even more vivid. It was from my old friend, colleague and countryman, Max Klang, with whom I had shared my first studio in Munich when I was still a first-year student at the Academy. In his letter he asked me whether I was the Ernest Stern he had known fifty years before in Munich, and suggested that if I were we should meet again. He had been a portrait painter in London for many years, he said, and he would look forward to seeing me. The letter was written in English, but it was still a foreigner's English, obviously shaky on grammar and idiom, and openly at war with orthography. In any case, as I remembered, Max's education had always been very sketchy. But as an artist he had been highly talented—and much more advanced than I had been in those early Munich days. I had completely lost sight of him, and somehow I had had the impression that he had gone to the States and settled down there.

I answered his letter at once and asked him to come to my flat, but the same night we were bombed out. A flying bomb wrecked our flat. Two rooms were completely destroyed, but, fortunately although my studio was damaged, none of my work was destroyed, and that was a great relief. As I have said, we slept in another flat on the ground floor and so we escaped injury. To our astonishment, we were not even greatly excited. It was just our turn. The next morning I even began to sketch the damage.

My meeting with Max Klang had been postponed, but a few days later he came along to the flat of some friends, with whom we had found shelter, and the delight at our reunion was great. We even assured each other that we hadn't changed much in those fifty years—he must have forgotten what the young curly-headed Ernest Stern, the first-year student at the Munich Art Academy, really looked like! We talked and talked; reminded each other of a dozen and one forgotten things, and laid great plans for the continuance of our renewed friendship. I showed him my work and I went with him to Burlington House to see his latest child portrait.

A few days later I read of his sudden death.

London, 1944. Bombed out!

In these memories of mine I have tried to show, in particular, how circumstances, and what often looked like chance, affected my life and helped to form my work and make it what it is. They are largely jottings, and often unrelated I know, and perhaps some readers will find their lack of strict chronological order and system distressing. Often, too, I have wandered off into anecdotal by-paths. At least I can point to the example of a greater man, Izaak Walton, who would excuse himself for similar digressions in some such fashion:

"But I am fallen into this discourse by accident, of which I might say more, but it has proved longer than I intended, and possibly may not to you be considerable."

Or interrupt a solemn dissertation on his art with the pleasant announcement:

"And now for my song."

STERN

INDEX